I0796457

The Road Was Full of Thorns

ALSO BY TOM ZOELLNER

Rim to River

The National Road

Island on Fire

Train

A Safeway in Arizona

Uranium

The Heartless Stone

The Road Was Full of Thorns

Running Toward Freedom in the American Civil War

Tom Zoellner

NEW YORK
LONDON

Published in the United States by The New Press, New York, 2025
Distributed by Two Rivers Distribution

ISBN 979-8-89385-008-6 (hc)
ISBN 979-8-89385-010-9 (ebook)
CIP data is available

The New Press publishes books that promote and enrich public discussion and understanding of the issues vital to our democracy and to a more equitable world. These books are made possible by the enthusiasm of our readers; the support of a committed group of donors, large and small; the collaboration of our many partners in the independent media and the not-for-profit sector; booksellers, who often hand-sell New Press books; librarians; and above all by our authors.

www.thenewpress.com

Composition by Westchester Publishing Services
This book was set in Adobe Caslon Pro

Printed in the United States of America

2 4 6 8 10 9 7 5 3

Contents

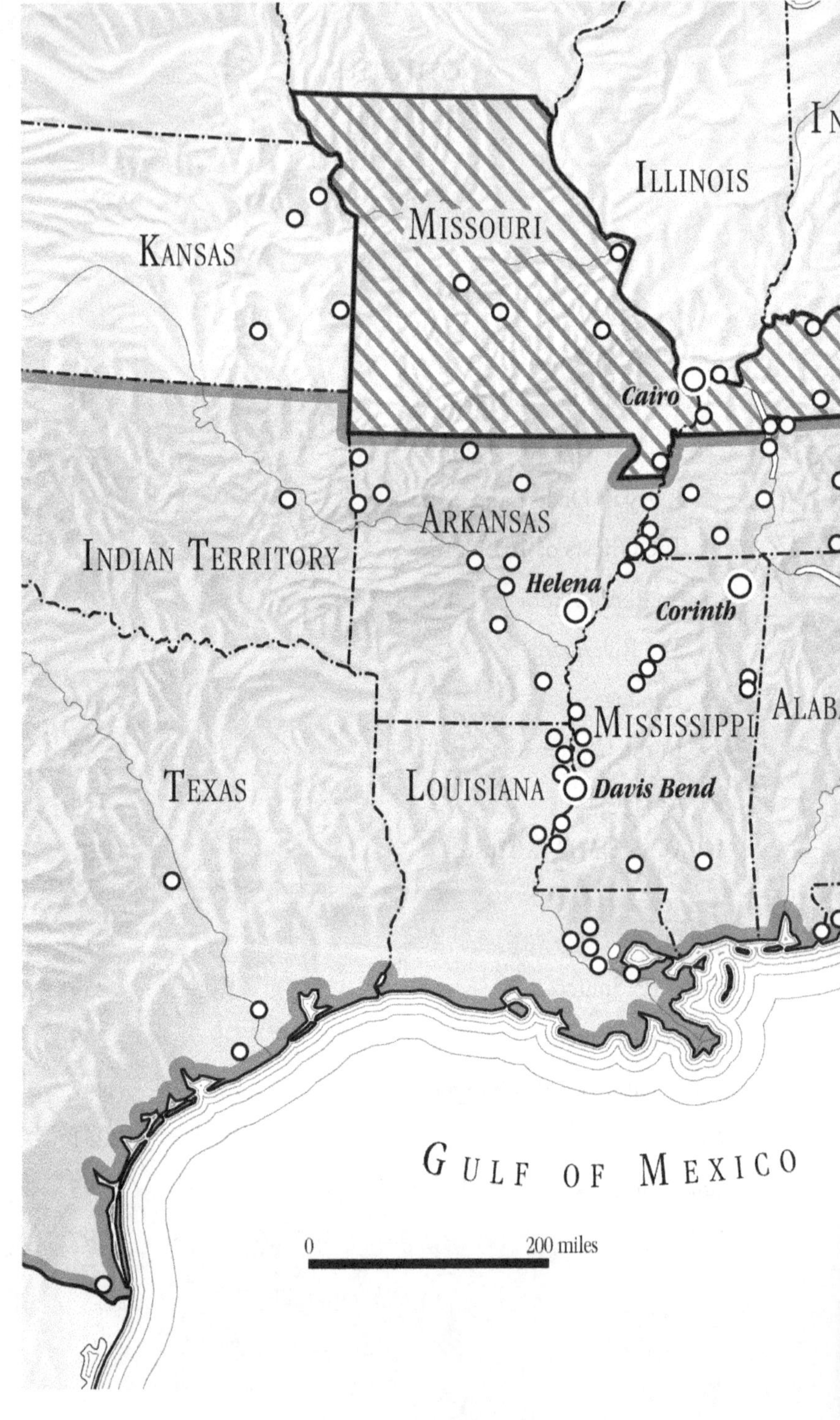

IN
ILLINOIS
MISSOURI
KANSAS
Cairo
ARKANSAS
INDIAN TERRITORY
Helena
Corinth
MISSISSIPPI
ALABA
TEXAS
LOUISIANA
Davis Bend
GULF OF MEXICO
0
200 miles

Contents

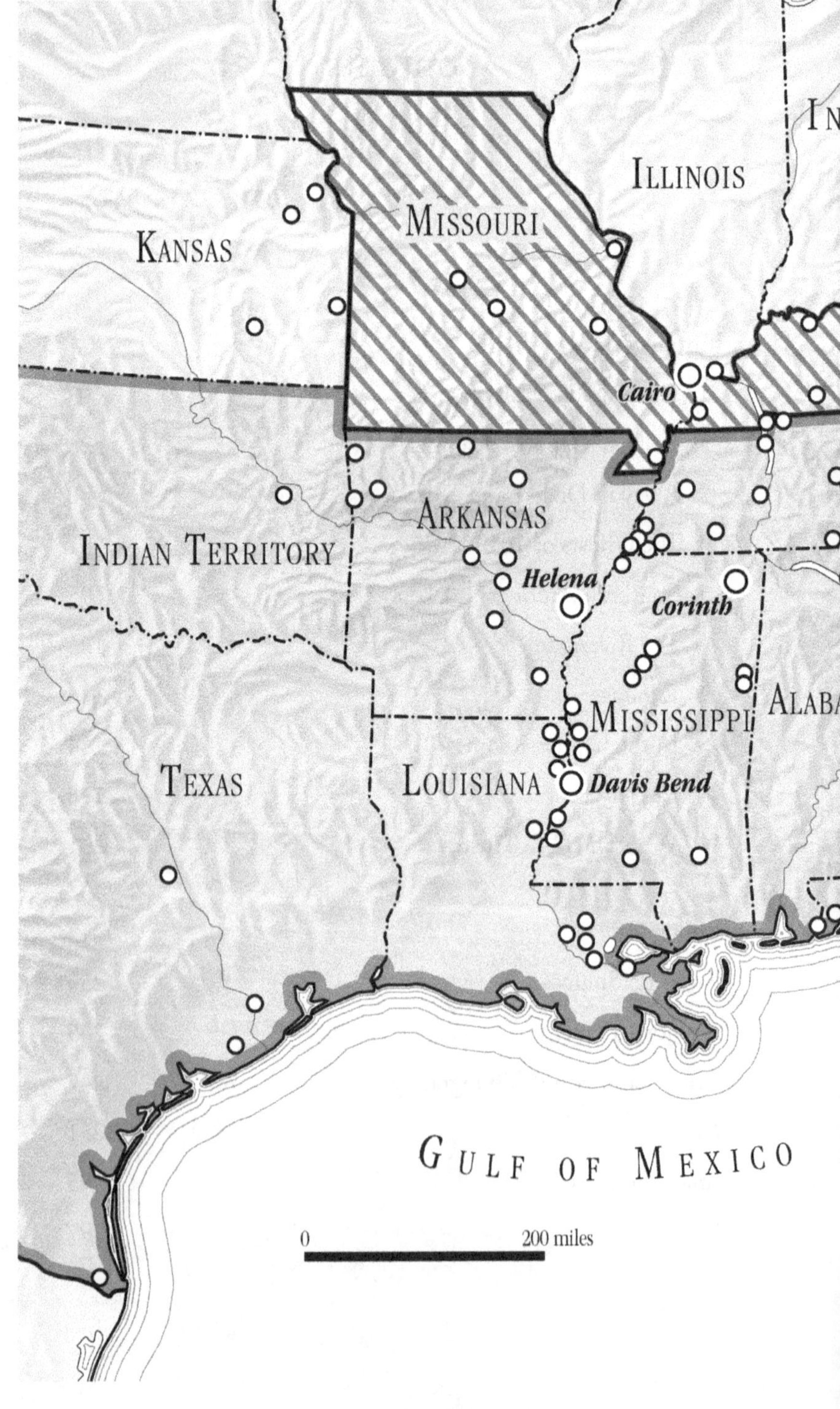

IN
ILLINOIS
MISSOURI
KANSAS
Cairo
ARKANSAS
INDIAN TERRITORY
Helena
Corinth
MISSISSIPPI
ALABA
TEXAS
LOUISIANA
Davis Bend
GULF OF MEXICO
0
200 miles

MARYLAND
OHIO
WEST
VIRGINIA
Statehood
in 1863
Camp Barker
DELAWARE
amp Nelson
VIRGINIA
Slabtown
(Hampton)
ENTUCKY
NORTH CAROLINA
NNESSEE
SOUTH CAROLINA
ATLANTIC OCEAN
GEORGIA
Port
Royal
N
W
E
S
FLORIDA
Union States
Border States
Confederate States
Major
Contraband Camps

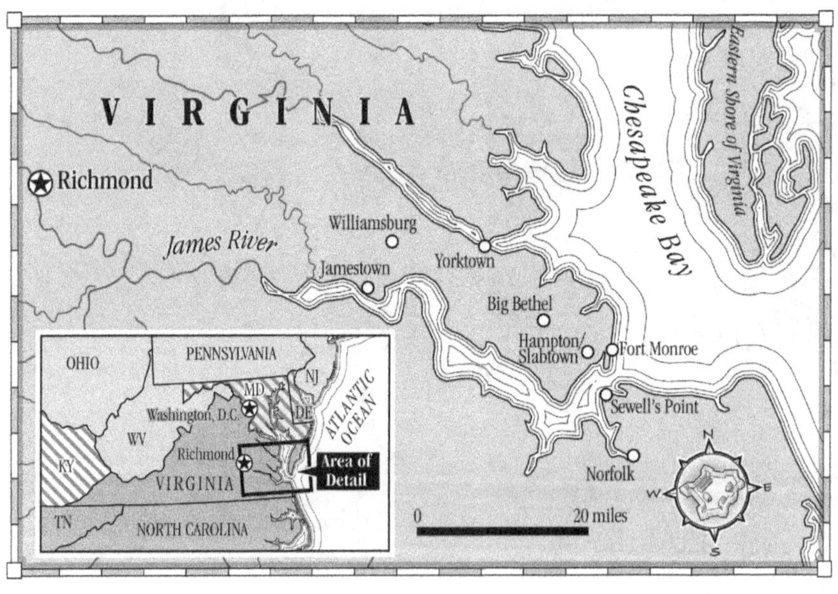
VIRGINIA
Richmond
James River
Williamsburg
Jamestown
Yorktown
Chesapeake Bay
Eastern Shore of Virginia
Big Bethel
Hampton/
Slabtown
Fort Monroe
Sewell's Point
Norfolk
0
20 miles
OHIO
PENNSYLVANIA
NJ
MD
DE
Washington, D.C.
ATLANTIC OCEAN
WV
KY
Richmond
VIRGINIA
Area of Detail
TN
NORTH CAROLINA

Introduction

Henry Jarvis ran away from slavery in the summer of 1861, terrified and chased by dogs. Such escape attempts usually ended in capture and further beatings. But Jarvis had heard a tantalizing rumor spreading through the plantation grapevine. He wanted to learn whether it was true that the U.S. Army was now offering protection for enslaved people at a nearby post called Fort Monroe.

Jarvis resolved to get there by any means possible. He lived under the whip of "the meanest man on the Eastern Shore" of Virginia, who might have killed him upon discovery. Jarvis was able to throw the dogs off his scent by crossing a stream, then hiding in the woods. Though he could not stay there forever, he decided to wait until his enslaver's birthday when there would be a raucous party at the plantation house—a big distraction.

"I knew they would all be drinking and carousing night and day, and all the servants kept home," he later recalled, "so I took the opportunity to slip down to the shore in the night, got a canoe and sail, and started for Fort Monroe," an installation at the strategic tip of land called Old Point Comfort.

A storm might have capsized his boat, or a Virginia naval patrol could have seized him at any point along the thirty-five-mile reach. Jarvis thought there was little chance that he would "ever get to land." But he asked the Lord to take care of him, and "by and by, the wind went down to a good steady breeze straight for Old Point, and I just made fast the sheet and drove ahead, and the next morning I got safe to the fort."[1]

The installation, Fort Monroe, was once the crown jewel of the U.S. system of coastal defenses, built on the edge of Chesapeake Bay at the mouth of the James River, opposite what is the present-day U.S. Naval Station Norfolk, to ensure that no foreign power could ever invade the country by sea. Its guns had always been aimed out at the Atlantic Ocean. But now the guns were pointed inland. Virginia had seceded from the Union on May 22, 1861, meaning that Fort Monroe was now a tiny blue island located deep inside rebel territory. People were calling it the Freedom Fort.

As Jarvis came to shore, he beheld an astonishing sight. Hundreds of men, women, and children who had run away from slavery were camped outside the gates of the fort, some inside army tents, others using blankets in the muddy clover fields near the town of Hampton. All of them had heard the same news as Jarvis: that U.S. Army general Benjamin Butler had sheltered three enslaved men who had run away from building a Confederate fortification and deemed them "contraband of war." He had put some creative legal reasoning into this definition of enslaved people as objects subject to capture. No army in its right mind would ever think of handing back rifles or cannons to an enemy. Why should Black laborers be treated differently, especially if they were being used to build gun platforms and battlements to be used against the Union?[2]

What started as an improvised military trick had unintended consequences. The news spread, electrifying the slave population of coastal Virginia. Within the week, the "contraband camp" at Fort Monroe was housing ninety people. By the middle of the summer, there were nine hundred men, women, and children living in an improvised village called Slabtown, most of them working for the U.S. Army as ditchdiggers, cooks, laundresses, stevedores, and valets. That was only the beginning of a movement that would change the course of the Civil War.

Contraband camps spread quickly throughout coastal Virginia and then sprung up within most every theater of the war. Wherever the U.S. Army traveled, torrents of people rushed toward the bluecoats in a bid to secure their own freedom. The effect was "like thrusting a walking stick into an anthill," in the words of one officer. Instant cities of refugees sprung up within the bombed-out rubble of what had been sleepy Southern crossroad towns.[3]

Some camps were clean and orderly, such as the village in a meadow northwest of the rail junction at Corinth, Mississippi. Others were filthy and miserable, little more than low spots in the brush, such as the sodden collection of huts to the south of Helena, Arkansas. Temporary encampments popped up in locations as diverse as Brownsville, Texas; Mound City, Illinois; Lick Skillet, Arkansas; nameless little islands in the Mississippi River; the fringes of city streets in Nashville, St. Louis, and New Orleans; and hundreds of other places in between. The United States had never had a refugee crisis of this scale. It hasn't ever since. As many as eight hundred thousand people—a fifth of the enslaved population of the entire South—left a plantation and lived in a contraband camp at some point during the Civil War, a number close to New York City's population at that time.[4]

The visibility of these camps put a powerful thorn in the conscience of the Northern public. Here was the very cause of the war at the doorstep, a national question that could no longer be deferred or squirreled away on distant plantations where its human face could not be seen. "What is to be done with the blacks?" demanded newspapers from Baltimore to Sacramento. General Butler's impulsive field decision and the coinage of the term "contraband" to refer to refugees may have been dehumanizing, but it proved an effective way of smuggling the dangerous idea of Black citizenship into the arena of possibility—especially in the mind of one man.

Abraham Lincoln rode past a crowded camp in Washington, DC, every day on his way to work in the summer of 1862; he sometimes ordered his carriage to stop so he could talk with the refugees. There is at least one recorded instance of him singing a hymn with them. While he invited none of them to the White House, or asked them their opinions on policy, his actions throughout the second year of the war demonstrate their influence on his thinking. He told visiting congressmen the war was heading toward emancipation because "slaves would come to the camps and continual irritation was kept up." In July 1862, he expressed doubt that "it would be physically possible" to break up the camps and return anyone there to slavery, which meant that a permanent solution had to be found. That same month, just weeks before he issued the preliminary proclamation of emancipation, he predicted that slavery "will be extinguished by mere friction and abrasion—by the mere incidents of the war."[5]

As this book will argue, Lincoln did not lead the process of emancipation so much as he trailed behind the fast-moving events like a streetsweeper behind a parade, seeking to legalize the realities forming on the war front and make the temporary freedom a permanent one. Like nearly everyone else in the government, Lincoln came to recognize that enslaved people could not be returned to their chains once they had been freed through military means. As he liked to put it, "broken eggs cannot be mended."[6]

When he issued the preliminary Emancipation Proclamation on September 22, 1862, the influence of the contraband camps could be seen throughout his language. Those "taking refuge within the lines of the army" were declared free, and if the Confederates did not surrender by the end of the year, the enslaved people still under their control would be "thenceforward and forever free." The Emancipation Proclamation made this federal policy by the beginning of 1863. While it did not actually free most of the enslaved people in the South, it steered the Union cause firmly in the direction of freedom, transformed the U.S. Army into a liberating force, and pointed the way toward a constitutional amendment to destroy slavery for good. Moreover, it was a knockout blow from a military perspective. The contraband camps became the primary recruiting grounds for the United States Colored Troops, whose regiments made up one-tenth of Union forces by the end of 1864, a rapid surge in power that spelled doom for the Confederacy.[7]

The destruction of slavery was a process, not a moment—it was "irregular, messy, and unpredictable," in the words of historian Joseph Reidy—and it unfolded in the chaos and suffering of war. New possibilities emerged from the disorientation. The collective flight of enslaved people *toward* white men with guns instead of *away* from them would have been an absurd proposition right up until the time Butler concocted his "contraband" loophole in front of a frustrated Virginia aristocrat.[8]

None of it would have been possible without Henry Jarvis and the others like him who took an enormous risk by venturing out in the chaos of warfare and attempting to find their way toward a U.S. Army position. They forded rivers, dodged patrols, traveled through woods in the darkness, stowed away in boxcars, often leaving family behind. Their collective flight toward the refugee camps was a grand act of defiance and hope. Previous generations of enslaved people had always resisted in various ways, including by running away, but now a new crack in the wall appeared. When they reached a blue-coated soldier, there was no guarantee of freedom: policies could vary from unit to unit, often dependent on the prejudices of the commanding officer, and many refugees were handed back to vengeful slave owners. What drove American emancipation in practice were the travels of eight hundred thousand people toward an undecided future—burdened, fearful, possibly limping or even carried by others, but willing to take a chance. "Instead of flowery paths, days of perpetual sunshine, and bowers hanging with golden fruit," wrote the formerly enslaved dressmaker Elizabeth Keckly of this experience, "the road was rugged and full of thorns, the sunshine was eclipsed by shadows, and the mute appeals for help too often were answered by cold neglect."[9]

Emancipation in the American Civil War often conjures a set of stock images: Lincoln signing a document at his desk, William T. Sherman promising forty acres and a mule, chains being snapped in two, a grateful freedman rising from his knees. But what it looked like, felt like, and smelled like for people like Henry Jarvis was a far different matter. Emancipation was a desperate flight across dangerous territory, and then a plea to convince the federal authorities that their interests were aligned. Emancipation was the taste of mud in the mouth; the sharp waves of the Chesapeake Bay; the terror of the slave patrols known as "paddy-rollers"; the bends of unknown rivers; the granite faces of Yankee provost marshals; a tenting site in mosquito-thick marshes; leg wounds that refused to heal; the groans of the dying; handouts of moldy biscuits; a sunrise to sunset job felling logs in the piney woods; the threat of Confederate snipers with orders to kill any runaways; the lessons of church missionaries bearing spelling primers; underground hymns sung in the open for the first time; and a profound mix of anxiety, disappointment, and hope shot through it all.

The overarching story embedded within those hymns was that of the biblical Exodus repurposed and fully present: a flight out of Egypt. The song "Go Down Moses," with its stirring admonition to "let my people go," began to find a national audience starting at Fort Monroe, amplifying a spiritual cause while also turning it into a political cry in which the enslaved people were key actors. "A keen observer might have detected in our repeated singing of 'O Canaan, sweet Canaan / I am bound for the land of Canaan,' something more than a hope of reaching heaven," wrote Frederick Douglass. "We meant to reach the north—and the north was our Canaan." When African Americans celebrated the Emancipation Proclamation in front of the White House on January 1, 1863, "any reference to the triumphant escape of the Israelites across the Red Sea and the destruction of their pursuing masters was certain to bring out a strong 'Amen.'"

This living metaphor came as a cognitive shock to white Americans who liked to think of *themselves* as the Israelites who had fought their way to the Promised Land to escape the oppressive British pharaohs. But had they turned into the Egyptians somewhere along the way?[10]

The story of how the "contraband of war" decision unraveled American slavery contains another remarkable irony. The spot where the legal trick was concocted—Fort Monroe at Old Point Comfort—happened to have been the landing site of the ships *White Lion* and the *Treasurer*, the first bearers of enslaved people to Virginia shores in 1619. The symbolic birthplace of slavery in America was also where it ended.[11]

The ironies went even deeper. A close look at the seventeenth-century origins of the South's "peculiar institution," detailed in this book, reveals a series of incremental measures designed to resolve short-term labor problems and placate wealthy actors. These measures built upon each other and picked up momentum, establishing a new on-the-ground reality. The half-decisions had erected, brick by legal brick, the cruel institution that would persist and sully the new nation of the United States. The institution would then be destroyed in similar mechanical fashion through a series of improvised half-measures and short-term military decisions that turned into legal realities, building upon one another, gaining speed, persuading the reluctant, transforming the ground with hard facts, knocking apart the bricks of slavery until the whole edifice came down. The American colonies had stumbled into slavery at the eastern edge of the Virginia Peninsula, and here, too, the U.S. would begin to stumble out of it.

When Henry Jarvis arrived safely at Fort Monroe after his night journey across the bay, the U.S. Army assigned him a place to sleep, gave him rations, and put him to work as a wage laborer. He did his job well. At over six feet tall, with "a well-set shapely head, a Roman nose, and the eye of a hawk," as an observer later described him, he was up to the physical challenge. But he wanted to do more than unload cargo ships and chop down trees. He asked for permission in late 1861 to be sent into the field as a soldier to fight the Confederates and, possibly, confront the man who had enslaved him on the battlefield.[12]

Benjamin Butler denied the request personally, telling Jarvis that "it was not a black man's war."

Jarvis's response was as brief as it was prophetic: "I told him it *would* be a black man's war by the time they got through."[13]

1

The Sound of the Hammer

Though he had grown up poor in a Massachusetts mill town, Benjamin Butler loved the peacocking that came with a military uniform. Denied admission to West Point as a teenager, he instead joined the merchant marine, settling on a naval uniform of his own design: a cocked hat with ribbons, an embroidered jacket, and a pair of pantaloons. "You look like a monkey," was his captain's only comment.[1]

A childhood friend recalled Butler as "a reckless, impetuous, headstrong boy" who would fling bursts of invective and peculiar twists of logic at his rivals, leaving them more confused than angry, a rhetorical skill he parlayed into a career as an attorney for impoverished clients.

Butler fashioned himself the champion of the armies of immigrant teenagers, most of them women, who ran spindles at the textile mills of Lowell, Massachusetts. His railing against the "quasi-slavery" in the factories and his calls for a ten-hour workday put him on the wrong side of the elite, who used their organ, the *Lowell Courier*, to slime him as a "demagogue, hypocrite, tyrant and liar."[2]

Butler fought back with relish, even though he yearned for their acceptance. His pugnacious streak was, he once theorized, an "unhappy condition of the mind which has ever led me to be with the under dog in the fight when I thought he had been wronged." One of his favorite techniques in the courtroom was to find a minor hole in the law and tear it vigorously until facts could fall into it. He once got a thief acquitted because he had stolen a key from a lock, which Butler argued should be defined as "real estate" and not personal property. Another time, he sued on behalf of a millworker for unpaid wages and was awarded the waterwheel that powered the mill—an irreplaceable asset that would shut down the factory.[3]

Though a Yankee down to his pegged leather shoes, Butler sympathized with the manners and economy of the South, whose slave-chopped cotton fed the looms of his hometown. But as Southern secession loomed, he accepted a post as brigadier general of the state militia. In the early days of the Civil War, a politician with no military experience could be made a general if he could assemble a few thousand recruits. Butler was just such a well-connected man. He brought another asset: his Democratic Party connections would make the Union war effort look more bipartisan.[4]

Butler traveled by train down to Washington in April 1861 wearing "a vast amount of sash, mountainous epaulets and a scythe sword with a railway curse in it," wrote an amused secretary. He nonetheless won an assignment to lead the 3rd Massachusetts Volunteers to Maryland to keep watch on a gang of secessionists, where he enraged the seventy-five-year-old commander of the U.S. Army, Winfield Scott, after he marched into Baltimore without orders to put down a riot. "I am carrying on the war now on my own hook," Butler bragged to his subordinates.[5]

Scott itched to fire him, but Butler had too much political value as a Unionist Democrat to be cut loose. He was instead sent to command Fort Monroe at the far end of the Virginia Peninsula, seemingly far from the action. "What does this mean?" Butler complained, feeling unappreciated. His wife, Sarah, told him to swallow his pride and accept what had been framed as a promotion.[6]

At 2 p.m. on May 22, the day before Virginia's official secession from the Union, and with war seemingly imminent, he stepped off the steamer *Cataline*, moved into the general's quarters, and assumed command of Fort Monroe, one of the most expensive military installations ever constructed on American soil. The British had embarrassed the young United States in the War of 1812 by sailing up the Potomac and sacking the capital city. Congress had resolved never to let it happen again and authorized a series of fortified gun emplacements at every strategic river mouth on the Atlantic coast. From Fort Monroe—a giant irregular hexagon surrounded by a moat—it was possible to look five miles across the mouth of the James River through a spyglass and see a buzz of construction at a place called Sewell's Point, where Confederate officials were scrambling to defend Virginia's access to the sea.[7]

Some of the richest local planters sent their enslaved men to do the labor of felling trees, planing boards, and nailing together oak platforms to support the battery of thirty-two-pound guns aimed at Fort Monroe from Sewell's Point, and they did their work diligently. The owner of at least three of the best workers, an attorney named Charles King Mallory, let it be known that he intended to take them down to North Carolina to armor up more rebel fortifications against the Yankees.[8]

The scene had turned violent on May 19, when the federal ships *Monticello* and *Thomas Freeborn* drew close and fired a barrage of shells at the four cannons rising from the defensive work at Sewell's Point, "throwing turf high in the air" and causing "momentary confusion in the breastworks." Rebel officers returned the fire and put five holes in the federal ship. The enslaved crews worked through the night making repairs to the gun platforms and filling in the bomb craters. When the sun rose the next morning, the federal convoy fired off a few more rounds before limping away.[9]

Three days later, three of the enslaved workers decided to make a gamble. Shepard Mallory, James Townsend, and Frank Baker slipped away from Sewell's Point and, with the aid of a borrowed vessel, crossed the wide channel of water, ditched the boat, and crept toward the main gate of Fort Monroe. A Boston newspaper gave a brief description: "They skulked during the afternoon and in the night came up to the Fort and delivered themselves to the picket guard." From there, they were brought to the grandest house facing the parade ground, one that might have been described as a mansion, where Butler decided to see them, even though it was only his second night at the fort. He was likely angling for a little intelligence about the enemy's activities.[10]

A woodcut drawing of this pivotal interview, sketched some months later, shows the enslaved men standing in the middle of Butler's quarters, their clothes torn yet their postures erect. The balding general sat at a desk facing them like a minor colonial of-

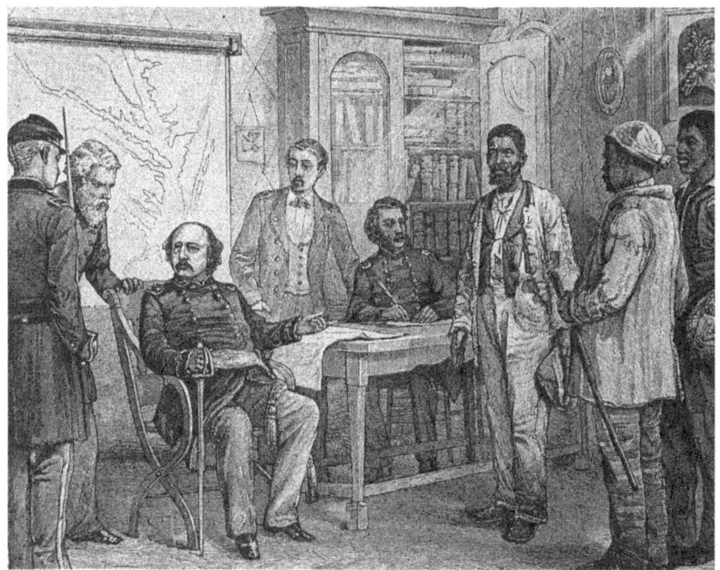

The interview. Shepard Mallory, Frank Baker, and James Townsend found their way to Fort Monroe the same day Virginia seceded from the Union. They would become the first of more than 470,000 escapees from slavery termed "contraband" by the government.

ficial or a county judge, a sword at his side, a map on the wall, and a portrait of a Roman military hero with a garland on the opposite wall.[11]

Butler wrote later that he interviewed them first as a group and then one by one, to check their stories: "Satisfied of these facts from cautious examination of each of the negroes apart from the others, I determined for the present and until better advised, as these men were very serviceable and I had great need of labor in my Quartermaster's Department, to avail myself of their services." In other words, they could help him dig fortifications against the rebels instead of being used as military assets against the Union.[12]

Another visitor came to call the next morning—an old friend, no less. This was John Baytop Cary, the head of the artillery unit of the 115th Virginia Militia, tall and dignified, though in command of only four hundred undisciplined men and engaged in a thousand tasks. Butler rode out on horseback at 3:30 p.m. and they met at the Mill Creek Bridge, which had been partially burned by secessionists the prior week. They knew each other from national Democratic conventions and greeted each other warmly—but with a certain wariness. Cary had orders not to give provocation to the Yankees but to burn bridges and fell trees if Butler should march on Richmond.[13]

The two men carried out their conversation on horseback, leisurely riding up the banks of Mill Creek as they talked. Cary first wanted to know if Butler would lift the blockade to permit families to move around, especially if they wanted to visit relatives in the North. Butler said he could not do anything about the naval cordon but affirmed his assent to freedom of movement by land, reasoning, he said later, that "the families of belligerents were always the best hostages for the good behavior of the citizens."[14]

Then came the heart of the exchange, one that Butler had been anticipating.

"I am informed that three negroes belonging to Colonel Mallory have escaped within your lines," said Cary. "I am Colonel Mallory's agent and have charge of his property. What do you mean to do with those negroes?"

"I intend to hold them," said Butler.

"Do you mean, then, to set aside your constitutional obligation to return them?"

Here was the opportunity for Butler the ruthless attorney to drive in the stiletto. "I mean to take Virginia at her word, as declared in the ordinance of secession passed yesterday," he said. "I am under no constitutional obligation to a foreign country, which Virginia now claims to be."

"But you say we cannot secede and so you cannot consistently detain the negroes."

"But you say you have seceded so you cannot consistently claim them. I shall hold these negroes as contraband of war since they are engaged in the construction of your battery and are claimed as your property. The question is simply whether they shall be used for or against the Government of the United States."

And so, that was that. The horseback parley was over. "Failing in the accomplishment of my mission," said Cary later, "we parted when it was quite dark, and returned to our respective posts."[15]

On the ride back toward the iron gates of Fort Monroe, one of Butler's aides, Peter Haggerty, questioned his boss whether such a thing was legal. The mill town brawler in Butler must have been privately rejoicing at his on-the-spot legal definition that left the Virginia gentleman stumped. "At any rate, Haggerty," he said, "it is a good enough reason to stop the rebels' mouths with, especially as I should have held those negroes anyway."

Within two days of this horseback ride, eight more enslaved people showed up at the gates of Fort Monroe, seeking protection. Dozens more followed in the week after that. They clustered in the anteroom of the general's office "seeking to get a new deal in the game of life," all eager to get the same interview with the general. "Here were seven of them, fine looking fellows, who stood with their backs against the side-wall, like so many Egyptian columns, waiting to understand their fate," wrote George Wilkes, a visitor to the fort.[16]

Amid the tantalizing promise of freedom lay a logistical mess. Fort Monroe was poorly equipped to handle the crush of newcomers. Theodore Winthrop, a committed abolitionist, wrote letters home to Staten Island, begging his old neighbors to send clothes. "Negroes come in every day from outside, and one day as many as forty came into the backyard; of all ages, from babies up to old men and women," reported Laura Wright Hildreth, the general's sister-in-law. "It was a ludicrous and the same time a sad sight to see the poor creatures, homeless, not knowing when or where they would get their next meal."[17]

Butler asked the War Department just how ruthless he could be when selecting which escapees to receive and which to refuse. The escapees showing up at the gates "are very numerous; and a squad has come in this morning to my pickets, bringing with them their women and children." He claimed to be in the "utmost doubt" over what to do about this tricky question. "As a political question and a question of humanity, can I receive the services of a father and mother and not take the children?" he asked rhetorically in his memo to Winfield Scott. "Of the humanitarian aspect I have no doubt. Of the political one, I have no right to judge."[18]

Without waiting for an answer, he made an order to Colonel John W. Phelps of Vermont that served both ends. "All able-bodied negroes within your lines are to be taken and set to work on the trenches and on the works," he wrote. "Rations will be served to them and their families." Unpaid for the time being, they were, in effect, laboring for a different master now.[19]

A terse communication from Secretary of War Simon Cameron on May 30 seemed to settle the matter of the contrabands—at least for the moment. "Your action in respect to the negroes who came into your lines from the service of the rebels is approved." Though Abraham Lincoln was not cited, it is unlikely the new president would have allowed the War Department to make such a monumental change in federal policy without direct oversight. Cameron further instructed Butler to "refrain from surrendering to alleged masters any persons who may come into your lines. You will employ such persons in the services to which they may be best adapted. . . . The question of their final disposition will be reserved for further determination."[20]

But Cameron did not anticipate how fast the news would travel. Within six weeks of this letter's arrival, nine hundred fugitives camped together in a muddy field within range of the artillery of Fort Monroe. Some arrived literally chased in by teams of slave patrolmen, who shrank away from the sight of U.S. Army sentries. "In all my life," reflected a soldier after watching one such pursuit, "I never saw creatures more rejoiced than they seemed to be when once inside our pickets."[21]

Butler had not used the word "contraband" in his earliest written communications, but it seems to have been picked up by the newspaper correspondents on the scene, most of whom viewed the general's decision as a card-shark trick—but a satisfying one. "The whole country laughed at the exquisite humor of the transaction," observed a Massachusetts writer.[22]

The episode also sparked laughter at the White House, starting with Winfield Scott, the aging hero of the Battle of Lundy's Lane in the War of 1812. Using the old nickname for Scott, Postmaster General Montgomery Blair related that "the President told me he had not seen old Lundy as merry as since he had known him, as he was this morning at your decision on the fugitive slave question. He called it Butler's fugitive slave law. The President seemed to think it a very important subject, however, and one requiring some thought in view of the numbers of negroes we were likely to have on hand in virtue of this new doctrine."[23]

The demi-slaves camped outside Fort Monroe, he told Butler, were "the essence of their military operations," and there was reason to think the whole Lincoln administration would soon be on board with this eminently utilitarian measure of robbing the South of a valuable resource, as well as hitting disloyal slaveholders in the pocketbook. As Dr. Henry West of the 125th Ohio Infantry would later calculate, each runaway cost the Confederates an average of $500, and the exodus was "sapping the very foundation" of the rebellion.[24]

* * *

A Confederate soldier found a copy of a newspaper at an abandoned Union post that seemed to hint Benjamin Butler was planning to march on Hampton and make it a haven for Black contraband. In fact, the opposite was true: Butler had ordered a retreat. But Confederate general John B. Magruder decided on a rash course of action nonetheless.[25]

A West Pointer nicknamed "Prince John" by his subordinates, Magruder was a theatrical personality and a heavy drinker. He had seen his share of burning villages during the Mexican-American War and had studied the scorched-earth campaign that drove Napoleon out of Russia. "When I found [Hampton's] extreme importance to the enemy and that the town itself would lend great strength to whatever fortifications they should erect around it, I determined to burn it at once," he wrote in his report two days after the event. A company of the Old Dominion Dragoon militia flooded into the graceful old downtown with torches and canisters of fuel to obliterate their own village, lest it fall into the hands of the Blacks.[26]

The destruction began at the home of Eliza Jones near the wharf and proceeded from there. Philip G. Gibson had spent the considerable sum of $28,000 on his three-story house, complete with a marble portico and gardens. It was soon reduced to a blackened shell. Recalled a young soldier named Robert S. Hudgins, "As the flames rose higher and higher and spread and brighten

[sic] the whole horizon, so did my boyish hopes mount upward—until my whole being was afire with enthusiasm at the part I was playing in the great drama."[27]

The Baptist church and the courthouse went up, and the smoke and fire made shadows on King and Queen Streets as the militia raced from house to house with their lit torches, consumed with mad glee. They broke picture windows with rocks and tossed flaming rags into the homes. A few burned down their own houses. "It seemed as if hell itself had broken loose," recalled Hudgins. There had been no rain for weeks and the plants were dried out. The spreading branches of the oaks caught flame and dabbled flames on roofs, goaded by a powerful night wind from the south. At one point, the light was as bright as midday, "a sublime and awful spectacle," said an Associated Press correspondent, reporting "the glare of the conflagration was so brilliant that I was enabled to write by it."[28]

Sons set fire to the same houses their fathers had built with their own hands. One Hampton native drew the job of destroying the house of Joseph Segar, the genteel owner of the Hygeia Hotel, whose wheatfields were now home to hundreds of refugee enslaved people camped out in the trampled crops. Inside the elegant house, one of Segar's loyal enslaved men was rushing to gather up what few valuables were still inside for safekeeping. "If you don't get out of here, I'll shoot you," threatened the rebel soldier. "I can't help that," replied Segar's man. "Got to get the master's things out of here." The soldier responded by firing his rifle; the shot missed; the enslaved man fled. Segar's house was soon in ashes along with the rest.[29]

St. John's Episcopal Church, a stoic old pile from a time out of mind, went up last, its roof aflame and the ancestral graves of its first families dusted with ash. The inferno became reflected in the waters of Mill Creek. Black refugees shouted and cursed, running in panic from the houses they had dwelt in during a few precious weeks of freedom. Some drowned trying to swim across the river to safety. Others died in the flames. The Associated Press correspondent thought it was the most "awful spectacle" he had ever witnessed.[30]

Hampton burning. Confederate general J.B. Magruder, acting on a false tip, ordered his soldiers from Hampton to torch their own hometown on the night of August 7, 1861, rather than let it become a refuge for runaway enslaved people.

Bugles sounded, calling the Dragoons to reassemble and march back in the darkness, away from the charred stumps and lone chimneys. Confederate sympathizers chased out of their homes, some too old or sick to flee the area, were told to move whatever furniture they could out to the garden before their houses were torched. A few of them hid in the swamps next to Mill Creek. The wounded had to undergo the humiliation of seeking treatment at the fort's hospital. One of them, the oldest resident in town, George L. Massenburg, "an undisguised secessionist," had to be carted over to the Yankee side in a wheelbarrow by his enslaved people. He had nowhere else to go.[31]

Only eight houses and hundreds of denuded chimneys remained intact, with smoke curling skyward from charred remains. A few curiosity seekers from the new Confederacy came in to gaze at the tableau of destruction, signifying the coming of total war to American soil, and, with it, a reinvention.

* * *

The rhythmic pound of hammers, the shouts of workmen, and the whine of a steam engine filled the coastal air as a team of freed enslaved people turned out planks from a sawmill in a forest six miles from the ruins of Hampton. Logs of white pine, spruce, and chestnut oak went into the saws at one end and came out as long boards, "slabs," where they were hitched up to horses and bound for the new settlement everyone called Slabtown, a brand-new version of the old coastal village whose economy had depended on slavery.[32]

The carpenters who had left slavery knew all about practical architecture, and their designs followed a standard. A family typically picked out one of the hundreds of brick chimneys sticking up around the flattened town like porcupine quills. Then they cleared all the burnt and broken wood, the shattered glass, and the wrecked furniture away from the footprint of the old house. In communal style, the carpenters and the new family put up the walls of a great room arranged around the brick pillar, and then topped it with a pitched roof covered with tar paper, or with sheet metal if available. A covered porch might be added, or new rooms could be fixed to the side to accommodate new family members. A side yard with a slat fence might hold chickens or a pig.

The New Hampshire soldier William Channing Thomas took a walk around Slabtown to gawk at the new houses and offered a description in a letter home. "They are of one story with one room which is kitchen dining room & parlor all in one," he wrote. "Their modus operandi is to select a good chimney & then build with mud & blocks or old boards a shanty by its side & they have not a house with a chimney but a chimney with a house." The hearth was, of course, the family center of socializing, cooking, and warmth. This was, for most, the first house they truly owned: a new manifestation of domesticity.[33]

Robert Hamilton, the publisher of the *Anglo-African*, the most prominent Black newspaper in New York, came down for a look. "The disruption of society is perfect," he wrote. "The surface of the country has been burnt over, so to speak, and to a certain extent literally. This therefore will at some time or other become a field for new settlers. The soil is excellent, the climate perfectly healthy and there are many attractions both to the enterprising man and him who would lie at his ease." Slabtown looked like nothing so much as a frontier town of the Old West, with new dirt streets named Union, Liberty, and Lincoln. The Virginia of tomorrow, Hamilton concluded, "will be in other hands."[34]

Where some saw hope, others saw an obscene upending of the social order. The Confederate colonel John Baytop Cary, who had failed to get the enslaved people back from Benjamin Butler, made a return trip to his former hometown under a flag of truce in January 1862 and saw, instead of the graceful homes of his youth, a raw village of two thousand Black men, women, and children. Charred stumps stood like tombstones where oaks had spread their branches.

Cary had trained up a generation of students at Hampton Academy, and he was also a classically trained aesthete who had hung a sign with the motto "Order Is Heaven's First Law" over the schoolhouse door. The disarray in the lunar landscape, the Black people walking about without passes, and the whole "scene of desolation" offended his sense of discipline and order. "Uncultivated fields, cattle roaming at large, ruined & burnt dwellings, all speak with eloquent tongue of the ravages of war," he wrote his wife that night. "They are evidently preparing to occupy Hampton," he wrote, "as the sound of the hammer could be heard from all quarters of the town clearly evinced. What then, we shall see if they succeed perhaps in advancing in another direction?"[35]

Cary's question was entirely prescient. What would happen if the revolutionary activity at Hampton should spread to other parts of the South, and the rest of the nation? The material of an entirely new society was being wrenched and nailed into place from the fragments of the old one. People who had never known what it was like to arise when they felt like it, go to bed when they needed to, or quit a disagreeable job and work for their own wages were now laboring for themselves and their new community, one of the most unusual in America.

* * *

There were oystermen and carpenters; field hands and house servants—most of them born into slavery and some who saw relatives for the first time in years among the muddy fields and torn tents of the camp sprawling outside Fort Monroe. Some of the arrivals, aiming for a homey feel, made small verandas of green boughs in front of their makeshift dwellings. Where they could find a patch of open ground, they planted gardens. Why had they come here? a visitor asked a group of refugees. "We wanted to do better, sir," was the simple answer.[36]

There was Jim Carey, a beautiful public speaker, who always drew a respectful crowd during prayer meetings when he preached of hell and salvation. During slavery, he had been allowed to sit in the balcony at a white church but once "got happy and shouted in a meeting," upon which he was dragged out and threatened with thirty-nine lashes for his exuberance. When Lincoln was inaugurated, his angry master told him, "*You* are the cause of this," to which he replied calmly, "It is only what I have been expecting a long time."[37]

There was Sally Walker, who had labored for years as a house servant for William Ham and his wife, both ardent secessionists, who worshipped at St. John's Episcopal Church and were fond of talking to their enslaved maid about spiritual matters. After Virginia seceded from the Union, Walker told Mrs. Ham she was praying that the Lord's will would be done, and Mrs. Ham grew alarmed and insisted that the prayer in her house be altered to one for the success of Confederate president Jefferson Davis. "She was evidently afraid that the Lord's will *should* be done," remarked a man who met Walker in the crowds outside Fort Monroe. She had made her way out of the Ham household to freedom. A relative of hers, Thompson Walker, later insisted that "we must trust in General Jesus, and not in armies and human arms."[38]

There was Robert Langley Brooks, a seventeen-year-old who had escaped from a Mathews County plantation more than fifty miles away, at a place called Winter Harbor where the soil was pancake-flat and often flooded. The native live oaks had been cut away to make boat hulls, and loblolly pines sprung up like weeds in the cleared fields. The year before, the master Jim Brooks had managed to raise $400 in corn by fertilizing the soggy ground with lime from oyster shells. Robert Langley Brooks lived in a one-room cabin with four others. When he heard he was going to be sold off and transported to the Deep South to pick cotton, he trusted the local rumors about the "Freedom Fort" to the south and stole away to join the refugees, paddling through the mouth of the York River in a stolen boat.[39]

There was a twenty-five-year-old man from the Eastern Shore of Virginia with a similar story. He told people that he fled to Fort Monroe as soon as he could to avoid being moved or sold farther south into the Cotton States, and that slave owners "don't think no more of separating us than a cow and calf." The purpose of the war had been plain to him and his companions from the start. "We knew all about it," he said. "We knew it was for the colored people."[40]

There was Joseph Corsey, who found his way to the fort from a plantation five miles from Hampton where he had often gone all day with nothing to eat but huckleberries and horse sorrel, working so hard in the fields that his malnourishment caused him to stagger home like a drunk. He could still remember the day when he and about a dozen others secured a piece of steak about the size of a human hand, and they "would sop their bread on it until the last bit of bread was eaten," greedy for every drop of protein.[41]

There was Waddy Smith, who walked in with useful military intelligence. "I came from York day before yesterday," he told his debriefer. "I have been at work on the batteries. The batteries are on the right side of the road going toward York. There is another further one left field before you get to town." They were guarded by 150 militiamen, said Smith.[42]

There was Edward Silence, who had details of a skirmish on the James River involving the steamer *Yorktown* that he watched from a battery on Mulberry Island.[43]

There was Israel Field, who had been forced to whip friends of his judged to be moving too slow, a terrible psychological torture. But this pain meant nothing to the enslaver James Downey, for "the black man was a dog in his eye." Field would be haunted the rest of his life by the sight of an elderly coach driver he had been ordered to lash 150 times until he lay bleeding and whimpering on the ground.[44]

There was Caesar Stevenson, whose master allowed him the opportunity to hire out for $150, but made his wife start work at 3 a.m. and refused to give their children any clothing until they were old enough to go to work themselves at the age of eight.[45]

All of them had taken astonishing risks to get here. A correspondent from the *New-York Tribune* watched as a group of enslaved people staggered into camp at Newport News after having rowed six miles "in open boats of the frailest sort," clinging to only a few meager possessions grabbed in haste. "It was a bold venture, that bordered on heroism," he wrote, "a push for little less than life itself."[46]

* * *

The *strangeness* of the experience, the abrupt departure from enslavement, shocked the consciousness of those who experienced it, creating a kind of daze that animated the residents of Slabtown as they built new homes around the bare chimneys of Hampton.

The slave owners' whips were gone. Extended family members saw each other for the first time in years. An unfamiliar lightness of being descended on them. John Quincy Adams had observed sixteen years prior that "the owner of a slave is the owner of a living corpse but he is not the owner of a man." Within the mud, squalor, and sickness of the contraband camps came the casting away of the former body and an emergence of a fuller kind of selfhood.[47]

Almost none of the refugees had been permitted to read or write on the plantation, and thus the precise nuance of their feelings is lost to time. What remains in the record comes filtered through the recordings of a few interlocutors, both white and Black, who noticed "the satisfaction, the sense of security which the sight of the fortress afford[ed]" to those who had fled in the direction of the American flag.

Fort Monroe with all its weaponry provided a particular sense of security. "Once under its guns, they begin a new life and are doubtless animated with new hopes never before cherished," wrote a sympathetic correspondent for the abolitionist-leaning *New-York Tribune*. The freed people "comprehend that a great event has happened, which, if it has not given them their freedom and permitted them to go wherever and whenever they please, has at least placed them beyond the reach of the danger from which they have fled."[48]

A Unitarian minister down from Boston named Arthur Fuller spent considerable time in Slabtown, listening to funeral orations and what he called the "rude and simple eloquence" of prayer meetings amid the tents. His view is colored by the characteristic romanticism of the nineteenth century, but he perceived a distinct difference between the Fort Monroe contraband and the Virginia slave. He wrote in his journal: "Now we may trust they are free from oppression, and that from their limbs their chains, and from their minds and spirits the shackles, have fallen forever. To-day these are not slaves, they are men."[49]

The singing at the evening prayer meetings was "more demonstrative than I am accustomed to or suits my taste," wrote the Harvard graduate, but he acknowledged it was a genuine spiritual outpouring. Male and female voices joined at sunset to sing verses "fresh and warm from the heart": *Shout along children! Hear the dying lamb.* Others sang of viewing the "Promised Land" from the top of Mount Pisgah, the biblical peak from which Moses viewed Israel. Some were improvised hymns rarely heard in the North, the kinds of coded musical messages that had been warbled for decades on Southern plantations making frequent reference to the Exodus story or of the freedom from sin promised by Jesus. In the ruins of Hampton, these verses were sung near the collapsed spires of churches where preachers had expounded on the moral correctness of slavery.[50]

I have a home above
From sin and sorrow free
A mansion which eternal love
Designed and formed for me.

A man in the crowd from New York City insisted the quality of the music was equal to anything he had ever heard in the Broadway theaters, even though the content was "generally of a devotional kind, the tunes being plaintive, and frequently imitations of well-known airs." The singing continued well into the night in smaller groups inside tents, where lamps and candles made shadows against the canvas and people strained to make out Bible verses in the dim light.

Thomas Wentworth Higginson spent his leisure time writing down the strange new lyrics in his journal. A prolific author of abolitionist poetry before he became a U.S. Army officer, his antislavery sermons had gotten him thrown out of his first pulpit as a Unitarian minister. Along the way, he developed a robust correspondence with the reclusive Amherst resident Emily Dickinson, whose verses he thought joyously bizarre and startling. He may have detected a similar type of rebellion against convention in the freed people's hymns. "When I hear a new one in the evening, I run out of my tent," he wrote in his journal. In the judgment of the Black-edited *Pine and Palm* newspaper, "the singing of the groups of colored people in Fortress Monroe" was "one of the most striking incidents of the war."[51]

One of the songs, which had been banned in slavery for its pointed content, left a deep impression on those who heard it, especially those who drew near and joined their own voices in the "singing amid the ruins of the war-destroyed church in Hampton." The missionary Lewis Lockwood thought it resembled the formal liturgy chanted at Trinity Church in New York—"heart worship with formalism." The refugees at Fort Monroe, he said, had "a deep impression they were the second children of Israel. And many of their songs were inspired by the spirit of liberty."[52] The song contained these lyrics:

When Israel was in Egypt's Land,
Let my people go,
Oppressed so hard they could not stand
Let my people go.

A freed man named Carl Holloway repeated the lyrics for Lockwood, who copied them down and sent them to his old employers at the Young Men's Christian Association in New York. By December 1861, sheet music for the song had been printed and circulated. A few white churches in the North adopted it for Sunday services. Although observers who heard it in the "gentle chanted style" in the evening firelight said nothing else like it had been heard before, a YMCA official named Harwood Vernon included a headnote to the lyrics explaining that the hymn was not new: "It is said to have been sung for at least fifteen or twenty years, in Virginia and Maryland, and perhaps in all the Slave States, though stealthily, for fear of the lash; and is now sung openly by the fugitives who are living under the protection of our government."[53]

The *New-York Tribune* reprinted the lyrics under its own titling of "The Contraband's Freedom Hymn," but without the music and without the aura and meaning brought to it by a live performance:

Go down to Egypt
Tell Pharaoh
Thus saith my servant Moses
Let my people GO[54]

The pointed emphasis on the last word, thought Lockwood, was "like a warning note in the ear of despotism."[55]

2

Let No Man Put Asunder

Benjamin Butler liked to go out walking in the afternoons among the muddy fields stretching away from the fort, dotted with makeshift tents of tattered canvas. Formerly enslaved people gathered around, eager to meet the man whose improbable field order had upended the social order within the space of a few weeks, casting them into an uncertain future.

"The General was proud of them, and they seemed proud of themselves, saluting him with a ludicrous mixture of awe and familiarity as he rode past," observed William Howard Russell, the celebrity journalist for the *Times* of London who had come by for a look. Butler seemed to relish the shouted greetings of the refugees living under his guns, as well as the thought that he had gained a significant advantage over the enemy with a courtroom maneuver.

"Just think," Butler confided to Russell, "that every one of these fellows represents some thousand dollars at least out of the pockets of the chivalry yonder."[1]

When an enslaved person managed to reach the Union lines, they were directed to speak with the regiment's provost marshal—the rough equivalent of a military police officer—who questioned them on their identity and the identity of their previous enslaver. In the early days of the war, when regiments were hastily assembled by local politicians, this official often had no special training. Some were given the job merely because they had legible penmanship; others came from educated professions.

One of them was Roswell Farnham, who would one day become governor of Vermont. At that time he was a thirty-four-year-old state's attorney who had volunteered with the Bradford Guards and been handed the job by surprise. "I hardly know what my duties are, except to have charge of all who enter and leave the camp," he wrote to his wife.[2]

He jotted down some brief impressions of the job, which gives a sense of the improvisation and rumors that characterized the first days of the contraband camps—a thrown-together atmosphere that would persist throughout the war.

> The greatest number of visitors are negroes,—slaves who want to leave their masters or who want to come in to sell vegetables &c. The masters have all left and the only trouble is that some of these colored men may be spies. Those who are able to do duty here are put to work, while those who are unable are sent to Old Point—that is Fort Monroe, and the report is that Gen. Butler intends to send them to Liberia. If that is the case this war will put a pretty effectual damper upon slavery.[3]

Though almost none of the Slabtown refugees were ever documented beyond a name in a ledger, and though they might have stood more as assets than as people in the eyes of Benjamin Butler and his U.S. Army superiors, a few of their individual stories were recorded piecemeal in the Black press and in government documents. We can still listen to their voices through these fragments.

The Slabtown pioneers included a spy sent south on a top-level mission; a preacher sent north to sway hearts and open wallets; an idealistic schoolteacher; a married couple with a gift for business; and a ditchdigger who yearned to fight his enslavers on the field of combat. And there were thousands more whose stories went unpreserved, but whose influence had begun to reverberate throughout the country.

"Out of this incident," wrote two of Lincoln's aides of the contraband decision at Fort Monroe, "seems to have grown one of the most sudden and popular revolutions in popular thought which took place during the whole war."[4]

* * *

During his brief return visit to his hometown after the fire and as he looked with dismay at the village of freed people, John Baytop Cary might have spotted an atypically large cabin with a yard big enough to hold six hogs and a front room stuffed with barrels and boxes.

This was not just a residence: it was also a general store well known to the soldiers at Fort Monroe as a good place to buy ginger cakes and other baked goods, and possibly some bootleg liquor. Behind the counter a visitor could expect to see Edward Whitehurst or his wife Emma, a couple who had moved to Slabtown with a chest full of money and an idea of how to secure their futures.

Edward Whitehurst was an example of the "enterprising man" described in the *Anglo-African*. He had been one of the many enslaved people in Tidewater country permitted to "hire out"—that is, do temporary paid jobs for various employers and kick back most of the money to the person who held them in chattel slavery. The oystering and fishing fleet of Hampton would have ceased functioning without this Practice. What tiny percentage of the wage the enslaved workers were allowed to claim for themselves could be spent on luxury goods or hidden away in the ground or another spot of safekeeping.[5]

With enough time and effort, an enslaved person might eventually buy their own freedom. Such capital deposits were treated with the utmost seriousness. Whitehurst was able to accumulate $500 in gold and silver coin by the time he was thirty-one years old. No bank would do business with an enslaved person, leaving Edward no choice but to keep it "in a trunk and with my wife." Emma worked at the Parrish plantation, likely tending hogs or doing various household tasks. Women were rarely part of the "hire out" economy. If Emma had been allowed to raise a small number of truck crops on provision ground and send them to market, she may well have contributed to the family's precious bankroll, which was likely concealed in the trunk under blankets, and never spoken about to others.[6]

On May 27, 1861, four days after General Benjamin Butler had looked at desperate men from across his desk, the Whitehursts unexpectedly found themselves free when, as Edward put it, "my master went off and left me." This was the case with the majority of Slabtown residents. "The number of slaves who run away is not so great as the number of those whose masters run away," noted an observer.[7]

Whitehurst had belonged to thirty-eight-year-old William Ivy, the son of a French Creole sea captain who had bought property in the area during one of his voyages. It was likely that Ivy's father had been employed in the busiest link in the domestic slave trade: the route from Norfolk to New Orleans. The younger Ivy moved permanently to Newport News in 1848 after marrying Ann Parrish, who died of complications from childbirth the following year. Her widowed husband stayed on the plantation to raise his infant son, Edward, who was now an heir to one of the First Families of Virginia.

The Parrishes had faded a bit in prominence and income since the heyday of the tobacco economy, but they still had a name. They came from Irish Puritan stock, but they shunned the colony in Boston and chose to migrate to the booming Virginia shore in 1697, where they were granted twenty-four acres of prime riverside land by the colonial governor. From that initial stake sprung a considerable amount of wealth and prestige. One of Ann's ancestors fought with George Washington. By the middle of the nineteenth century, the family had choice lands stretched in a line along the northern edge of the James River. One of their estates bore the name Cherry Grove. Another held the family cemetery and a small brick house that had stood there since 1750.[8]

The tobacco furrows had been plowed under long ago, but the family still raised a substantial harvest of corn, sweet potatoes, and hogs with the labor of one hundred enslaved people, about half of them children under twelve. A few of them—possibly including Emma Whitehurst—stood by holding pitchers of liquor whenever William Ivy's father-in-law threw one of his legendary summer evening parties. Smart young people came down on the steamboats from Richmond or Baltimore to be "entertained lavishly" at Ivy's house on the river, yellow lamplight reflecting on the water.[9]

Not every gathering was so civilized. Edward Parrish was fond of inviting neighbors over to whip enslaved people for entertainment. Charles Smith, tied to a tree, was whipped with great enthusiasm "for alleged offenses." He managed to dodge a number of the strokes, which stripped the bark off the tree in multiple places. The slashed tree later withered and died. Smith survived.[10]

The twenty-one enslaved people owned by Edward Parrish found themselves abandoned to freedom when William Ivy enlisted with the 3rd Virginia Cavalry and went with his regiment into the forest hoping to lure Union troops out of Fort Monroe. His commanding officer was none other than Charles King Mallory, whose three runaway enslaved people had set the example by seeking protection at Fort Monroe. Ivy's teenage son Edward may have fled with the rest of the Parrish family to Henrico County near Richmond to wait out what many of the slaveholding gentry felt would be a brief unpleasantness.[11]

The U.S. Army gave Edward Whitehurst a job immediately on arrival. "Work was at the root of it all—the very thing that made their presence a 'necessity' militarily," wrote Amy Murrell Taylor, who first wrote of the Whitehursts in her book *Embattled Freedom*. "It was why these refugees were allowed into the Union lines in the first place, and it was the basis for any kind of relationship they would forge with the U.S. Army." Because of his knowledge of the surrounding geography, he and Charles Smith—who had been savagely whipped at the tree as public entertainment—were put to work as army guides. Then, Edward volunteered as a nurse at the Hygeia, the once-elegant hotel turned into a hospital for wounded troops. Perhaps at the age of thirty-seven he was judged too old to be tasked with the hard labor of digging fortifications. At any rate, Edward and Emma showed an evident desire to forgo a government job and make their own living at the general store.[12]

They were hardly alone. An observer in September 1861 said that a multitude of freed people were "industriously contributing toward their own support," declining the handouts of rations in favor of "fishing, clamming and oystering," not just for their own food but to sell the catch to others. The *New-York Tribune*'s correspondent wrote of the commercial activity among the formerly enslaved, "Many of them do washing, and some carry on a brisk business in selling pies, cakes and other things to the soldiers."[13]

The Whitehursts joined this emerging shopkeeper class as soon as they could. Edward reported that they "went over near Hampton & in Hampton and started a store and Bake House," a move made only "by permission of General Butler." His friend Charles

Smith, who had been whipped at the tree by Edward Parrish's neighbors, likened it to a "country grocery store."[14]

With Smith's help, the couple soon became prosperous and joined the ranks of leading Black businesspeople amid the flattened houses of Hampton, where a transhistorical dynamic seems to have applied: after disaster comes economic opportunity. Theirs was not the only pop-up business in Slabtown run by emancipated people. A soldier of the 9th New York Regiment, John England, marveled at the array of "little restaurants where they sell ice cream, lemonade, meals &c."[15] According to a document later filed with federal authorities, the storehouse, livestock yard, and cropland of Edward and Emma Whitehurst included:

> *Six hogs*
> *50 bush. corn*
> *2000 lbs. fodder*
> *40 bush. potatoes*
> *2 barrels flour*
> *40 pound butter*
> *2 barrels ginger cakes*
> *20 acres of corn*[16]

Altogether, this inventory was worth an estimated $722 in the summer of 1862. How much of the commodity wealth was drawn from the original liquidity that the Whitehursts had carefully sequestered in their trunk, and how much of it they may have earned from a year's work selling retail goods to a reliable customer base around Fort Monroe, is impossible to say. The Whitehursts may also have set aside some of the gold and silver coins in the trunk as savings, choosing to invest only a portion of their nest egg.[17]

Their savviness with money was not unusual among enslaved people, and their mercantile impulses were in line with what historians have called the "internal economy" of slave states before the Civil War, in which a substantial amount of currency passed through the hands of people in captivity. The exchange among those in bondage, resembling an underground economy, was not without controversy: it was technically illegal under a 1798 Virginia law that prohibited enslaved people from dealing in "goods, wares, or merchandise." But such commerce was widespread and impossible to stamp out. Some masters thought the tiny measure of independence that came from earned income undermined the plantation economy and its necessarily strict hierarchy. Others thought the psychology of private ownership was a morale booster and an incentive for more enthusiastic toil.[18]

The money for refugee enterprises came from multiple places: the sale of vegetables planted in modest gardens; quilts and scarves sewn in the evening; discreet gifts from sympathetic humanitarians; tips given to household servants; the occasional theft from an unwary master; a kicked-back portion of "hiring out" money for spot jobs on neighboring properties. The most well-to-do were permitted to tend their own livestock, deal in cash crops like tobacco, or run their own fishing boats in the Chesapeake Bay. A few country stores in the region kept separate account books for enslaved people, who typically came in to shop on designated Sunday afternoons, when some courthouse squares and churchyards were also open for "slave markets," buzzing scenes of bartering, socializing, and gossiping. The goods available ranged from staples like flour, cheese, and bacon, to luxury goods like rum, candy, dishware, necklaces, and silver-tipped walking sticks.[19]

The vibrant parallel economy of the upper slave states had allowed couples like the Whitehursts to develop what one historian has called a "dual work ethic"—one for the master, often halfhearted; and the other for themselves, far more energetic, conducted during whatever time could be finagled away.[20]

The abrupt crash of freedom, however precarious and provisional, had now opened a new economic horizon built on the remnants of the old ways. Where did the Whitehursts acquire the "corn, hogs, fodder, potatoes, flour" for their country store? At some point in the summer of 1861, Edward made the decision to travel back to the Ivy plantation with a wagon to claim "the property taken from the farms I raised" to build up his inventory.[21]

This kind of disaster commerce was characteristic of the contraband camps springing up all over the South. Before the Union navy captured the key town of Port Royal, South Carolina, on November 7, 1861, secessionists had tried to destroy their own property by setting it on fire. "Let the torch be applied to wherever the invader pollutes our soil, and let him find, as is meet, that our people will welcome him only with devastation and ruin," exulted the *Charleston Mercury*, praising the "patriotic flames ascending from burning cotton." But they abandoned a wealth of household goods, and it all went to their servants. A correspondent from the *New York Evening Post* watched refugees enter the camp at Port Royal offering for sale "a turkey, a shoulder of bacon, or two shoulders and a brace of hams in the shape of a struggling porker." Those who had horses or a mule could ask for higher wages. Improvisational capitalism was as much a feature of the camps as labor on behalf of the military.[22]

Whitehurst also paid a visit to the sutler at Fort Monroe, John Moody, who sold him additional goods from the fort's general store, presumably at a lower cost than Whitehurst thought he could charge amid the new jerry-built houses and squatter shacks of Slabtown. Moody had become notorious for selling bootlegged whiskey smuggled in via steamship and packed out of the store in bottles squirreled away inside discreet packages, raising the possibility that Whitehurst had an arbitrage sideline in liquor—albeit one that could be conducted openly in Hampton rather than illegally at the fort. Whitehurst acknowledged, too, that he had been partially supplied "in Baltimore," suggesting that he traveled there himself on a wholesale buying mission. Whitehurst's country store occupied an important commercial niche, providing staple foods to refugees beyond the hardtack and stale bacon handed out by U.S. Army soldiers.[23]

With their retail business growing and their social status rising in the improvised community of freed people, Edward and Emma made a renewed commitment to each other by getting married in a church ceremony and having their names recorded in a "government book." Their previous bond seems to have been in the custom of slave marriages with no legal standing, and thus able to be snapped off at will should the master decide to sell one of the partners. The union might have been sanctified by an informal ceremony in which the couple jumps over a broomstick, or been as practical and unfussed as them moving into a cabin together. But this could be a setup for pain, given the looming threat of separation.[24]

"I made some inquiries as to where the husbands or wives of the slaves I conversed with were," wrote a correspondent for the *Boston Traveller* who mingled in the crowds at Hampton in the summer of 1861. "In many cases they would tell me that their husband or wife had been sold off some years ago, and they had never heard of them since. They made the same statement about their children, who are often sold off at about the age of eight years." But in the crowded penumbra radiating from Fort Monroe, the freed people encountered a new reality: a government with an interest in joining freed couples "under the flag."[25]

Among the people from the North the Whitehursts encountered in the summer of 1861 was Lewis C. Lockwood, a white minister sent down by the American Missionary Association (AMA) with a huge job description: distribute clothing, build schools, baptize converts in the waters of Mill Creek, promote Christian morals, and plead with the high command at Fort Monroe for better conditions. He had formed an important partnership with Mary S. Peake, a schoolteacher in Hampton whose now-destroyed house had been a social center of Black intellectual life.

Lockwood venerated Peake as a kind of living saint. "In her presence I was a learner," he wrote, "and, under the inspiration of her words and example, obtained new strength for fresh endeavors in the cause of God and humanity." He may have met Emma and Edward Whitehurst through Peake. In any case, the couple is listed as among the first that he conjoined in a Protestant ceremony on September 29, 1861. He later married Henry Jarvis to a woman named Nellie.[26]

Lockwood did his best to make the ceremonies both divine and personally meaningful. He first preached on the miracle of Jesus turning water into wine at a wedding festival. Then there was an exchange of vows. Because so many couples had told Lockwood how terrified they were of being separated by their master selling one of them off to Alabama or Mississippi, he put "great stress" on the closing phrase of the ritual, often to the point of shouting it: "What God hath joined, *let no man put asunder*."[27]

He then offered separate prayers for each couple, reemphasizing the wish that "no power on earth" could then break the bond of love, and "gave each of the parties a certificate, in handsome form, which they seemed to prize very highly. It appeared to have a most beneficial effect upon the parties themselves, and the whole population." A hundred more engraved certificates had to be shipped down from a printing shop on Brooklyn's Nassau Street to meet the demand. The correspondent from the *Pine and Palm* invited to witness the ceremony when the Whitehursts were married described "ten or twelve couples at the African meeting-house, who desired this sacred service to their domestic union."[28]

Beyond the piety and romantic love behind this rite, U.S. Army policy played a crucial role in this wave of marriage sanctifications in the contraband camps. General Butler had worried about the preponderance of women and children eating up rations and offering no hard construction labor in return. As the historian Stephanie McCurry has argued, marriage was a way to fold women as dependents into a system that imagined men as the chief value units of military emancipation, even though most were "arriving out of slavery inhabiting a multiplicity of family forms" in which sanctified marriages were almost unknown. Northern Christian conscience lined up nicely with what the U.S. Army thought would be most efficient in its war machine.[29]

Lockwood had grown up in rural western New York and was working at the Young Men's Christian Association in New York City when he answered the religious call to the South. His writings paint a picture of a man given to emotional outbursts, struggles with despair, and a feeling that he was the answer to prayers. He worked himself ragged, often walking dozens of miles a day between encampments, and said prayers at up to seven funerals a day. Lockwood's sole vice seems to have been tobacco, and he was forced to make a written apology to his superiors for sneaking cigars when he thought nobody was looking—they soothed his asthma, he claimed.

His dispatches to the New York headquarters of the AMA contained frequent pleas for more clothing, at least $5,000 worth, as some of the Union soldiers were trying to make pocket money by selling shirts and pants to the near-naked refugees. He also lapsed into sermon language at the slightest prompting. A routine note about travel arrangements could swerve into a prayer like "O ye weary sin-laden souls, come to Christ for rest."[30]

Under the leadership of hard-driving businessman Lewis Tappan, the AMA insisted the Constitution had intended to eradicate slavery and preached a gospel that was as much about political salvation as the hereafter. Tappan was already semi-famous for assembling the legal team that argued the 1841 case of the *Amistad*, defending a group of kidnapped Mende people who had revolted on a Spanish ship and ended up in U.S. waters. The Supreme Court ruled they had acted as free men in international waters, establishing an important legal precedent.

Tappan made sure the case received publicity in the *National Anti-Slavery Standard* and turned it into a fundraising machine for antislavery churches on the Western frontier that attracted idealistic young ministers. Many of them were graduates of Ohio's Oberlin College, where both Black and white were trained in the muscular gospel that engaged the roiling issues of the day, appealing to the creed that God "hath made of one blood all nations of men."[31]

On his first night at Fort Monroe, Lewis Lockwood had wandered through the refugee camps and into a meeting in a long building. The worship leader was praying in "a sing-song manner," but the content of his prayer was "very scriptural and impressive." Lockwood then asked for the room's attention. "I told my mission in a few words," he reported, "and my remarks were received with deep, half-uttered emotions of gladness" by people who "felt assured that some great thing was in store for them." Despite his sentimentality and paternalism, attitudes which would be held in low regard today, Lockwood could see what others could not. With its mingling of poverty, hope, oppression, and striving, Hampton was the early blueprint for an America freed of the curse of bondage.[32]

Not every white minister who responded to the emergency call for charity was as optimistic or welcoming. One strict Baptist had worked as a plantation overseer in the South and, because of this experience, professed to hate the institution of slavery. But he retained a dislike of Black people, reported a fellow missionary. He refused to eat with the refugees, let them call him "brother," shake hands with them, "or in any way put himself on a level with them."[33]

Others came down to Hampton expecting to find the pliable cherubs of abolitionist literature or the happy slaves of Southern propaganda, and were shocked to find complicated people with all the standard virtues and failings of human beings, some of them personally likable, others more ill-tempered, all of them hungry, tired, and a bit dazed. "There are some professed friends of the contrabands who came here with great expectations," reported Lockwood, "looking for that on earth which can truly be found in Heaven—they did not think the people would steal or break the Sabbath—and when they see them so much like white people—say 'well, maybe slavery is best for them.'"[34]

Such differences reflected a cultural split among the missionaries, who didn't always get along with each other. Tappan had founded the AMA as a coalition of Congregationalists and Presbyterians who were unreservedly opposed to slavery. But not all of them were willing to let go of white supremacy. A class divide among the donors also complicated the picture: the Bostonians tended to be hardheaded businessmen and university graduates, and there were even some Christ-denying Unitarians in their midst. The New Yorkers and Ohioans were more evangelical and working class, less likely to have attended college or studied Latin or Greek. The New Englander Susan Walker, who had shared a boat with the frontier evangelicals for several days, concluded there was "no congeniality of taste and sentiment" among them.[35]

Lockwood was firmly in the camp of the evangelical New Yorkers. He also had a problem kowtowing to earthly authority. His outspokenness got him into trouble on multiple occasions. When he shielded a freed enslaved man named Brother David from being reclaimed by a master loyal to the Union, one of the fort's medics, Dr. McKay, threatened to have him brought up on charges of "negro stealing." Lockwood also clashed with a quartermaster named Tallmadge, a virulent racist who withheld rations from the freed people. "What more could you expect of old Pharaoh slavery revived under the Stars & Stripes?" remarked Lockwood acidly. He threatened to leak the "whole iniquity" before the press, which irritated the wrong people, and resulted in his ejection from Fort Monroe.[36]

But the blowup had a salutary effect. The War Department moved Tallmadge to another post; and the AMA successfully placed Rev. Charles B. Wilder as the superintendent of contrabands. The missionaries were permitted to claim military rations and use government ferries and railcars at a discount rate. Lewis Tappan professed he didn't want theocracy, saying only it was "the province of the Church to act beneficially on the State." But dynamic events in Slabtown had set another standard. Union commanders were now recruiting pastors from the AMA to manage the camps and giving them government titles—a mingling of church and state that might not have been legally palatable in ordinary times. But within the storm cloud of war, the consilience of abolitionist activism with U.S. policy was gathering force.[37]

The high profile of the controversial AMA at Fort Monroe, in fact, was one of the strongest early indications that the abolition movement was on a shaky path of convergence with the policy of the U.S. government. Wilder knew that his federal appointment only strengthened Washington's entanglement with the cause of freedom, creating an existential threat to Southern slavery. "Every slave drawn from rebellion weakens their cause," he wrote.[38]

* * *

The praying and the singing that was now done out in the open in Slabtown and other contraband camps had been a secret affair on many plantations, where the slave owners viewed such gatherings as potential crucibles for insurrection.

Enslaved people who wanted to worship outside the view of their enslavers had to do it in isolation, typically on Sunday evenings in a wooded spot known as a "hush harbor." A call to worship might be given in an audible code, such as the singing of a particular field song like "Steal Away to Jesus." An ex-slave from Maryland named Peter Randolph said that to fool the patrols, the hush harbor was rarely held in the same place. A scout would mark the site by "breaking boughs from the trees and bending them in the direction of the selected spot," thus giving it an aura of a mobile tent revival, or a universal church in the forest, cloaked by walls of leaves. Eliza Frances Andrews recalled hearing the singing through her bedroom windows at night, "a sort of weird chant that makes me feel all out of myself when I hear it way off in the night, too far off to catch the words."[39]

Plantation owners were entirely correct to be wary of the hush harbor, and not necessarily because plots were being hatched. Here was the unfolding of the real interior-life of the slave, where the servile personality could be set aside and the spirit set loose. After 1861, the hush harbor was where the feigned prayers for the Confederacy mouthed during the master's daytime service could be "corrected" into more heartfelt prayers for the U.S. Army. An enslaved person could hear the roughly told stories of Hebrews set free from Egypt and of the prophecies of freedom to come, driven home by the preacher's exclamations of "Now didn't He say it?"[40]

The ability to read from the Bible, so crucial to a Protestant understanding of salvation, was viewed as a security threat. Most Southern states had passed anti-literacy laws in response to the underground circulation of the pamphlet *An Appeal to the Colored Citizens of the World* in 1829, in which the abolitionist David Walker had called for enslaved people to rise up. "America is more our country, than it is the whites," he wrote, "we have enriched it with our blood and tears." Panicked Virginia lawmakers had given free Black teachers a year to leave the state or be sold into slavery.[41]

But through a combination of determination and the willingness of a master's family to allow it, an enslaved person might learn to read. One such person was William Roscoe Davis, who had been conceived around 1812, when a white sailor raped his mother on a slave ship traveling from Madagascar to Norfolk, Virginia. Davis was sold in succession to three different masters before coming to live at Wesley Armistead's farm outside Hampton, Virginia, at the age of six.[42]

Even then, he showed an independent streak. When the overseer came to whip him with a long cowhide, Davis told him: "No, master. I'll die first." Three hulking white men were then sent to teach him a lesson, and he again resisted, threatening to slaughter at least one of them with a corn knife on his way to the hereafter. After that, nobody tried to whip him. Armistead developed a strange respect for the pugnacious slave, especially when he heard secondhand over the breakfast table that Davis had told people he would go down fighting if anybody attacked Armistead's family. The expression of loyalty had surprised and touched him.[43] When Davis became a driver himself, he refused to use the lash against his fellows.

Neighbors noticed the Armisteads' exceptionally well-kept farm, and Davis told them people worked better "when led, not driven." He enjoyed liberties not given to others, such as being allowed to operate a pleasure boat at Old Point Comfort and keep some of the profits himself. "Still," wrote an acquaintance, "he hated to be a slave and talked like a philosopher about his rights. No captive in the galleys of Algiers, not Lafayette in an Austrian dungeon, ever pined more for free air."[44]

Perhaps because of his favored status, and despite his ambition to be free, his master's son had slipped him a primer and a Bible. "You shall know," he told Davis. One evening, in an experience that combined a conversion with an earthly resolve, Davis knelt before the book itself "and prayed that God would teach me to read it, if only a little." Painstakingly writing out the words of Scripture in a shaky hand, he gradually taught himself to read and write within a year. He thought that the love he had for his wife and children was "the standard of my best feelings," but as he read more of the Bible, he realized he loved Christ even more than his own family, and that "the reading of that freedom-inspiring book" provided an "increased longing after liberty, and an expectation that the day of deliverance would soon come."[45]

Davis became technically free when the Armisteads ran away from Hampton in the days before Magruder burned down the city, resisting the family's pleas to move farther south with them. He moved his family into the new schoolhouse at Woods Mill, and the forty-seven-year-old with "high cheek bones" and "distinct copper coloring" started speaking to the crowds in the open air in Slabtown and other places outside Fort Monroe, bringing the hush harbor practices out in the open. Listeners described him as "an Apollos" who "melted every heart" with his sermons on holiness, deliverance, and the U.S. Army as a vessel of providence "striving to put down rebellion in this land."[46]

Slabtown. Freed people built their own homes in the ruins of Hampton, often using the chimney of a former home as a central hearth.

These were more than stock exhortations. Davis had perceived the society coming into being in the ruins of Hampton as the messy birth of a new America. If his fellow pastor Jim Carey was consumed by signs in the night skies and fiery calls of repentance, Davis was preaching a sunnier kerygma of deliverance. He urged the crowds gathered around him to embrace and enjoy the gift of liberty they had been given because "the virtual emancipation of fifteen or eighteen hundred" at Fort Monroe was actually "the promise of the emancipation of four million."

He assured them: "The Lord works from little to great."[47]

After hearing this extemporaneous sermon on the grass, Lewis Lockwood of the AMA recognized a golden fundraising opportunity. It would be one thing for a white missionary to make a speaking tour of Northern churches to ask for money on behalf of the needy freed people, but if a Black speaker—one with the credibility of having been enslaved himself less than a year ago—could make the same plea, it would be far better. Lockwood wrote to his superiors in New York: "I hope that some benevolent individual will take this man of genius and piety under his patronage."

The AMA found the money, and Davis and Lockwood took the train to New York in the winter of 1861 to begin a speaking tour that included Boston and more than a dozen cities in Massachusetts. They were joined by the Rev. W.L. Coan, who was impressed with Davis's eloquence, concluding he "can do a work such as *no* man who has appeared before the public can do." But it was a difficult trip. A few Southern partisans showed up to throw eggs and verbally abuse Davis with racial slurs. He got a chilly reception in Boston, where missionaries to the Black community were regarded as low on the social scale. Coan blamed "negro hating and Secesh sympathy" for some of the disappointing turnout, though the Beacon Hill clergy also may have played a role by gently badmouthing the effort among their congregants. "If Boston ministers are representative men, then God help the black and the AMA," lamented Coan's colleague Michael Strieby.[48]

Rain chased most of the expected crowd away on January 15, 1862, in New York City, where Davis stood before a quarter-full room at the Cooper Institute, in the same spot where not even two years prior the Illinois lawyer Abraham Lincoln had gone before a skeptical audience in a poorly fitting suit to make a case that the expansion of slavery into western territories was against constitutional principles and ought to be vigorously resisted. He was not then a candidate for president but would soon be nominated by the Republicans. Now here stood a forty-seven-year-old former enslaved man from the Confederate states, whose presence might have been called a direct consequence of those events. Lockwood introduced him, awkwardly, as "one of Uncle Sam's slaves."[49]

If the term bothered Davis, he didn't show it. Instead, he disarmed his listeners with a confession that he was "embarrassed at speaking" because "he had but little education and that he stole." Then came a brief version of his life story that he had practiced for white audiences—the fight armed with the corn knife, the encounter with the Bible, the thirst for learning. He painted a picture of the South's distinctive feature that was well known to the abolitionists in the audience. "What did a slave work for but the grave? That is all I am sure of, except for the lash," he said, in an account published the following day in the *New York Times*. "But he rejoiced in God that there was a day when they would be released from the yoke of Slavery—a day in the distant future."

He finished with a line from "Go Down Moses," the new hymn from Fort Monroe, stating a "hope that the Government would 'let the people go.'"[50]

The most successful of Davis's speaking events, though also one of the most uncomfortable, was at Plymouth Church in

Brooklyn. Its senior pastor, Henry Ward Beecher, was a celebrity who had made his name by emphasizing a loving, tolerant, and even playful God over one of briny judgment. In the words of a later biographer, he was "the most famous man in America," with a talent for showmanship, and a keen awareness that all history is made of publicity. He had already clothed himself in controversy by underwriting an antislavery colonization mission to Kansas in which the free state settlers were issued prayer books, hymnals, and Sharps rifles—the latter for intimidation purposes only, he insisted. He had delighted in the emergence of Slabtown. "You may call them 'contraband,'" he sermonized, "you may with dexterity call them ingenious or evasive names, but the Southern law that said Slave! is broken! Slaves in the possession of the government of these United States can be nothing less than men. They are emancipated."[51]

Another of Beecher's high-profile acts was to occasionally hold "reverse slave auctions," in which a person under bondage would be displayed before the Brooklyn congregation and a collection plate passed to buy their freedom on the spot. Plymouth Church, he bragged, was among the "best slave-auction places anywhere to be found—that better prices were obtained for slaves that were put up for sale here than for any others."[52]

Davis's wife, Nancy, joined him on this occasion, bringing two of their youngest children as props. They had been freed eight months prior by Butler's contraband decision, so it was nothing more than a stunt for raising money for the rest of the Hampton refugees. Davis played a "reluctant role" in the demonstration, throughout which his son Andrew "alarmed the church with screams of protest."[53]

Though it had come with its share of humiliations, Davis's tour was a material success. The AMA shipped hundreds of barrels of clothing down to Hampton during the winter months of early 1862, where Charles Wilder said it had made the difference between life and death. The ladies' sewing circle at Beecher's church had been one of the biggest contributors. One woman sent a check to the AMA's office at 61 John Street with a cover note: "I pray this may be the beginning of the emancipation of the African race." A Chicago couple mailed in their life savings of $300.

Another donor sent two dollars cash with the admonition, "Be sure to take good care of the poor 'contrabands' for God has opened up a new field."[54]

This conspicuous show of support convinced the U.S. Army that the missionaries were competent agents of relief and that handing off that responsibility could free them to prosecute the war instead of caring for the unexpected explosion of refugees. From the teeming camp at Port Royal, South Carolina, Gen. William T. Sherman observed that the AMA could "relieve the Government of a burden that may hereafter become insupportable and to enable blacks to support and govern themselves in the absence and abandonment of their disloyal guardians."[55]

Davis was not the only freed enslaved man on the abolitionist lecture circuit that first winter of the Civil War. "A regular Virginia plantation slave passed through here last week on his way to New York in search of his wife," reported the *Reading Journal* in Pennsylvania. The man, John Parker, told a story of being forced into the construction service of the Confederate army—exactly the kind of military action that Butler's contraband decision had been gauged to prevent. He said he helped three other unwilling men aim cannons at the Battle of First Manassas, though he claimed they deliberately elevated the screws so that the cannons would fire over the heads of Union troops. He also built breastworks for the anticipated defense of Richmond. Here was news to chill Northern audiences: "the South sought to turn its economic slave power toward forced military service.[56]

When a chance came to escape, Parker took it. Like thousands of others, he found his way to the pickets of the U.S. Army, where the soldiers called out, "Come on! Come on! Don't hurt him!" He kept going northward into Pennsylvania, he said, until "I thought when I saw the big barns that I was in another country." Frederick Douglass spotted the story about Parker in the *Reading Journal* and asked him to speak about his experiences at the Cooper Institute four weeks after William Davis's speech. "A rebel negro, in his regimentals, a deserter from Dixie, will be exhibited," promised one advance notice.[57]

Parker and Davis were paraded as curiosities before Northern urban audiences, and there was a strong element of patronizing pathos behind the effort. Yet, when combined with the extensive press coverage of the contraband camps and the AMA's efforts through its monthly magazine to put a human face on the refugees, the effect was galvanizing.

* * *

Wherever William Davis went in the North, he told people about the hunger of freed people to learn how to read and write. "We want to get wisdom," he said at the finish of his stump speech. "That is all we need. Let us get that, and we are made for time and eternity."[58]

This thought electrified a young man in the audience in Boston, a free man of color named John Oliver, who walked out of the church that evening burning with determination. He was a native of Petersburg, Virginia, who had left the South because he had been denied an education. Though he worked at it every day, spelling out sermons by hand, his grammar was still imperfect. He was determined to not just improve himself but improve others.

"Since I have heard Mr. Davis speak of the condition and educational wants of the slaves who are constantly coming into Fort Monroe and other places in the line of our army, I have felt a desire to go and help teach them," he wrote in a rather stiff letter to the AMA's headquarters that amounted to a job application. "And with my knowledge of both slavery and the slave and the condition in which the former has left the latter, I believe that I would be of great service to that people."[59]

Though trained as a carpenter, Oliver had been studying to be a pastor for two years but was willing to interrupt his education, provided he could be paid enough to care for his widowed mother at a salary of $25 a month. Eager to have a Black seminarian from New England as an inspirational figure for the students, the AMA accepted his offer. The leaders of the organization believed in giving physical relief but also put a premium on education, for salvation lay through the ability to understand Scripture, and awakening came "not only by the lips of the preacher but by the evangelist teacher in the school." But Lockwood passed on a warning that life would not be easy for Oliver and that he would have to "rough it" in chaotic conditions down at Fort Monroe. "If he waits to have the way smoothed for him," he told an associate, "he will have to wait a good while."[60]

This was no exaggeration. Oliver arrived at Fort Monroe in May 1862, took a few days to look around, and then went by horse ten miles to the other side of the peninsula, arriving at an encampment of refugees living in cast-off tents with poles stuck at angles in the mud. Most were coughing, sneezing, and generally miserable. Oliver counted 140 children, all sick with whooping cough, dysentery, tuberculosis, or measles, or some combination of those infections. Those without identifiable maladies were "wast[ing] away seeming to have no disease," an apparent sign of malnutrition. An average of three of them died each day. And yet there was a marked absence of crying or distress, as though the brutality of slavery had defeated even the capacity for sorrow. "They will continue to suffer, and even die, and there will not be much murmuring among them," noted a disconcerted missionary.[61]

When J.N. Bebout, a colleague of Oliver's, visited the tumbledown camp on nearby Craney Island, he found 1,800 people suffering there, mostly women and children. But many of them said the portion of freedom they were most eager to claim was not even material comfort but the ability to read. "When I went round among the tents, either day or night, I found them busy with their books," wrote Bebout. "Sometimes ten or twelve would be standing at the end of a barrack or beside a bank where the sunshine made it comfortable to learn their letters from one another, and at night I would find them crowded around almost every fire."[62]

Oliver tried to organize basic reading lessons in the open air, but he found many of the students "rude and inert." He seemed to be doing more shouting than teaching. At some contraband camps, Northern teachers were stunned to learn that a few children released from slavery had not been given names or could not remember them. So they were made up on the spot. The teacher Elizabeth Bouten had to keep changing her roll call lists because the children kept changing their names. A boy named Quash switched his name to Bryan and threatened to "mash [the] mouth in" of anyone who called him the former name.[63]

Unable to find sleeping quarters, Oliver made do by shifting as a guest from tent to tent. The situation grew worse when troops under the command of General Ambrose Burnside occupied the area in preparation for a march up the peninsula to Richmond. Discipline had reached a low point. "I have never seen worse management," complained General John Ellis Wool to the War Department. "Supplies of every kind are scattered in all directions." Soldiers seemed to take the disorganization as license to appropriate their own materials. They dismantled the hand-built wooden shelters of the freedmen so they could use the lumber for their own quarters, uprooted the corn and potatoes planted by ex-slaves for their own use, and, in Oliver's view, acted "more like wild animals than civilized beings."[64]

More thefts and indignities followed. Two Black men were killed in scuffles. The men from General George McClellan's failed Peninsula Campaign forced laborers off their jobs at gunpoint and turned them into personal servants without pay. The army physicians refused to treat Black children, saying their jobs attending to the military were more pressing, but they would occasionally relent if Oliver pestered them. "Good God," one ex-slave lamented, "if this is the way we are to be treated we may just as well be in slavery."[65]

Arthur Foreman had been enslaved but had found freedom after the U.S. Army captured Norfolk. In the middle of the war, he made a living as a freighter, taking pride in his ownership of a shallow draft barge, which he called *Humbug*. He used it to haul driftwood across Norfolk Harbor to fuel the ovens of the army's bakeshop, considering himself "a true friend of the Union cause, always ready to do what I could to aid it." Then, a quartermaster named Captain Dodge said he was requisitioning the *Humbug*—Foreman's only means of income—to help repair a canal. Dodge and his men wrecked the boat; Foreman was ruined. "He never paid me a cent for the use of the boat," he complained. The art of boatmaking was a point of pride among Tidewater freed people, who inherited the skills from their West African ancestors along the Gold Coast.[66]

Over at the town of Portsmouth not far from Norfolk, Warren White had escaped imprisonment in a Confederate labor camp felling timber in a swamp. He found his way to Union lines and was put to work as a nurse for $10 a month. During his off-hours, he cut wood to supplement his income, managing to get ownership of five hundred cords of standing pine and red oak until the day he got cleaned out by the 11th Pennsylvania Cavalry and the 18th Indiana Infantry, who stole his planks and firewood, plus his horse for good measure. The theft landed as not just a financial but an emotional shock to White. Despite this betrayal by federal troops, he swore that "from the beginning to the end of the rebellion, my sympathies were constantly with the cause of the Union. I never did anything to injure it but did all in my power to help it."[67]

John Oliver tried to maintain his idealism in the face of all this trouble, allowing himself to be heartened by the thirst for learning he saw all around him. When Hampton's teachers made an improvised school and chapel out of the Old Courthouse near King and Queen Streets, where a public whipping post used to stand, Oliver came up from his post at Newport News to speak at the rededication, remarking on the irony of how the "slavery Bastille" had been "changed into a place of peaceful worship dedicated to God."[68]

Like the other teachers around Fort Monroe, Oliver was working mainly from printed cards that spelled out the alphabet and a common textbook called the *Union Primer*, published by the American Sunday-School Union. Grubby used copies were carefully passed around at Hampton, a single one shared by perhaps a dozen students, and the AMA put out a call for more than a thousand of them to be shipped down. The *Union Primer*'s method was for the teacher to write out simple words on a blackboard—DOG and CAT were the first examples—and call out the letters individually so that students could distinguish the marks, see how they came together as words, and then make out rudimentary sentences: *The ox is fat; he cannot run. The dog is lying in the sun. Tom loves to run, and skip, and jump. And follow Peter round the pump.* "It is as easy to teach a child to read in six months as in six years," assured the preface. "The great point is to *begin right*." But there were no blackboards at Hampton, no easy way to display the letters or words to a group, and teachers had to improvise.[69]

Though the times were cruel, the answer still seemed as simple to Oliver as when he first heard William Davis put words to it in the winter of 1861. The government need only dot "this Barbaric corner of Virginia over with schoolhouses" to "redeem the land which has been so long cursed by the slavery of their race." The James River could provide them plenty of fish and oysters, and the freed people who had grown up tending livestock and plowing fields knew how to manage their own farms. "Only let them know they are free," he said, "and I have no fears about their future."[70]

3

Away in Dixie Land

Mingling among the crowds at Fort Monroe was a man with a secret.

Abraham Galloway had been born a slave on the banks of the Cape Fear River in North Carolina, but he had escaped his servitude four years before the war began. He had smuggled himself to Philadelphia in the hold of a cargo ship and made his way to Canada, where he could have stayed for the rest of his life. But he paid close attention to the extraordinary news from Fort Monroe and, in May 1861, went to see the action up close.[1]

Galloway had guts and charisma. A writer for a Black newspaper, *New National Era*, who met him later, said he was "tall and rather portly, quadroon complexion, dark eyes, and with a handsome suit of jet black hair. His features partook strongly of the Comanche." He could not read but he was a commanding speaker who had learned to use his voice like a musical instrument, dropping it or raising it to emphasize a point. A New York journalist would later write of his "twinkly and slippery eyes" that squinched closed when he laughed. But when he needed to, Galloway could fall silent and blend easily into crowds, just as he had at the Wilmington docks. Slavery had taught him how to flip an invisibility switch. Even his appearance seemed oddly indeterminate; some described him as light-skinned, but a Massachusetts abolitionist who met him in 1863 said he was "coal black." He kept quiet about his real reason for coming back: Galloway was here to meet General Benjamin Butler.[2]

An abolitionist friend of Galloway's named George Stearns had recommended him as a Union spy and may have hoped that Galloway would be sent behind Confederate lines to spark an uprising among enslaved people against their masters, just as he had hoped John Brown would touch off a revolutionary insurrection. But

Butler had other ideas. No record exists of their first meeting, nor did Butler ever write down anything about Galloway's service—he was too discreet for that—but it was clear that the twenty-four-year-old ex-slave would report directly to the general and that he would perform scouting missions in Tidewater country, posing as a local and almost certainly carrying forged papers identifying him as a free person of color or a slave with a traveling pass.

A sign of his clandestine activities appears in the private diary of Corporal Edmund J. Cleveland, who helped occupy Beaufort, South Carolina, after its capture. Galloway, he wrote, had been assigned to "scout marine landings" for the successful mission to shut down blockade-running ports in North Carolina during the spring of 1862, traveling undetected through swamps and small fishing towns in the marshy lowlands. He put himself in immense danger, as slave patrols were able to identify local enslaved people by the way they talked and comported themselves. The customary penalty for spying was an immediate hanging.[3]

But cold-blooded nerve was ingrained in Galloway's persona. There is no record of him hesitating in his bid for the job at Fort Monroe. And it doubtless helped that his upbringing on the Cape Fear River not far away had given him a local accent and familiarity with Outer Banks customs, along with his proven ability to melt into his surroundings. Much of what he did had to be kept quiet, but rumors about his activities reached the attention of Robert Hamilton, the editor of New York City's *Anglo-African* newspaper, who decided he had to see the legendary Union intelligence operative for himself.

Perhaps second only to Frederick Douglass, Hamilton was the most prominent Black American editor of his time. His brother Thomas had founded the *Anglo-African* in 1859 as a journal of poetry, fiction, essays, and lively debate over the fraught question of whether free Black people should give up on the U.S. entirely and leave for another country. Thomas Hamilton fell too sick to work in the spring of 1861 and sold the paper to James Redpath, a Scottish-born immigration agent for the government of Haiti, who changed the name to *Pine and Palm* to symbolize the botanical continuum between the pine trees of the northeastern U.S. and the palm trees of the Caribbean.[4]

Redpath turned what had been an intellectual salon into a promotional tool for Haiti, "unquestioningly the most fertile island in the New World" and capable of supporting a population of tens of millions—"a natural paradise, requiring only intelligent labor to develop its exhaustless resources." Though the breathless prose drove away many subscribers, he kept up robust coverage of Southern slavery in the first months of the war, at a time when most mainstream publications were prone to ignore it in favor of troop movements. The paper heaped scorn on the Confederacy with a regular column called "Away Down South in Dixie!" detailing slaveholder atrocities. The poetry was equally unsparing. One poem began: *Curses on you, foul Virginia, Stony-hearted whore!*[5]

Dismayed at what had been done to their paper by the hotheaded Redpath, the Hamilton brothers re-founded the *Anglo-African* with a renewed mission to document the monumental changes unfolding in the country, including the growth of the contraband camps. Which is why Robert Hamilton took a steamer to Hampton to meet Galloway in the winter of 1862. Though the button-downed editor and the hardened espionage agent might have seemed an odd pair, Hamilton was no cloistered aesthete. He cited a lesson his father taught him during an anti-abolitionist riot thirty years prior when he had taken his sons to a hardware store on Broadway "and bought us a pistol with the necessary 'fixens,' and told us to do the best we could with it if we were attacked."[6]

The two men went on a walk around the burned areas of Hampton, and Galloway showed him the tentative rebirth happening across Slabtown. Hamilton saw hope in the rubble.

"The houses are not as good nor as large as people desire; but when the war is over and they are assured that the property which they now cultivate is theirs, a very different prospect will present itself to the eye from that which is now seen," he wrote. "Log cabins and slab houses will then give way, and beautiful houses will rise from the ruins of this once beautiful village." He may also have visited a grocery like the one owned and managed by Emma and Edward Whitehurst. "Many of our people have started little stores which will soon grow into large ones if we are true to each other."[7]

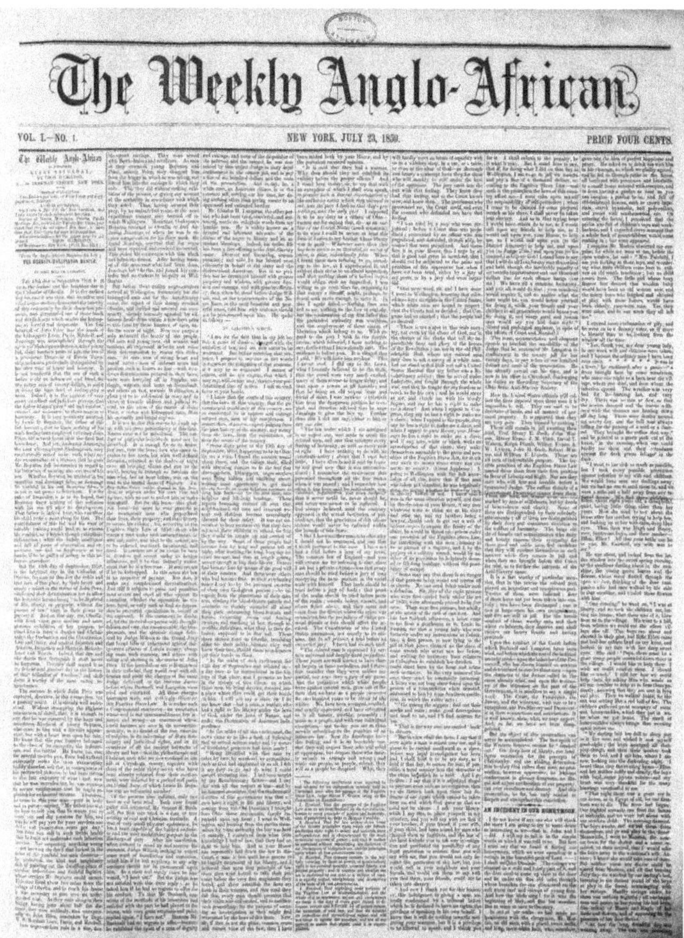
The Weekly Anglo-African

VOL. I.—NO. 1. NEW YORK, JULY 23, 1859. PRICE FOUR CENTS.

The *Weekly Anglo-African* was the nation's premier Black-owned newspaper and the one that most understood the contraband camps as a serious social and political challenge to the North.

Hamilton also went to Portsmouth to visit John Oliver's schools and was delighted to hear the singing. Possibly they performed some of the hidden songs of the plantations such as "Go Down Moses," and he shared with them some popular tunes from the Broadway theaters. Hamilton wrote that he "spent some time in speaking to, and singing with the children, and found that they acquired our tunes with the greatest ease."[8]

The spy and the journalist went into the new First Baptist Church, where William Taylor, a formerly enslaved carpenter, took the pulpit and preached an energetic sermon before eight hundred people just out of bondage. He then introduced Galloway and Hamilton to the crowd. Whatever Hamilton said must have been well received; fifteen people bought subscriptions to the *Anglo-African* that night. And what he saw there gave him hope for the future.

"Although many things are to be seen which make the heart sad," Hamilton wrote, "yet the joys of the present moment must obliterate all sorrows of the past."[9]

* * *

Not long after Henry Jarvis arrived at Fort Monroe from his journey across Chesapeake Bay, the U.S. Army gave him a job. The twenty-seven-year-old field hand likely became one of the hundreds of former enslaved people doing combat engineering in the contested precincts on the Virginia Peninsula. He told a later interviewer that the labor suited his abilities, and he was "getting on very well."[10]

Digging military entrenchments and erecting fortifications took muscle and determination—it was more demanding than field work. Blocks of stone had to be shouldered into place, trees had to be felled, platforms had to be elevated and shaped, and embankments had to be fortified. At coastal locations and on the edge of creeks, men often toiled for ten hours in waist-deep water, slogging through mud. Teams of five dug the ditches, with one man breaking apart ground with a pick, three shoveling away the debris, and one packing the loose dirt on the banks and on the ground. Through this approach, an average of one cubic yard of the sandy soils of coastal Virginia could be moved per hour.[11]

Behind Confederate lines in Virginia, enslaved people faced significantly worse conditions, with meager rations and the threat of whipping. Robert E. Lee, trained as an engineer, was such a proponent of entrenchments that his men called him "the king of spades," and he made heavy use of slave labor to harden Confederate targets. The three original freed people at Fort Monroe—

Shepard Mallory, Frank Baker, and James Townsend—knew exactly the kind of sandhog jobs they were abandoning when they applied to Butler for their freedom. They may have worked in essentially the same role for the federal government, perhaps alongside Henry Jarvis.

In the autumn of 1861, the U.S. Army became fixated on the idea of throwing up improvised fortifications. Classic Napoleonic tactics emphasized slowing down enemy advances while holding strategic ground, but modern improvements had changed the game somewhat. The invention of a cylindro-conoidal bullet nicknamed the "Minié ball" in 1849 meant that a musket rifle could now fire at double the range of an old smoothbore rifle, creating the need for thicker fortifications. A Minié ball could pierce three feet of dirt, or twenty inches of stacked elm boards.[12]

The West Point engineering professor Dennis Hart Mahan laid out recommendations for the coming war in a manual called *A Treatise on Field Fortification*, which was embraced by most Union commanders, some of whom had never received formal training. Mahan emphasized preparing the battlefield ahead of time, erecting parapets of dirt and oak logs, perhaps reinforced as thick as twenty feet to survive a direct artillery shot, with a raised platform called a "barbette" for soldiers to ascend, squeeze off a round, then duck back to safety. All trees in front of a parapet should be chopped away with stumps no higher than two feet to create a "kill zone" of about a thousand yards, the range of a good Minié ball, and the ground in front scattered with barriers of sharpened logs, or palisades, and staked telegraph wire crisscrossed at knee height to trip up advancing troops.[13]

The effect of building "defense in depth" was not only tactical but psychological: it gave regiments a sense of confidence and safety. "We worked all night throwing up fortifications," wrote Col. Daniel Harvey Hill to his wife after he reached Yorktown in the summer of 1861, and "are now in a very strong position and I have not the slightest uneasiness." As they dug into the sandy soil, his crews found "human bones, powder, cartridges, bombshells," and other artifacts from the siege of Cornwallis during the Revolutionary War eighty years prior. Miniature cities of redoubts and parapets went up across Virginia, with the bulk of the work accomplished by Black men on both sides. Enslaved people working alongside Black convicts put up a chain of field fortifications for the Confederate army around Richmond that stretched twelve miles.[14]

Many Union soldiers were delighted to see formerly enslaved people doing the hard preparatory labor of war, relieving them of the burden. As a private in a different theater would later observe: "One hour's digging in Louisiana clay under a Louisiana sun and we are forever pledged to do all we can to fill up our ranks with the despised and long neglected race." At Fort Monroe, a particularly brutal sergeant named Smith was prone to use a slaveholder's whip on those he thought were working too slow or who asked impudent questions about when they would get paid. Some received less than 50¢ a month, far less than the promised $10. "The men in the employ of the government need the money they so industriously earn to provide necessities for their families," protested a missionary. "Why is it withheld?" Hundreds of freed people gave up on working directly for the government and hired themselves out as servants to the officers, who were more likely to pay cash. "He can brush a coat, black boots, take charge of a wardrobe, drive hard bargains with the sutler, explain the geography of the country for fifty miles around, tell at any time just where the enemy is posted and in what force, and withal—as I am informed by his present possessor—can concoct every sort of beverage known in the Virginia vernacular, with consummate skill," wrote an admiring Captain Timothy Gordon of the new personal valet to Company G of the 4th Massachusetts Regiment. "If such a piece of property isn't contraband, what is?"[15]

Despite the intermittently odious terms, the freed people worked hard for the U.S. Army. "They are faithful, cheerful and even zealous," reported an observer. Every morning he watched men taken out on work details "always marching in regular order, under the direction and leadership of one of their number." A visiting member of a Northern Sanitary Commission described the laborers as "quiet, respectable, industrious, but depressed folk, with far more agreeable expressions than one could ever hope to see in a low white laboring class." A Union sergeant was duly impressed with those working under his direction. "Fifty of them will do more work in a day than a hundred of the white men he used to have." Despite the hardships, only a handful said they were too sick to work. The vast majority were up at dawn every morning, ready to lift, dig, and sing work songs in cadence. Thanks to their construction of defenses, wrote a *Chicago Tribune* correspondent, "Fortress Monroe may safely be set down as impregnable."[16]

The wood that went into these fortifications denuded forests in every direction, a common landscape feature of the Civil War. A piece of countryside could look as though a battle had been fought there before a single shot was fired. Locals had no say in this sudden militarization of nature. "The 96th Regiment cut down about 15 acres of heavy timber yesterday, mostly beech nut," wrote Private Joseph Whitney. "It was the prettiest grove I ever saw. The man that owned it was a rebel colonel. His wife offered our colonel five thousand dollars if we let it stand, but no, it was military necessity."[17]

While freed people were generally kept away from combat at this stage of the war, military construction duty was not without its hazards. Injuries from falling logs or collapsing ditch walls were commonplace. Workers risked losing fingers in the saw, or injuries from tools that caused infected wounds and resulted in crude amputations. A fort-in-progress also served as a ripe target for guerrilla attack, and the freed people had no weapons to fight back. In Elizabeth City, North Carolina, Major J.W. Wallis sent a dozen Black laborers recently free from slavery to help soldiers gather wood. Confederate raiders attacked the party, killing one and wounding two. Such ambushes were a feature of the remaking of the coastal landscape.[18]

A new commander at Fort Monroe, John Ellis Wool, tried to bring some order to the construction sites. He came into his new post in the first week of September 1861 at the age of seventy-seven, after a career spent in virtually every U.S. military theater of the nineteenth century. He had been shot through the thighs by British snipers while leading a commando raid in Canada during the War of 1812; hustled the Cherokee out of Georgia on orders from Andrew Jackson; fought the Mexican army with Zachary Taylor in the mountain notch at Buena Vista; and cracked down on American settlers' persecution of the Yakima and Cayuse in Oregon Territory.

Wool grew up as an orphan on the streets of Troy, New York, and had taught himself how to be a lawyer without an apprenticeship. He had a lean face, a stern disposition, and could still mount a horse without assistance. "General Wool looks vigorous and active—by no means as old as some of the papers represent him to be," enthused a writer from the *New-York Commercial Advertiser*, perhaps hoping to curry favor with the new commander from the Empire State.[19]

When Wool arrived at Fort Monroe the first week of September 1861, he found a four-month-old refugee camp sprawling in all directions with vague promises of work, wages, and freedom going unfulfilled by sullen quartermasters. "We have now too many crazy people at this post," he confided to a fellow general. Wool did not much care for Butler's term "contraband," and he thought Slabtown was a disgrace. He issued General Order No. 34, which established two classes of workers: "able-bodied" men who were to receive $10 per month, and "Negro boys from 12 to 18 years of age and sickly and infirm negro men," who got $5. But the payments, which included food and clothing, could be withheld by the quartermaster and were intended not to establish a foundation of an independent life but rather as "an incentive for good behavior." Wool's preferred term for the escapees of plantation life was one ripped from the poorhouse laws of his native Troy: "vagrants," people too drunk or shifty to hold a steady job or care for their families.[20]

Trouble persisted. If anything, Wool's new orders made life worse. The War Department did not provide nearly enough money to pay those men who were digging trenches, unloading ships, and building bridges. The directive made no provisions at all for women. Quartermasters were withholding wages based on a whim and putting the limited money into a community chest called "the contraband fund." People like Henry Jarvis had risked their lives to reach Union lines and chafed at being treated as wards of the state.

If the freed people were dependent on the beneficence of the U.S. government, the dependence ran both ways, because within the space of six months, the U.S. Army had become reliant on the muscle and sweat of those who had found their way into the pickets. A visitor thought "it would be difficult to get along without them, so useful and almost indispensable have they become on the docks, in the making and working of the railroad for the transportation of government stores, and in a variety of avocations." The army, he went on, could more easily spare an equal number of white soldiers than it would be able to give up what amounted to several regiments of Black combat engineers. Should the contraband camps be suddenly evacuated, the government would be "seriously embarrassed" and operations at the post would grind to a halt.[21]

Pressures mounted on Wool. He rethought General Order No. 34 and came out with a new directive four months later, appointing a commission to investigate the wage complaints and naming Charles B. Wilder to the new position of superintendent of contrabands. This was a significant move because Wilder was no soldier. He was a pastor in the employment of the American Missionary Association.

Wool had been far more receptive to the offer of direct charity than had General Butler, mainly because it would take the responsibility off his hands and let him fight a war. His biggest priority was getting the fort ready for a massive influx of troops that would march up the Virginia Peninsula, capture Richmond, and end the rebellion as soon as possible. "I have urged for months Fort Monroe as a basis of operations against the Army of the rebels," he assured General George McClellan, the commander of the Army of Potomac. Wool was now as aware as anyone of the importance of the freed people's labor, and how the AMA had eased their jarring transition into a troubled state of semi-liberty.[22]

Wool left almost no reflections in his personal papers regarding the status of freed enslaved people, but he told the missionaries he respected "the principle that Black People should have the same rights as white people," and he was firm in his conviction that no rebels should be allowed to recapture their human property. "General Wool is friendly," reported an AMA representative in a hopeful tone.[23]

This was made clear by one of Wool's only recorded conversations with a former enslaved person, occurring after his owner showed up at Fort Monroe demanding his return.

"Are you willing to go back?" Wool asked the refugee.

"I do *not* wish to, sir."

"Then you shall not be forced to go, and if any man attempts to molest you, come to me."[24]

The general's house was a five-minute walk from the eastern edge of Old Point Comfort, where ocean waters lapped at the shore and where visitors with a sense of historical imagination took seaside walks there in quiet moments, trying to visualize what the shore must have looked like 250 years before, when English sails first appeared on the horizon.

The fishhook-shaped spit was known for more than just being the home to Fort Monroe. Educated Americans of the time knew it as the same spot where the ships *White Lion* and *Treasurer* landed in late August 1619 with the first enslaved people from Africa to be brought to the Virginia Colony. The broader truth about North American slavery was more complicated: it had flourished under European powers in the Caribbean far longer than that. Hundreds of enslaved Africans had been brought to Florida by the Spanish as early as 1526. But as a symbolic point of entry for the Anglo-American colonies, Old Point Comfort loomed in the popular imagination as the birthplace of the peculiar institution.[25]

A correspondent of the Black-edited newspaper *Pine and Palm* made the connection plain to its readers. America's first village of freed people living under military protection was "within sight of the spot where the first slave cargo was landed in this country."[26]

4

The Ghosts of 1619

On the afternoon of April 26, 1607, a pillar of woodsmoke rose above the blanket of cedar and cypress trees near a peninsula where Algonquin-speaking peoples launched birchbark canoes into the ocean.

A small party of fishermen was barbecuing oysters over an open flame when rustling in the woods startled them: a creeping sound of unseen strangers approaching, crashing through the brush. The hunters ran away frightened. Minutes later, a band of men from the Virginia Company of London, dressed in plate armor and carrying swords, happened upon their abandoned feast in the clearing.

They helped themselves to the abandoned food. The oysters, reported George Percy, "were very large and delicate in taste."[1]

He had other reasons to be dazzled. The company's three ships—the *Susan Constant*, the *Discovery*, and the *Godspeed*—had hit a violent storm on their way from England and been knocked off course. The ablest soldier among them, John Smith, had been suspected of plotting mutiny against the Virginia Company and was locked up in a ship's cargo hold. The attempt by a joint stock company to establish a trading beachhead on the far side of the globe might well end in starvation and failure. But now here was a place where fisheries seemed abundant, with, Percy wrote, "fair meadows and goodly tall trees with such fresh waters running through the woods," and fields with "fine and beautiful strawberries four times bigger and better than ours in England." One man took a handful of dirt to his mouth, tasted it, and proclaimed the new earth fertile, even "spicy."[2]

The woods held unknown entities, making noises as the light disappeared from the treetops. "At night when we were going abroad," wrote Percy, "there came the savages creeping upon all fours from the hills like bears, with their bows in their mouths." After a hail of arrows and a brief skirmish, they melted back into the cypress.

Two days later, Percy and the rest of the party crossed the wide mouth of the river and came ashore on the coastal spit. "We rowed over to a point of land where we found a channel, and sounded six, eight, ten, or twelve fathom which put us in good comfort," he said. "Therefore we named that point of land Cape Comfort." The name would eventually change to Old Point Comfort.[3]

The swash and backwash of ocean waves coming at the shore at oblong angles throughout the Ice Age had pushed trillions of sand particles above a layer of sedimentary rock. The steady creep of sand over eighteen thousand years had also brought in a scattering of skeletal debris: diatoms, shark teeth, whale bones, which all hardened into an angular berm marking the entrance to an estuarine river draining the uplands.[4]

Twelve fathoms would be deep enough to accommodate a large cargo vessel, and it meant this river, which they named James after their king, could be an ideal entrepôt for accessing the wealth of the interior. The shareholders in London had instructed them to build their stronghold on a river bending to the northwest—as this one did—in the belief it would lead them to "the other sea" that went to India. John Smith, once released from the brig, esteemed the point's strategic value as "a little island fit for a castle."[5]

Five members of the Powhatan band hesitantly approached the men from England at Old Point Comfort, not knowing what to expect. Captain Christopher Newport held his hand over his heart in a wordless sign of friendship. "In all your passages you must have great care not to offend the naturals if you can eschew it," the orders from London had instructed. The advance party laid down their bows and bid the English to come visit the village called Kecoughtan, "Great Town," where they were fed a supper of corn cakes and offered draws on a copper pipe stuffed with astringent tobacco. A temporary friendship was forged.

But the English kept seeing pillars of smoke rising above the treetops. They pressed forward through the columns and up the river looking for "the strongest, most wholesome and fertile place" to build a fortress, as the shareholders had directed them. On May 8, 1607, they spotted another Powhatan town whose leader seemed unaware of the peace made at Old Point Comfort. He demanded to know why they were there and aimed a notched arrow menacingly at them, "willing us to be gone." The explorers put their hands over the hearts and withdrew.[6]

Five days later, after erecting a cross at the entrance to Chesapeake Bay, they found a spot on the northern shore of the river that seemed right, loaded their casks ashore, and started putting up a crude log palisade to ward off possible attacks. The men slept under tattered tents, or out in the open, while Newport continued upriver to look for the rumored Appalachian Mountains and the passage to the fabled other ocean.[7]

The first residents of Jamestown could not have known it, as all the evidence had been concealed, but their spot had been damned by an event 35 million years prior. A meteor-like object called a bolide had slammed onto the planet's surface at a spot twenty miles to the northeast of Old Point Comfort, digging a shallow crater that would become the Chesapeake Bay and destroying the natural aquifers in the substrata that would normally hold vaults of fresh water. The bay's placid surface gave no hint of the geological trauma buried beneath its sandy bottoms, covered with a carpet of eelgrass and teeming with oysters and crabs.[8]

The Jamestown colonists puzzled at their inability to find natural springs at any spot in the woods around their fort. Salt water kept leaching into any well they tried to dig. They were reduced to drinking the brackish water from the James, full of "slime and filth." Parasites crept into men's intestines. John Smith went off to broker a renewed peace with the Powhatan and trade iron hatchets for bundles of corn, and returned to the squalid fortress littered with new graves and men so lethargic they could barely be roused to plant life-saving crops in time for the upcoming winter. These were soft-handed gentlemen adventurers, unaccustomed to hard labor.

Venturing forth to plant seeds in the marshy ground required nerve. When they wished to make a territorial point, the Powhatan emerged from the woods with a moss-stuffed effigy of their god Okeus as a warning. They danced in front of it, said Percy, "so strangely painted, grimed, and disguised, shouting, yelling, and crying as so many spirits from hell could not have showed more terrible." As hoarfrost crept into the shortening nights of 1607, Jamestown teetered on the edge of extinction. A strange disease, probably typhoid fever, ran through the encampment, bred from the warm and stagnant waters of Chesapeake Bay—the "Great Water," or K'tchisipik in Algonquin. "Our men were destroyed with cruel diseases as swellings, fluxes, burning fevers and by wars," wrote a despairing Percy in a memoir published in London the following year. "There were never Englishman left in a foreign country in such misery as we were in this new discovered Virginia."[9]

John Smith had a touch of grandiosity and he looked about at the woods with a prospector's vision. There was, he wrote, "more land than all the people in Christendom can manure, and yet more to spare than all the native of those countries can use." He tried to persuade the Powhatan not to kill or maim the English when they ventured outside their flimsy log walls to plant corn or beans. As a witness to an earlier conveyance of this message, Percy said the inhabitants "murmured at our planting in the country." But Parahunt, son of Wahunsenacawh, chief of the Powhatan, argued for letting it happen. "They take but a little waste ground which does you nor any of us any good," he reasoned.[10]

The directors of the Virginia Company had been clear in their charge letter: be subtle regarding the long-term purpose of the colony. Do not build the fortress too large or alarm the Natives with the idea that you mean to usurp their lands. Stay on amiable terms and trade goods with them "before they perceive you mean to plant among them." Let the troubling idea edge gently forward in the mind. Smith had given assurances to his hosts that he and his friends were only seeking temporary refuge from a Spanish naval assault—not exactly true—and would be on their way shortly.[11]

Parahunt's dismissive assessment seemed correct. The English were too sloppy to make anything they achieved seem lasting. The "starving time" of 1609 had left only thirty-eight men alive, and John Smith gravely injured. He had gone to sleep on the deck of a small boat when a stray spark or ember set off a pouch of gunpowder fastened to his belt, nearly blowing off his genitals.

Whether it was a freak accident or an assassination attempt was never established. Smith returned to England for treatment, and while there he published a detailed map of Virginia that explorers used as a standard for the next seventy years.

Persuaded their investment was in trouble, the London directors paid 1,500 pounds for the construction of a new supply ship to ferry emergency food and at least five hundred migrants. The *Sea Venture* ran into Atlantic thunderheads that "beat all light from heaven, which like a hell of darkness turned black," and violent waves crashed over the gunwales, nearly sinking the ship. Water leaked through the gaps in timbers that hadn't set; passengers frantically tried to plug them up with rags and hunks of salt beef, while others bailed water to the point of physical collapse. The storm receded but the waterline crept upward. After an "Egyptian night of three days of perpetual horror," the structural wound apparently fatal, the exhausted travelers resigned themselves to a water grave and pulled cherished bottles of liquor out of their cabins, drinking toasts to one another in hopes of meeting again in a different world.[12]

Then came a salvific cry of "Land!" from Captain George Somers. The doomed vessel had drifted miraculously toward the palm-fringed edge of Bermuda. Somers aimed the prow straight for the beach and ripped open the hull on a set of reefs. The survivors crafted makeshift vessels from the remains of the *Sea Venture* and staggered into Jamestown nine months late. William Strachey, a writer who had been a passenger on the ship, wrote a dramatic account of the wreck and self-rescue in a letter to the London office, which leaked to the public.[13]

News of the spectacular voyage captured the imagination of Britons. The overseas territory of "Virginia" had been a distant fantasy since the days of Elizabeth I, when her favored subject Sir Walter Raleigh had directed the planting of the Roanoke colony in 1585 and named the unknown lands to the northwest for his Virgin Queen who had tried to unite the nation's religious factions under the *Book of Common Prayer*. A 1605 comic play called *Eastward Hoe* used Virginia's promise as a major plot point—a sunny character named Captain Seagull avers, "We should find ten times more comfort of them there than we do here," in a land "without any soldiers or lawyers or taxmen."[14] Strachey's letter caught the interest of William Shakespeare, who had friends inside the Virginia Company's boardroom. One of his last plays, *The Tempest*, tells the story of an aging magician on a New World island who encounters the aristocratic Italian survivors of a shipwreck. In an early scene, the windbag Gonzalo imagines what kind of society he would create if he were made king over the island: a blessed anarchy without the need for money, laws, or the compulsion of labor.

> Letters should not be known; riches, poverty,
> And use of service, none; contract, succession,
> Bourn, bound of land, tilth, vineyard, none;
> No use of metal, corn, or wine, or oil;
> No occupation; all men idle, all,
> And women too, but innocent and pure;
> No sovereignty.[15]

The chance of a fresh start, a reborn country, was enormously appealing to some Londoners sick of polluted streets, religious strife, capricious government, and bone-breaking work. Shakespeare seemed to recognize the hunger for a tabula rasa and reflected it back in a form of science fiction. Yet he also recognized the worm in the apple—the possibility that corruption and sin would only be replicated in the unsullied new place. It could go either way; the die had not yet been cast. The magician Prospero—the name a cognate for "prosperity"—had for his companions a poet named Ariel and a rough laborer called Caliban. Forced to haul wood, pick berries, and other rude chores, Caliban calls Prospero a "tyrant" and yearns for freedom.

At the moment Shakespeare was writing, the Virginia Colony was on the edge of a significant change. One of the passengers on the *Sea Venture* had been a young striver from Norfolk named John Rolfe who had brought an illicit treasure with him: a pouch of tobacco seeds of the coveted Orinoco strain then being grown by Spanish overseers in the colony on the island of Trinidad. Mindful of their monopoly, the Spanish authorities threatened the death penalty on any foreigner caught exporting the seeds. The sweet-flavored tobacco took easily to Virginia soil and soon became an edgy consumer craze back in England. Jamestown had found its economic footing.

Rolfe helped ease local tensions by marrying Pocahontas, the high-spirited daughter of the regional leader Wahunsenacawh, and bringing her to England to meet King James at court under her baptized name Rebecca. Though she died of an unknown illness and was buried at Gravesend before she could return home, the marriage created a period of tranquility that opened the way for the English to plant more settlements in the James River corridor. Rolfe, also a trusted deputy of Virginia Company director Edwin Sandys, sent handwritten updates on colony doings.

In January 1620, a letter from Rolfe arrived with the following news:

> About the latter end of August, a Dutch man of war of the burden of 160 tons arrived at Point Comfort, the commander's name Capt. Jope, his pilot for the West Indies one Mr. Marmaduke an Englishman. They met with the *Treasurer* in the West Indies, and determined to hold consort ship hitherward, but in their passage lost one the other. He brought not anything but 20. and odd Negroes, which the Governor and Cape Merchant bought for victuals (whereof he was in great need as he pretended) at the best and easiest rates they could. He had a large and ample Commission from his Excellency to range and to take purchase in the West Indies.[16]

The ship that had landed at Old Point Comfort with the "20. and odd Negroes" to trade for food was the *White Lion*, an English privateer vessel in violation of a 1604 agreement between England and Spain to stop the pirating and raiding that had plagued the Caribbean during the reign of Elizabeth I.

The human cargo were people from the Kingdom of Ndongo in present-day Angola, refugees from a war started by Imbangala mercenaries in partnership with Spanish slave merchants. The captives had been shackled by the neck, loaded aboard the *San Juan Bautista*, and set on a hellish journey across the Atlantic. "They are so tightly packed, so nauseated, and so maltreated," wrote a disgusted friar of the conditions on a typical vessel. "They lie with one head to another's feet and are imprisoned below deck, closed off from the outside, where they do not see the sun or the moon. There is no Spaniard who dares to put his head through the trapdoor without vomiting, nor stay below for an hour without the risk of serious illness. Such is the stench, oppressive crowding, and misery of that place."[17]

Nearly half the oceangoing prisoners died en route from starvation and disease, and the captain sold twenty-four children away from their parents during a Jamaica layover, before the ship was intercepted by the *White Lion* and the *Treasurer* off the Bay of Campeche in Mexico and relieved of its remaining human cargo as plunder.[18]

The *Treasurer*'s role in this hijacking would become crucial, as it was partly owned by Sir Robert Rich, the Earl of Warwick, an ambitious and handsome adventurer who had started to colonize Bermuda. He didn't mind flouting the new restrictions on piracy. Nor did he have any scruples against imitating the Spanish practice of enslaving Africans. He wrote his brother in 1617 that Bermuda had a "good store of neggars which Mr. Powell brought from the West Indies," where transatlantic slavery was already flourishing. Now it seemed Rich wanted to export slavery to the Virginia Colony, where he had an important connection: the other part owner of the *Treasurer*, Samuel Argall, was a former governor and could be expected to make sure the ship wouldn't be turned back.[19]

The writer and Virginia politician John Pory complained about the piracy, as well as Argall's implicit participation in the slave trade. "He more for love of gain, the root of all evil, than for any true love he bore to this plantation, victualled and manned her anew, and sent her with the same commission to range the Indies." Pory also worried that the unsavory commerce would lure Spanish warships to the colony.[20]

The startling new development at Old Point Comfort did not necessarily square with contemporary English sensibilities. While it was true that Queen Elizabeth I had licensed a gangster-like noble named John Hawkins to conduct three raids into the interior of Africa in the 1560s to round up "Saracens," the Vatican's term of art for Muslim captives turned into slaves, the Protestant English still fancied themselves morally superior to the Spanish and viewed slavery as just another Catholic barbarism. Royal Navy sailors lived in dread of being put in coffles themselves by Moorish privateers. John Smith wrote with contempt of watching his kinsmen "all sold for slaves, like beasts in a market-place."[21]

The centuries-long eclipse of feudalism had created a distinct notion of English freedom. In the widely read proto-encyclopedia of the *Holinshed's Chronicles* in 1577, contributor William Harrison could note with a touch of nationalistic pride: "As for slaves and bondmen we have none, nay such is the privilege of our country by the special grace of God, and bounty of our princes, that if any come here from other realms, so soon as they set foot on land, they become so free of condition as their masters, whereby all note of servile bondage is removed from them." The body of custom and statute known as English common law had oriented itself around the principle, later given voice by John Locke, that humanity is born inherently free. Government policy should lean *in favorem libertatis*—in favor of liberty. King James I himself appears to have been unenthused about getting involved in the trade in forced labor, then seen as a distasteful business of the Spanish and Portuguese. When he granted a patent to an outfit called the Company of Adventurers of London Trading into the Parts of Africa in 1618, the king specifically mentioned gold but pointedly excluded human beings.[22]

As flawed as its leadership might have been, the Jamestown colony had been founded on similar principles. The settlement promoter Richard Hakluyt had been adamant: there was to be no forced labor demanded of anyone in this "most godly and Christian work" that was to take "gentle course without cruelty or tyranny." Rather than get bogged down in a war with the Spanish over control of the North American midcoast, the English would use the soft power of humane example to win over the Indians and enslaved Africans suffering under their Spanish oppressors and thus turn them to Protestantism and an alliance with His Majesty's government.[23]

Such was the politics of 1606. Thirteen years later, the suffering Virginia Colony learned the realities of frontier survival. The settlers desperately needed labor. The Orinoco strain of tobacco had flourished in cleared patches of forest along the James, but required constant watering, weeding, and tending before harvest. In the same year that the *White Lion* and *Treasurer* arrived, the colony had shipped twenty thousand pounds of tobacco back to England, a volume that would double the next year. The *White Lion* likely did not deliver the first Africans to Virginia, nor were its cargo of captives from Ndongo easily classifiable as "slaves" once they were led ashore. A census taken that year of the 978 people living in the colony notes thirty-two Africans under the heading "Others not Christian in service of the English"—a grouping that almost certainly included the first arrivals apparently put to work chopping tobacco. Other enslaved people who may have arrived earlier went unrecorded.[24]

On September 29, 1619, only a month after the *White Lion* and *Treasurer* dropped off its human cargo at Old Point Comfort, the Rev. Richard Burke preached inside the thatched chapel within the Jamestown fort, focusing on a piece of Scripture in the lectionary of the *Book of Common Prayer.* The verse for that day read: "But they that will be rich fall into temptation and a snare, and into many foolish and hurtful lusts, which drown men in destruction and perdition." Believers had to be on guard. Three years later, the metaphysical poet and dean of St. Paul's Cathedral John Donne preached a sermon to a group of wealthy emigrants as they prepared to depart London for Virginia, warning them to conduct themselves in a holy and modest manner lest they bring disgrace upon themselves. "Infamy is one of the highest punishments the Law inflicts on man; for it lies on him even after death," he warned.[25]

The Africans thus emerged into a mercantile environment in which everyone seemed to be grasping for advantage. Would-be tobacco lords who couldn't finagle land for themselves planted seeds at the edges of Jamestown's muddy streets and at the sides of cabins. The fever was justified. Smoking tobacco had become a fad in London's smart set, even though—or perhaps because—King James I hated it, saying "there cannot be a more base, and yet hurtful, corruption in a country than is the vile use (or other abuse) of taking tobacco." Younger cosmopolitans rolled their eyes at their stodgy sovereign and let smoke curl out of their nostrils.[26]

The English appetite for the sweet leaf (*Nicotiana tabacum*) meant that if a Virginian could work four acres, he could clear an annual profit of between 225 and 300 pounds, which was more than ten times the net income the average English farmer could expect to earn on the traditional staples of vegetables and cattle. Within a decade of its founding, Jamestown had taken on the characteristics of what would become a prototypical American boomtown: heavy drinking, ostentatious dress, a fearsome mortality rate, and new arrivals looking to get rich fast. The company's directors complained of "too much drunkenness and that all kind of riot both in apparel and otherwise." Hasty orchards were planted less for edible fruit than for produce to be fermented into hard liquor.

When the Virginia Company appointed a minor aristocrat as governor, people grumbled he wasn't high enough on the social register, even though most of their houses were merely log posts covered with boards. They were concerned not with the casteless paradise dreamed up by Shakespeare's Gonzalo, but of replicating Albion on fresh shores, only with the younger offspring of wealthy families, or "second sons," playing roles they had been denied back home, even though some had studied at Oxford to be clergymen. The arriviste settlers took to wearing silk stockings, scarves with gold lace, beaver hats, gilded belts, pearl earrings, slashed sleeves, and ornamental swords. The opulent clothes were not merely expressions of pride; they were reproductions of overseas class systems. Pory found himself so bothered by the spirit of conspicuous fashion that he took to wandering under the sweetgum and white oak trees to seek peace in "these crystal rivers and odoriferous woods," free of the "expense, envy, contempt, vanity and vexation of mind" represented by Jamestown and its new arrivals.[27]

Unlike the dissidents in the Massachusetts Bay Colony more than a thousand miles to the north, the Virginians did not see themselves involved in a grand project of founding a New Jerusalem. They saw themselves as everyday Anglican businessmen, out to extend the reach of their estates. A lack of guidance from London had made it all the easier for the American colonies to set their own rules. The royal treasurer for Charles I, Lord Francis Cottington, summarized the general attitude of the metropole when he observed that the settlers of Virginia and Massachusetts "plant tobacco and Puritanism only, like fools."[28]

When Sir William Berkeley ascended to the governorship in 1641, he settled at a riverside plantation called Green Spring and solidified a Royalist class system at which propertied gentlemen—the cavaliers—controlled the export commodities, bank credit, and the levers of political power, while an underclass of lowborn servants from southern and western English counties harvested the tobacco, cleaned the houses, unloaded the ships, and repaired the tools. Those councillors who attached themselves to Berkeley became known as the Green Spring faction, one of America's first political parties.[29]

The faction was ambivalent about opening Indian lands to newcomers, but enthusiastic about bringing in new laborers: a paradox that would result in an eventual explosion. If the English had initially been ambivalent on racialized slavery, they had long been comfortable with other types of unfreedom such as hard labor as punishment for a crime, or the ancient serf-lord agricultural bond, which was by then largely relegated to national memory but still could be found in countryside pockets and remained enshrined in common law. Serfdom and outright bondage had flourished in Wessex, Sussex, Staffordshire, and other regions of southern and western England, the homelands of most of the Virginia elite, whose bonds through intermarriage, in the words of one historian, were like "a tangle of fishhooks so closely interlocked that it is impossible to pick up one without drawing three or four after it."[30]

The settlers grabbed the most fertile land beside the major Virginia rivers—the James, Rappahannock, York, and Potomac—through land patents granted by the royal governor, usually through a chain of aristocratic friendships. Deep draft clippers could dock at a private wharf next to an estate, unload servants, bring on tobacco, and create more market isolation for the few towns that sprung up. Only about one hundred "great planters" really controlled Virginia by 1640. They held multiple colonial offices and kept accounts with London trading houses. On plantations that averaged nine hundred acres in size, they erected brick manors reminiscent of Gloucestershire, created deer parks in the forests for hunt parties, and planted hedgerows that concealed the row of plain boxy cottages known as "the quarter," where the Black and white servants dwelled, with terms of employment already blurring into permanent attachment to the estate.

Under a 1618 law, anyone who paid for the transportation of new settlers across the Atlantic could claim fifty acres of land per head for themselves—a "headright." In this way, the emerging tobacco elite were able to consolidate big tracts of land even as they claimed tyrannical rights over their workers. The new head of the Virginia Company, Sir Edwin Sandys, started a charity drive with the aim of shipping street urchins to the tobacco fields of the New World as a way of developing their moral character—"one of the best deeds that could be done," remarked an associate. A young man or woman would agree to a term of between four to seven years of labor in exchange for passage.[31]

The stories of abundant deer in Virginia, the plentiful oysters, the sturgeon that would practically jump into a frying pan, the easy work—all these turned out to be advertising fables. The newcomers instead discovered "want of houses, pestilent ships, shortness and badness of food"—in short, a hellhole—and they shivered in lean-tos in the forest. At least one thousand perished within a year. A company investigator, George Larkin, thought a poor newcomer "had really better be hanged than become a Servant into the Plantations."

The number of laborers from the British Isles went into steep decline after 1665. Replacements had to be found. English ships arrived in greater numbers from Barbados—and, eventually, directly from Congo, Biafra, and Angola. In 1671, Berkeley reported the presence of "2,000 black slaves," imported under the corrupt headright system and designated as on unequal ground with white migrants, who were called "Christian servants for a short time." The defining institution of the South was taking shape.[32]

No coherent legal definition of slavery existed; this was an act of improvisation that built upon itself, compromise upon compromise. In 1640, a runaway Black servant named John Punch was sentenced to work for his master "for the time of his natural life." By 1655, Henry Whistler could write in Barbados of "miserable Negroes born in perpetual slavery," promoting the righteous belief that, for some, bondage was both forever and hereditary. The ethos crept into Virginia as ships packed with African captives sailed into Old Point Comfort with the relentlessness of the waves and the sand particles that built the spit over the accretion of years. Within seven years of Whistler's observation, the Virginia legislature made slavery an officially hereditable condition, passed down from mother to child.[33]

There was no single transformative moment when the English colony in America resolved to embrace the labor customs of the Spanish; no one flashpoint of change. Slavery had crept into Tidewater Virginia as a gradual and improvised response to a labor shortage. The laws came only after the praxis had set in and cemented. Virginia might well have changed its course in the early seventeenth century and gone the way of moralistic New England, consigning racialized slavery to an outlier practice. But by 1667, that moment had passed. It was the year the Virginia Assembly passed a statute, probably written by Sir William Berkeley, making it clear that Christian baptism did not set "slaves by birth" into a condition of freedom, even as the words "negro" and "slave" were becoming synonymous.[34]

Here lay a tricky point. Prior ethics borrowed from the Spanish made it acceptable to fasten the yoke on heathens from Muslim or animist backgrounds. But did the equality of all people under God promised by Christianity result in a literal freedom to people under bondage? These questions troubled the Virginians until Berkeley's 1667 law cleared the colony's race policy of any of its religious overtones. Distinctions of servitude withered away, replaced by hardened racial categories. Tobacco barons in search of a revised verdict from heaven cited the biblical "curse of Ham" passed down from one of Noah's disobedient sons onto the dusky races of Africa, fating them to be servants. The Virginia Assembly soon made it legal for a master to beat a slave to death "by mistake" and to be free of accusation, "as if the accident never happened."[35]

The planter Nathaniel Bacon gathered a mass of embittered white servants and free Blacks around him in 1676 to chase the seventy-one-year-old Berkeley out of Jamestown, demanding access to Native lands for those who could not afford the riverside estates favored by the elite. He promised "liberty to all Servants and Negroes" who helped him. The alarmed colonial government, fearing a united front of the dispossessed, responded by doling out more land grants to poor whites in a nakedly political effort to split their interests away from indentured Blacks. Now there was even more of an imperative to push English settlement farther inland to seize Indigenous territory. Any entrepreneur who bought an African at Old Point Comfort could claim fifty acres of new Native land under the headright system. He would also own that laborer for life—a double incentive.[36]

This became the key to American politics for many years to come: the splitting of the common interest between poor whites and poor Blacks, with race as the fatal blade. "As more Africans arrived and the commitment to the economic system of slavery grew deeper," wrote the historian Annette Gordon-Reed, "the perceived differences between whites and blacks provided a workable excuse for widening the social gap between indentured white servants and blacks, until that gap became a yawning chasm."[37]

Virginians soon began to speak of "whiteness" as an essential condition that cleaved humanity in terms of ability and divisions of labor. The influx of white indentured servants went into a steep decline when prices in the scaled-up transatlantic slave market suddenly became affordable for a wide range of New World buyers. In 1705, the embrace of slavery became unquestioned when the legislative body of the Virginia Colony, the House of Burgesses, approved "An Act Concerning Servants and Slaves," establishing lifetime property rights for masters and permitting the open sale of Black men and women, not merely a brokerage of their hourly toil.

By that point, half the labor force of Virginia was enslaved. Ships were delivering more than a thousand new arrivals a year who had been kidnapped from West Africa. Yet many landowners still found it necessary to use euphemisms like "my field hands" or "gardeners" to convince themselves that what they were doing was simply a version of countryside labor back in England—another extension of the ancient class system, even though nothing like this had ever been done back home.[38]

The Virginians liked to cite an ethos called "patriarchism," in which the head of an estate, like a biblical patriarch, provided material sustenance for his family and his servants, who in turn allowed themselves to be ruled with a strong hand. It was a racialized extension of the Lockean social contract. "I must take care to keep all my people to their duty, to set all the springs in motion, and to make everyone draw his equal share to carry the machine forward," wrote William Byrd II to a friend in 1726.[39]

But the system had built-in flaws. White Virginians had to be always on their guard against revolts. Lower-class whites were made junior partners with the landed aristocracy in policing Black laborers, walking the night roads in militia companies and making sure that Black people understood their place in the New World hierarchy. "Our poor negroes are freemen in comparison of the slaves who till your ungenerous soil; at least if slavery consists in scarcity and hard work," wrote Byrd to the Earl of Orrery, with as much self-deception as pride. Cruel punishments for Black disobedience mounted, outpacing anything seen in contemporary England: whipping, castration, amputation, burning at the stake. "Numbers make them insolent & then foul means must do where fair will not," reasoned Byrd.[40]

More than the pleasures of dominance, more than the economic advantage, more than the forced sexual relations with enslaved women, of all the grim and illogical reasons why slavery may have crept into the colonial mainstream, no explanation may lie closer to the truth than the simple grasping for status that led the English planters to seek new frontier fortunes. The urge to flaunt ostentatious property and be thought a gentleman proved a durable motivation. As a Kentucky man would later say: "You might have any amount of land; money in your pocket or bank stock and while travelling around no body would be any wiser, but if you had a darkey trudging at your heels every body would see him and know that you owned slaves."[41]

* * *

The United States were never as unified as myth and popular imagination implied. The geographically dispersed British colonies on the Eastern Seaboard found themselves in a constant state of quarrel and mistrust from the 1620s onward, except in times of existential threat. Four New England settlements had barely managed to hang together to fight King Philip's War in 1676, and they pushed against King Charles II when he tried to herd them under a united dominion.

In the next century, during a period of tax protests and military heavy-handedness, delegates to the first Continental Congress in Philadelphia argued bitterly over the Articles of Association, which would have sacrificed a season's worth of Virginia tobacco to a trade boycott against the British. States without western land reserves feared permanent victimhood. "The continent is a vast, unwieldy machine," lamented John Adams, who saw in his more pessimistic visions a grouping of distinct nations with different religious traditions, economies, and temperaments—a kind of Europe in the bush. The Rev. Jonathan Boucher said he more expected to see "the wolf and lamb to feed together, as Virginians to form a cordial union with the saints of New England." George Washington's continental army was seen by most as a temporary and emergency measure, and a dangerous instrument of central oppression to keep lying around after royal governors had been sent home.[42]

The Constitutional Convention in the summer of 1787 was no less torn with factional suspicion and jealousy. Slavery was not even first on the list of points of difference. Questions of trade, taxation, and representation split the delegates, leading to the murky bicameral compromise of the House and Senate to give smaller states a veto power over ideas contrary to their interests. A body as aristocratic and obstructionist as the Senate seemed the only way to placate regions of the continent as different as "Russia and Turkey," in the words of slaveholding delegate Pierce Butler, who demanded a clause that would require Northern states to return escaped refugees. Yet contradicting his own argument, he pushed for more clout for South Carolina by proposing to count its enslaved people as full citizens.

Here was the explosive problem that Benjamin Franklin had suggested the Founders allow to "lie over for the present." The peculiar institution of slavery that would soon be eradicated from the North formed a crucial economic base for Southern states whose delegates were threatening to walk out of the convention unless they got what they wanted. Hence the notorious compromise that counted "three-fifths of all other persons" in matters of representation and direct taxes, and also managed to keep any form of the word "slavery" out of the Constitution, though it hovered unspoken. A statement released in Thomas Jefferson's name before the 1800 presidential election stated: "the Constitution has not empowered the federal government to touch in the remotest degree the question of the condition of property of slaves in any of the States."[43]

The deliberate silence was necessary to hold the Union together and guarantee an orderly settling of seized Indian lands to the west. "Convinced that slavery was already doomed by the laws of political economy and the progress of morality, it was easy for the men in Philadelphia to conclude that nothing significant was sacrificed by compromising with slavery to create a new nation," writes the historian James Oakes. They could not have foreseen the oncoming boom in cotton, beginning in the 1790s, that would make slavery an indispensable economic tool to the hungry young country, sealing its future into seeming eternity.[44]

Numerous Founders soon professed gloom over the future of the Constitution. The man who wrote most of it, Gouverneur Morris, thought New York and New England should break away, leaving the plantation South to the "privilege of strangling commerce, whipping Negroes and bawling about the inborn inalienable rights of man." Even George Washington thought internal feuds were creating "confusion and anarchy" within a hopelessly heterodox nation "moving by hasty strides to some awful crisis."[45]

The differentiated settlement patterns of the seventeenth century were now baked, awkwardly, into the American way of government. The prevailing Virginia ethic of "liberty" meant that white planters had the economic liberty to exploit Black labor as well as the liberty to live within a universe of racial hierarchies. In his 1785 *Notes on the State of Virginia*, the only book he ever wrote, Jefferson judged enslaved people "in reason much inferior" to whites, and "in imagination dull, tasteless and anomalous." They were capable, he thought, of bursts of sentimentality but nothing beyond "plain narration."[46]

Even so, Jefferson lived in philosophical turmoil. "The whole commerce between master and slave is a perpetual exercise of the most boisterous passions, the most unremitting despotism on the one part, and degrading submissions on the other," he famously wrote in his book. The fulsome champion of Virginia liberty Patrick Henry acknowledged the practice was "as repugnant to humanity as it is inconsistent with the Bible, and destructive to liberty." But he would own sixty-seven enslaved people in the course of his long life, forcing them to pick crops at his Pine Slash Farm and other properties. Making first-class money in Virginia society was not possible through other means. "I am drawn along by the general inconveniency of living without them," he admitted.[47]

Jefferson, Henry, and their fellow gentlemen farmers fancied themselves a better class of slave owner, far more humane than the vulgar *arrivistes* of the Deep South. They liked to see themselves as country squires with conspicuous shelves of books, even if unread; enlightened guardians of the interests of their enslaved people, the old *patriarcha* idea propelled into a new century. They reigned over their estates with a vague idea of authoritarian benevolence. The term "First Families of Virginia" was so overused that it became an abbreviation, FFV, and then a national joke.

A massive portion of America's wealth had been amassed through a crime whose real and symbolic beginnings lay with the First Families of Virginia in their backyard, at Old Point Comfort, the sandy spit overlooking the mouth of Chesapeake Bay. The strategic value of the "little isle fit for a castle" first noted by John Smith in 1609 hadn't gone overlooked by future generations, who erected a succession of forts there, variously destroyed by fires and hurricanes. Tobacco growers complained about the duties they were forced to pay for the upkeep of a gunnery aimed out at the ocean.

Only an undefended lighthouse stood at Old Point Comfort during the War of 1812, when a trade dispute with Britain culminated in renewed hostilities. On the morning of June 25, 1813, a group of marauders from the Royal Navy came ashore and made quick work of the Virginia Militia by firing Congreve rockets into their line of defense, and then—enraged by a lucky shot from the Virginians that killed the illegitimate son of George III—sacked the town, using St. John's Church as a temporary barracks. "Every horror was committed with impunity, rape, murder, pillage; and not a man was punished," a British sailor reported, with disgust. Many Africans who fled to the British redcoats, hoping for liberation, were instead transported to sugar estates in the West Indies. Even after news of these betrayals spread, Royal Navy captains reported shock at how many Africans still tried to swim out to the warships, gambling their lives. "A great many black slaves, with their families, used to take advantage of our visits to come away with us," wrote William Stanhope Lovell. "Some of their first exclamations were, 'Me free man; me go cut massa's throat; give me musket.'"[48]

None played on this potential advantage more than Vice Admiral Sir Alexander Cochrane, who had detested Virginia and its settlers ever since his brother was killed by George Washington's army at Yorktown. "They are a whining, canting race," he said of the Americans, and felt they "must be drubbed into good manners." A year after the spectacle at Hampton, he had a thousand handbills printed up and posted around Chesapeake ports promising "FREE" settlement in the West Indies to anyone who wanted to join "His Majesty's Sea or Land forces." The offer made no direct mention of enslaved people, but it was clear to everyone what he meant to convey in capitalizing the explosive word. In his private correspondence, he was explicit. "Let the Landings you make be more for the protection of the desertion of the Black Population than with a view to any other advantage," he instructed a subordinate. The British took in enough refugees to form several corps of Colonial Marines who, thought Cochrane, performed "unexpectedly well."[49]

Cochrane was operating within a tradition more than two thousand years old: flip the enemy's human property and convert them into weapons. During the Peloponnesian War, the Spartans had promised freedom to Athenian slaves if they dropped their tools, picked up swords, and joined their legions. And there was an American precedent, too. In 1775, a band of enslaved men in Williamsburg approached the royal governor Lord Dunmore with information about their disloyal masters. Dunmore mustered up a three hundred–strong Ethiopian regiment, declaring "all indented servants, Negroes, or others, free, that are able and willing to bear arms." Irony ruled the hour. The British still governed eleven sugar islands in the Caribbean, where the brutality was worse across the board than in Virginia, but they twice appeared as liberators within the context of war's demands and could even then claim a moral cause to the fighting. As an enslaved man would go on to tell the Boston lawyer George Smalley: "When my master and somebody else quarrel, I'm on the somebody else's side."[50]

The experience provided an unforgotten lesson to enslaved people, but also to the Virginia planters. The Blacks among them were, in the words of historian Alan Taylor, "an internal enemy" in danger of rising against them, especially with the help of a foreign army. And in the War of 1812, the British dealt another lasting psychological shock: a 4,500-man expeditionary force led by Major Gen. Robert Ross and accompanied by two corps of formerly enslaved Colonial Marines marched into Maryland and encountered a militia that "ran like sheep chased by dogs," to the delight of a group of enslaved Blacks nearby. "They were of course, rejoiced beyond measure at the happy change in their circumstances, and manifested their joy, in a thousand extravagant ways," said one of the British soldiers. As it turned out, false reports of a slave uprising had spread, convincing the Americans they would be fighting on two fronts. A general in the militia, Walter Smith, observed that "each man more feared the enemy he had left behind, in the shape of a slave in his own house or plantation, than he did anything else." It was an astonishing confession.[51]

Ross's army marched on Washington, DC, and occupied it for twenty-six hours, setting fire to the Capitol and the White House. Most of the three thousand books in the Library of Congress were turned to ash. The attack revealed the porous character of the Atlantic coast, the relative defenselessness of the young republic, and the grave danger of an invading army turning unhappy enslaved people to its side. After the war, President James Madison appointed a Fortifications Board to study the vulnerabilities and make recommendations. Baltimore had been spared the torch only because of Fort McHenry's ability to withstand a shelling, as Francis Scott Key watched from onboard a ship in the harbor and admired the young republic's ability to withstand enemy munitions and the power of the "hireling and the slave" the British had drawn to their side. The phrase, which appears in the third verse of his baroque poem "The Star-Spangled Banner," is a reference to the threat posed by escaped field hands who had become Colonial Marines.

Hardening the coast against future onslaughts, the Fortifications Board concluded, would require dozens more facilities like Fort McHenry, with higher walls and far more guns, placed at every significant river mouth. This could cost tens of millions of dollars. Congress quailed at the expense, along with the troubling idea of keeping a "standing army" on American soil, an allergy that dated to the Revolution. The U.S. Army Corps of Engineers conceded that the spending would be a drain on the Treasury but argued it would be "a trifling sum if compared with the magnitude of advantages which will be procured and the evils which will be averted." The muscular foreign policy of the incoming Monroe administration, with its declaration that the Americas were henceforth off-limits to new European colonies, only made the prospect of invasion more likely.[52]

Monroe sold the fort-building as a peace plan—"the best expedient to prevent war," he said. In light of how the Royal Navy had been able to sail unmolested up the James River and other arteries, the first and second generations of coastal defenses at the mouths of American rivers now looked little better than the pathetic wooden palisades of Jamestown. A third system of fortifications was now necessary.

But America lacked skill in this art form. The French were the acknowledged global leaders of military technology. The Napoleonic Wars had provided a superb continuing education in siege and defense. West Point professors assigned textbooks written in French; the U.S. Army adopted many of the French architectural terms of forts rather than create translations: *embrasures*, *bastion*, *casemate*, *caponier*, *place d'armes*, *ramparts*, *banquette*, *counterscarp*.[53]

Then came the opportunity to hire a world-class expert. Simon Bernard had been born poor in the French country town Dole. At the age of sixteen, he walked more than 150 miles to Paris so he could attend the École Polytechnique. When he later joined the army, Napoleon Bonaparte listened to him give an explanation of

Fort Monroe. One of the most expensive military installations of the nineteenth century. One of its engineering supervisors, Robert E. Lee, told the Confederacy not to bother attacking it, even though it lay deep in rebel territory.

how the general should besiege Vienna, and quickly ordered him away from the front to ensure that such a clever asset wouldn't get shot. Bernard stayed by Napoleon's side at Waterloo, which made him intolerable to the restored King Louis XVIII. His appointment to the U.S. Fortifications Board came as a relief to both himself and the French throne.[54]

Bernard shared a hatred of the British with his American employers, but he didn't speak English. Some of his new colleagues grumbled that the biggest national security project the country had ever seen shouldn't be in the hands of a foreigner. But he set out to create his masterpiece at Old Point Comfort.

Crews began digging out a moat, laying bricks, building earthen walls, and extending wharves. Bernard recommended an irregular hexagon design to provide wide angles for guns to lay down flanking shots and cross-fire on anyone who tried to ford the seawater ditch. More than forty cannons could be simultaneously fired at a water-level target out in Hampton Roads, dooming an approaching ship within seconds.

Laborers loaded large boulders into skiffs, rowed them out two thousand feet to the south, and dumped the rocks onto a shoal to create an artificial island. They called it "Rip Raps" for the amusing sound the boulders made when they landed on the growing underwater pile. When it was finally complete, they fixed it with more gunnery. An impassable gate of cannon fire could now be thrown up at the mouth of the James River.[55]

Costs ballooned. The budget climbed to $1.8 million, an extraordinary sum at the time. The fort named for the president who commissioned it took fifteen years to complete, serving as one of the country's first gargantuan defense outlays on a single project. Congressional debt hawks kept complaining Fort Monroe was a spectacular boondoggle: "a useless waste of money," "a mammoth," for which "an immense sum" had to be raised. Rep. George Kremer of Pennsylvania, who was particularly acid about the "monuments of our folly" that Bernard was erecting all over the coasts, urged his colleagues to "strangle the monster" and kill the fortification plan, even if it meant half-built installations had to go to ruin. The U.S. Corps of Engineers told Congress it was "too late to remedy the evil" and America could not afford to "come down from the exaggerated school of warfare to which Europe was then accustomed." One of the young engineers from West Point who oversaw its finishing touches, Robert E. Lee, told associates that no invading army could breach its walls.[56]

Whether congressional skeptics liked the result or not, the United States had created an extraordinary military asset, the equivalent of ten fully armed battleships. Fort Monroe was then the biggest militarized structure on the globe that did not also enclose a civilian town. Whoever controlled this spot now took effective control of the Chesapeake Bay. There would be no more sackings of the U.S. Capitol.

Then the most expensive military installation in the country fell into a peacetime slumber. Among the young privates posted here was a restless eighteen-year-old Edgar Allan Poe, who scribbled poems in his frequent tobacco breaks between artillery drills, and applied for an early discharge, fearing "the prime of my life would be wasted," as he pleaded in a letter to his stepfather. When the Englishman James Silk Buckingham came by for a visit in 1841, he was allowed to walk around at his leisure because nobody was there to stop him. He found "barracks for the troops, officers' quarters, spacious parade ground, forges, armory, ordnance depot, magazine, and workshop of every kind"—but nobody around except construction workers. The sense of security in coastal Virginia was such that its biggest fort didn't even have a permanent staff.[57]

* * *

The nearby village of Hampton had always fancied itself as the gentle side of the South. The era of the Jamestown tobacco plantations was a distant memory, and the smaller farms here in the nineteenth century had assumed more of the yeoman character envisioned by Thomas Jefferson. Even the richest planters working the same soil once plowed by John Rolfe seldom owned more than twenty enslaved people. The soils had become exhausted from overwork; consequently, the commodity-scale production that had so delighted the brokers of London and Cádiz was no longer possible.

Though packet ships down from Baltimore still landed daily at Old Point Comfort, the harbor on Mill Creek had accumulated enough silt to make it impractical for the big ocean vessels that had once ferried local tobacco and cotton to Europe to call there anymore. A shift in the countryside toward lower-intensity crops like melons, peaches, wheat, and cherries had left the region with a surplus of enslaved people.

Corseted ladies still showed up for tea at the Hygeia Hotel, a graceful resort built just opposite the landward side of the fort, on the spot where the *White Lion* had landed its cargo of kidnapped Africans in 1619. The hotel had white columns and broad verandas, and advertised itself as a healthful place to rest in the torpor of a Virginia summer. Pleasant beachside temperatures brought "tonic invigorations," the managers proclaimed, "and the nights are few when a bed-covering is not found an agreeable necessity of repose." Edgar Allan Poe gave one of his last public readings here before he died of a rabies-like disease in Baltimore. Soldiers at Fort Monroe still threw oyster shells into the moat as Poe had done as an unhappy private; there were generations of shells stacked up three feet high under the brackish water.[58]

At the center of Hampton, just west of the intersection of King and Queen Streets, was St. John's Church, the oldest

Anglican parish on the continent, where the graves of some of the first English settlers rounded the weathered brick sanctuary, and the communion silver had been cast at the same time the King James Bible was being translated. Within the social hierarchy of the Old Dominion, the term "First Families of Virginia" was both a self-aware quip and an ironclad reality. Seniority really did matter, and some of the true antediluvian names in the state traced their lines back to these fields at the easternmost tip of the peninsula: the Carters, Byrds, Parrishes, Armsteads, and Wyths.

Nearby Jamestown had turned into a deserted ghost village, its imported European bricks long burgled for other projects and its church crumbled into an Acropolis shell. The painter John Gadsby Chapman depicted its fall in warm romantic light in his 1834 *Ruins of Jamestown*, draping it with the honor of antiquity. Hampton, as its erudite promoters liked to remind visitors, had now become the oldest English-speaking settlement in North America.

The local postmaster would deliver mail on slow days by walking about the oyster houses and butcher shops with letters stuck in the brim of his hat, handing them to the familiar faces he recognized on the streets. Crime was rare. The courthouse jail was almost never occupied, its few cells overgrown with cobwebs. The weather was mild and Mediterranean with, as one resident put it, "brilliant coloring and golden, semi-tropical sunshine" for eight months of the year. The major excitement came in the form of periodic cholera outbreaks, or when the tides came up from the wharf and made ankle-deep floods around the courthouse. "No one could desire to live in a more favorable place," reflected George Benjamin West.[59]

When soldiers from Fort Monroe went into Hampton on leave to drink and fraternize, they walked down dusty roads paved with cracked oyster shells past the homes of the Southern petite bourgeoisie, their carriage lanes lined with fruit trees. One family kept a garden with over two hundred varieties of roses. "Several old houses with spacious rooms and high ornamented ceilings gave evidence at one time they had been occupied by citizens of considerable rank and taste," wrote a lieutenant. Most of them had at least one wooden cabin, the slave quarter, set discreetly to the side and in varying states of repair.[60]

Northern visitors to the Hygeia Hotel sometimes brought up the delicate question of slavery. The people of Hampton would respond that the abolitionist propaganda was not true and that slaves in the town lived in a state of gratitude. “Even the darkest aspect of slavery was softened by a smile,” remarked one reluctant defender of the milder form of bondage—a clear sign that race relations lay uneasy.[61]

The 2,417 enslaved people of Elizabeth City County, of which Hampton was the seat, shared both last names and occupations with the whites. Some worked, as Robert Engs has noted, in jobs “that were potentially undermining to the slave system: some were fishermen and boat pilots with access to vessels that could carry them to freedom.” Others were trusted to market their master’s crops and given watch over significant cash assets. Enslaved people were known to hire themselves out as virtual freelancers, paying their owners a cut of their wages—an arrangement that prefigured the sharecropping system of later years.[62]

The enslaved people were sometimes mistaken for free people of color, who lived in cordial homeostasis with their white neighbors, though their subordinate role was never forgotten. A familiar face around the Hygeia Hotel was that of Thomas Peake, a light-skinned Black man with blue eyes, a jolly disposition, and a head for Bible quotations, who had met his wife, Mary, during his days sailing with the merchant marine. She was the offspring of a mulatto mother and a French-born father of a high social class who had sent her to a school with white teachers.[63]

The Peakes, who in the 1860 census were reported among the town’s 201 free people of color, were a leading family of what passed for a Black middle class in Hampton. They lived near Fort Monroe in a house that cost $2,200, a substantial sum, though Mary was in the habit of draining the family budget through promiscuous almsgiving. As an acquaintance reported: “A very old man, in the suburbs, often came to her door, and never went empty away; and frequently at evening she would go and carry him warm tea, and in the winter she brought him wood in small armfuls.” Any friend of hers who seemed in danger of perdition was certain to hear her urge repentance. In her spare time, she donated time to the Daughters of Zion, a ministry to the poor and sick, which left her with tuberculosis. She earned a living through dressmaking and—discreetly—teaching enslaved children how to read. This was technically illegal but tolerated in Hampton, where most of the red-letter racial laws of the past had yellowed with age. The literacy rate here among enslaved people was among the highest in the South.[64]

But slavery was still slavery, even in a sleepy coastal town dreaming of past centuries. The census of 1860 showed Virginia was home to more enslaved people than any other state. Many were the offspring of a white ancestor who had taken part in the common—but rarely commented upon—practice of visiting enslaved women at night for compulsory sexual relations. Female beauty could be an awful inheritance. "In those days, if you was a slave and had a good-looking daughter, she was taken from you," said Robert Ellett. "They would put her in the big house where the young masters could have the run of her."[65]

The constant degradation broke spirits and bodies. During harvests, William Corsey and John Wood, among others, frequently got by on three hours' sleep a night, subsisting on a diet of cowpeas and wild blackberries. In the view of Charles Grandy, who had been taken to the supposedly easier climate of Hampton after laboring in the Mississippi cotton fields, the work was just as miserable and the beatings were equally harsh. "It was slavery no matter where you were," he said. Grandy was once whipped so savagely that he stole the bullwhip and hid it in the woods in a futile attempt to save himself further injury.[66]

No amount of decayed gentility could efface the presence of the whipping post in front of the courthouse, conceal the manacles applied to harvesters in the wheatfields, or hush the anguished screams of mothers when a young male was sold off to a broker—euphemistically called "a Georgia trader"—who handled the business of transferring enslaved people from one part of the country to another. Tidewater Virginia had, in fact, made an uncomfortable turn away from tobacco into exporting human beings.[67]

After clearing Louisiana of British influence in the War of 1812, Andrew Jackson adopted a successful program of Indian removal through a series of sham treaties in the lowlands of what would soon become Mississippi and Alabama. Two federal gunboats destroyed a holdout called Negro Fort on the banks of the Apalachicola River, killing 270 with a single flaming cannonball that made a direct hit on an ammunition storage magazine. "In an instant, hundreds of lifeless bodies were stretched upon the plain, buried in sand and rubbish or suspended from the tops of the surrounding pines," wrote Marcus Buck, a U.S. volunteer, in a letter to his parents, later published in the *Virginia Argus*. He added a prophetic footnote: "N.B. First rate land in Florida can be purchased for 50 cents per acre. What speculations if it should ever be ours, which I think will be the case."[68]

The opening of the Old Southwest and the establishment of Alabama, Mississippi, and Arkansas created immense fortunes for some of the federal agents charged with distributing the land. They made corrupt deals with speculators, who in turn flipped them sight unseen to multiple unwitting buyers who had to untangle the mess themselves, sometimes at the point of a gun. The migrants who were able to secure bank credit, consolidate large parcels of land, lay out surveyor's stakes, construct levees, sweep out the choking stands of cypress, loblolly, and sweetgum, and acquire a measure of political influence were assured of fortunes in short-staple cotton if they imported enough enslaved people. The ban on the overseas slave trade in 1808 made the Upper South the logical place to turn, especially since tobacco exports had withered. Indians had been forced out of the Deep South; now Blacks would be forced in.

While traveling through Virginia for a series of articles for the *New York Times*, Frederick Law Olmsted watched the exodus up close. "I have not been on or seen a railroad train, departing southward, that did not convey a considerable number of the best class of negro laborers, in the charge of a trader who was intending to sell them to cotton-planters," he wrote. Prices for a healthy young man rose over the thousand-dollar mark, and some traders turned to kidnapping free Blacks. The mass transfer of nearly 1 million enslaved people—on miserable transport ships sailing in domestic waters from Norfolk to New Orleans; inside darkened railroad boxcars; yoked in shuffling coffles driven along by mounted drivers holding whips—consisted of a Second Middle

Passage, in the words of Ira Berlin, the largest human migration yet seen on the North American continent.[69]

Forced family separations became commonplace, a looming threat to maintain the precarious social order that depended on a climate of fear. Charles Ball was not permitted to say goodbye to his wife and children before his hands were lashed together and he was marched away. "I felt incapable of weeping or speaking, and in my despair, I laughed loudly," he recalled. Nobody knew when a sale might be coming; enslaved people dreaded the summons of a master to go into town with him, or even returning from work to find a spouse or child had been sold off to cotton country. Viney Baker went to sleep one night next to her mother and awoke to find her gone, sold to a speculator who "wanted to buy a woman."[70]

At the age of seven, Elizabeth Keckly watched a horrific scene. Her master, Colonel Burwell, couldn't pay the bills for a new flock of hogs and decided to sell Little Joe, his cook's son, to save himself from the embarrassment of being thought a deadbeat. He told Little Joe's mother to dress him up in his best Sunday clothes. "When her son started for Petersburgh in the wagon, the truth began to dawn upon her mind, and she pleaded piteously that her boy should not be taken from her; but master quieted her by telling her that he was simply going to town with the wagon, and would be back in the morning," said Keckly. "Morning came, but little Joe did not return to his mother. Morning after morning passed, and the mother went down to the grave without ever seeing her child again. One day she was whipped for grieving for her lost boy." Keckly knew the agony all too well: her own father had been taken from her.[71]

Westward expansion intensified the cruelty of slavery, spreading it across the vast tablelands where the large-scale production of bulk commodities fundamentally reshaped the master-slave relationship. In places like Hampton, it was within the realm of possibility that an enslaved person could hire out on fishing boats, hear the latest seaboard rumors, gain some literacy, acquire a little money, plant a garden, and have some regular social contact with free people of color and small-time white farmers. Not so in the Southwest. The work gangs were bigger and the hand-blistering field days lasted from sunup to sunset, with violence simmering closer to the surface. The high productivity depended, in fact, on systemic punishment, which quickly became a perverse kind of management science.

A significant number of pioneering Delta planters had leveraged their slave assets to buy the auctioned Indian land, and their exposure was considerable. Bankruptcy and social disgrace would be their fate if their enslaved people failed to deliver a satisfactory crop in a seesawing market. Errors and dawdling were not permitted. A new variety of bullwhip with a long lash and a lead-weighted handle ensured that drivers could crack down on malingering with greater force than before. And a toxic symmetry developed. The angrier the driver became, the more work slowed down, and the more brutal the abuse. Complaining about his enslaved people, one owner said they gave him "all the trouble that they can which keeps me one half my time in hot blood."[72]

After being sold down the river, Charles Ball struggled to meet the daily fifty-pound quota under threat of shame and torture. The plains around him were frosted with cotton tended by bent-over enslaved people, with virtually nothing else in sight: no barns, no melons, not even livestock. "It was manifest that I was now in a country where the life of a black man was no more regarded than that of an ox, except as far as the man was worth the most money in the market," he wrote.[73]

The rise of the cotton frontier came as a direct result of the spinning mills of new English cities like Manchester, which developed an insatiable appetite for upland cotton (*Gossypium hirsutum*), a species of the plant that flourished in the loamy soil of cleared Indian lands near the Mississippi River. Tough, cheap, and easy to loom, the new short-staple bolls with creamy lint were the seeds of a boom that boosted production from a few thousand bales at the time of the Revolution to more than 4 million bales per year, with a commanding presence—57 percent—in the nation's portfolio of export products. Upland cotton needed no apprenticed skills, only a machine-like body, destroying the artisan class of carpenters, wheelwrights, and machinists who could at least take a small pride in the work. Armed patrols with torches and pistols prowled the night roads slicing through the furrows.[74]

Few of these unpleasantries were discussed among the polite Hampton gentry, who learned to avert their eyes from the children being torn away from mothers when a Georgia trader came to town. They may have deplored the tacky wealth and the conspicuous cruelty of their brethren in the Cotton States, but they banked the new cash brought to them by Georgia traders, and both groups shared a collective dread that the wages of violence and family separations would rebound to them. This reason alone made them terrified of emancipation. "The question of slavery, as it is called, is to us a question of life and death," said the eminent Virginia politician John Randolph. "You will find no instance in history where the two distinct races have occupied the soil except in the relation of master and slave."[75]

There it was again: the peculiar idea of freedom that seemed as durable as the seaward banks of Old Point Comfort. The Constitution protected the right of a man to grow his own crops with his own enslaved people, and did not extend to the enslaved. Nat Turner's 1831 revolt, waged less than a hundred miles away, had never left the consciousness of white Virginians, just as all remembered that the enslaved people of Saint-Domingue had slain their masters as they lay abed.

The doctor Jesse Torrey related the story of a Virginian who slept above a trapdoor in the attic with an ax at his side in case his enslaved people should revolt in the night. Many others, he reported, posted "armed sentinels" keeping constant watch over the slave quarters, a strange manifestation of the blessings of liberty. Sleeping in a low-grade state of fear, doors and windows locked, was part of the routine on a Virginia estate, especially after an uprising in Jamaica had convinced members of the British Parliament to do away with the institution throughout their empire in 1834, spawning the perilous notion of universal liberty as a contagion threatening to spread throughout the Americas. Southern newspapers pushed the insistent myth that enslaved people were happy and peace loving, even as the paranoia over abolitionists and revolts grew more intense.[76]

As the cotton frontier extended, the capital links reached deeper into Wall Street, which flourished off the dynamic combination of new Southwestern lands and field slaves forcibly marched there from the Chesapeake. At one point a single firm, the New York and Mississippi Land Company, controlled 10 percent of all the land given up by the Choctaw. Brokerage houses pooled enslaved people together as assets and chopped up their value into percentage bonds, thoroughly commoditizing the practice, and making the trade even more valuable than railroads. A few blocks from the New York banks lay the South Street countinghouses with traders peering at bills of lading, and, beyond them, the docks on the East River servicing packet vessels stacked with clothes, whips, hoes, manacles, and every other kind of manufactured product necessary for the maintenance of a Southern plantation.

The trade route to New Orleans was particularly well traveled, and visitors disembarking there would have stepped off the boat in the French Quarter not far from a group of banks and brokerages clustered around the St. Louis Hotel and Exchange, featuring a gorgeous rotunda where "auctions of every conceivable form of property, including enslaved human beings, were conducted beneath the 88-foot-high dome surrounded by towering Tuscan columns, like a scene out of ancient times." The seventeen banking institutions here catered almost exclusively to sugar and cotton plantations, exchanging credit and up-to-date market information with their partners in Manhattan. "What would New York be without slavery?" asked the editor of *De Bow's Review*, an influential business magazine for slaveholders. He then answered his own question: "The ships would rot at their docks; grass would grow in Wall Street and Broadway, and the glory of New York, like that of Babylon and Rome, would be numbered with the things of the past."[77]

On this question, the nation had been united by more than the constitutional silence, but by the monetary bonds stretching from the far side of Texas to the tip of Maine. God was in heaven, the slaves knew their places, and cotton was the white King of America. Cotton's reach had woven slavery into the fiber of the nation, and into the homes of nearly all its citizens through the garments that they wore. The everyday links didn't stop there. Sugarcane chopped and boiled by enslaved people was on the breakfast table. Rice grown by forced labor was in the pantry. Tobacco harvested by enslaved people was in the vest pocket. Slavery may have been tucked out of sight for most, but it was omnipresent in daily national life. James Henry Hammond proclaimed in 1858 that the South was "satisfied, content, happy, harmonious and prosperous."[78]

Southern gentry talked of slavery as an almost mystical gravitational force. When the system came under threat, they responded by doubling down on the principles that had sustained them since Jamestown and gave distinctive shape to the economy and the social order. Northern coercion could never break the ancient order. Behind all politics loomed a hierarchy lodged in the mind: the pull of patriarchism. After a failed attempt to reform the system in 1798, the discouraged Virginia abolitionist Francis Asbury concluded, "Slavery will exist in Virginia perhaps for ages; there is not a sufficient sense of religion nor of liberty to destroy it."[79]

One of the premier agrarian intellectuals of the Tidewater, Edmund Ruffin, had inherited prime riverfront property along the James River whose patent dated to the colony's earliest days. As editor of the *Farmer's Register*, he had distinguished himself as a soil scientist and a prime advocate for sprinkling exhausted soil with doses of lime and oyster shells to bring it back to life after two centuries of tobacco had stripped it of nutrients. Ruffin concluded from his historical studies that slavery had been "established by the wise and benevolent design of God," just like marriage and family, and that it had been a blessing to the nations everywhere it spread. "To the direct aid of domestic slavery, every cultivated portion of the earth owes its first improvement, and every civilized people their first emerging from barbarism," he wrote. Mass enslavement was a *protection* against savagery, he reasoned, not one of its marks.[80]

No person or force seemed able to prevent the American system of slavery from going on and on. To many in the South, the institution appeared capable of projecting itself centuries into the future, perhaps as long as time itself might last.[81]

5

Southern Ardor

In the spring of 1861, Hampton residents witnessed a bizarre new apparition atop the western walls of Fort Monroe. A battery of cannons had been erected on a set of wooden platforms, their muzzles pointed not at the ocean, where the threats to America were supposed to have been coming from, but inland toward Virginia.

The fort's commander, John W. Phelps, then ordered the sluice gates cranked upward to let water fill the moats—a telltale sign of war preparation. That Phelps was an easygoing Vermonter who held frequent concerts for the local gentry on the parade ground made it all the more surreal. Those who lived nearby could hear sentries crying out the passing of hours all night long, a conspicuous change in their routine.

Among those who noticed these developments was the retired tenth president of the United States, John Tyler, an aristocratic planter who had a cottage less than a mile from the fort. He complained publicly about federal weapons aimed at "the sacred soil of Virginia."[1]

The distinct cleavage in the former president's choice of words—Virginia pitted in opposition to the U.S. Army—represented a new tic in popular conversation. Through all the talk of disunion that occasionally rippled through the nineteenth century, Virginia showed little collective enthusiasm for breaking with the republican faith of its native sons Washington, Monroe, Madison, and Jefferson. While it may have been an economic linchpin of the Old South and the birthplace of its signature institution, it had also provided nearly half of the land cradle of the national capital and an equal portion of its presidents. The thought of splitting from the Union seemed a fantasy, as did the idea of Fort Monroe hurling shells at its neighbors.

In order to get California admitted as a free state in 1850, Northern Whigs and Democrats had to agree to the Fugitive Slave Act, which forbade anyone to help an escapee anywhere in the country, at the penalty of a $1,000 fine or six months in jail. Abolitionists swore not to obey it, claiming fidelity to a "higher law." Brooklyn's star preacher Henry Ward Beecher called the fugitive act "the monster iniquity of the present age," and Vermont established its own judicial process to handle such matters. Some Northern juries quickly acquitted those accused of breaking the despised federal law, regardless of the evidence.

Nullification of unfavorable mandates from Washington had previously been a Southern specialty. Now it was practiced everywhere. On the Fourth of July in 1854, William Lloyd Garrison set fire to a copy of the Constitution before a crowd and declared, "So perish all compromises with tyranny!" to wild applause. The founding document was drenched in blood, he said, because it allowed for slavery.[2]

Congress, meanwhile, had descended into shouting and physical violence. Among the most brazen of Southern bullies in Congress was Henry Wise, who went into session with a pistol in his pocket—occasionally waved around for effect. When the English novelist Charles Dickens visited the U.S. Capitol in 1842, he asked to be introduced to Wise, whom he described as "a wild-looking, evil-visaged man" who appeared to have been suckled by a wolf, with a persistent "great ball of tobacco in his left cheek." Vain and loquacious, rail-thin, sporting long hair over a high collar, Wise was said by an acquaintance to have preferred brawling to eating. He bragged that he could make anyone "hate him with a bitter hate," dishing out a stream of biting insults to Northerners that made his constituents love him even more. His marathon speeches drew bigger audiences than Richmond playhouses featuring the leading actors of the day. One editor thought he "would have kept the crowd, if he had spoken for a month." Heckling, catcalling, and bell ringing often accompanied his public remarks. Secessionist politics had merged with entertainment.[3]

Henry Wise was a walking and shouting manifestation of the performative tendencies that had taken over Congress, concurrent with the rise of regional partisan newspapers that thrilled to rambunctious disputes. Members spent more time on their images than on legislating, fashioning themselves as folk heroes battling for the noble cause of their side. They clipped their speeches out of newspapers to show them around; fed gossipy items to favored reporters; and paid close attention to how they were portrayed. Almost no factor could make or doom a career more than living up to standards of "manhood." Southerners viewed their orderly aristocratic governance as superior to that of the dirty North, with its harebrained ideas of women's rights, industrialism, social reform, immigrants jabbering in foreign tongues, and, most intolerable of all, abolitionism.

When Frederick Law Olmsted was making his tour of the Cotton States for the *New York Times*, he grew depressed after a conversation with a slaveholding Yale graduate named Samuel Perkins Allison, a carrier of pistols and Bowie knives who told him he "couldn't imagine that the North would be governed by any purpose beyond a regard for self-interest." Like many of his wealthy friends in Nashville, Allison believed in a theory of the universe, somewhat like an Aristotelian chain of being, in which cultured gentlemen like himself were destined to hold the benevolent levers of power over lower-class whites, enslaved people, and especially those who wanted to end slavery for selfish economic reasons. "Allison & his friends evidently had no power of comprehending a hatred of Slavery in itself," wrote Olmsted. These Southern grandees thought the North was devoid of philosophy or culture, dedicated only to making money.[4]

While the official *Congressional Globe* shied away from making detailed descriptions of the frequent brawls on the tobacco-stained rugs of the House and Senate, preferring to allude to "sudden sensations" or discussions that became "unpleasantly personal," newspapers on both sides of the divide gave extended and immediate coverage to the exchange of insults and fists. "The only persons who do not have a revolver and a knife are those who have two revolvers," observed James Henry Hammond of South Carolina. After his colleague Preston Brooks gave Charles Sumner of Massachusetts a beating with a gold-tipped cane on the floor of the Senate on May 22, 1856, for the crime of insulting his uncle in a speech called "The Crime Against Kansas," the

New York Evening Post asked: "Has it come to this, that we must speak with bated breath in the presence of our Southern masters? . . . Are we to be chastised as they chastise their slaves?" Brooks left the fragments of his shattered cane on the Senate carpet; admirers sent him dozens of replacements. One came with the note "Hit him again." The Southern culture of honor confirmed by violence saw an apex expression in its politics.[5]

Events accelerated. On March 6, 1857, the Supreme Court finally issued a verdict in the case of Dred Scott, an enslaved man who had been taken to the free state of Wisconsin by his owner and claimed that the period of residency in that state made him free by default. But Chief Justice Roger Taney called African Americans "beings of an inferior order . . . and so far inferior that they had no rights which the white man was bound to respect, and that the negro might justly and lawfully be reduced to slavery for his benefit." Slave owners rejoiced at the confirmation of what they had always claimed: that the Constitution not only enshrined the peculiar institution but sanctioned its spread. "We demand it; we mean to have it," said Senator Albert G. Brown of Mississippi.[6]

Abolitionists fought back. A group of patrician Bostonians later called the "Secret Six" gave money and weapons to the farmer-activist John Brown, who plotted a messianic act to end slavery by trying to spark a race war. His quixotic vision ended in a blaze of gunfire at the federal arms depot at Harpers Ferry, Virginia, on October 16, 1859. He went to the gallows six weeks later.

The most ardent Southern secessionists saw the strange incident as a premonition of more terrorism to come, and a sign that sharing a country was no longer possible. The *Charleston Mercury* had fulminated the year before that the North and South were "rival, hostile Peoples," and now even Republican leader William Seward predicted "an irrepressible conflict between opposing and enduring forces," saying that a revolution was at hand. "I know, and all the world knows, that revolutions never go backwards." He had toured Virginia and found little there to admire, summing it up as "exhausted soil, old and decaying towns, wretchedly neglected roads, and in every respect, an absence of enterprise."[7]

Thousands of young Northern men joined a militaristic club called the Wide Awakes that staged torchlit parades, in which they marched in formation against the power of Southern slavery, proclaiming the inflammatory creed of abolitionism to crowds of onlookers, most of them wary but some privately thrilled at the show of force against the bullies. The Wide Awakes were known to carry knives under their coats. Southern editors demonized them as a threat to civilization. "These semi-military organizations, the sport of the hour, shall erect the guillotine, tear down the temples of justice, sack the city and overturn society," worried one newspaper editor in Georgia.[8]

The Democratic Party Convention in April 1860 turned into a disastrous split, ending in separate nominating conventions a month later. Inflammatory rhetoric grew overpowering, to the point that anything less than flagrant war talk seemed hopelessly weak. Alabama congressman Jabez Curry said the South would endure "a Saturnalia of blood" rather than submit to "the abhorrent degradation of social and political equality." As the Mississippi delegation to Congress paraded out of the U.S. Capitol for what they thought was the final time, former attorney general D.C. Glenn told the Northerners: "It is right that we should part. Go your way, and we will go ours." His home-state ally Jefferson Davis had already pledged in a fit of rage that if Mississippi's interests were threatened by a Republican president, he would tear its star from the American flag and proclaim it "a sign round which Mississippi's best and bravest should gather to the harvest-home of death." His wife, Varina, took a more thoughtful view. Even as Washington felt like "a great mausoleum" as Southerners fled, she paid President James Buchanan a goodbye visit, having already gifted him a pair of slippers for Christmas. "I love the dear old man and would like to forget that I do," she wrote, secretly believing the South was doomed.[9]

The nominee of the new Republican Party, the affable Illinois lawyer Abraham Lincoln, had campaigned as a moderate, pledging not to interfere with slavery where it existed but to delimit it in new western territories. He received almost no votes in Hampton or anywhere else in the rest of the South, which split its choice between Stephen Douglas and John Breckinridge among the Democrats, with a significant percentage going to the third-party candidate John Bell. Lincoln squeaked into the presidency with just 39.8 percent of the popular vote.

Many slaveholders considered it the final insult. South Carolina called a secessionist convention and voted 169–0 to leave the Union without waiting to see what Lincoln would say in his inaugural address. "The Union Is Dissolved!" blared the *Charleston Mercury*, prematurely, as bonfires and colored lanterns lit the night and bands played into the morning hours. "I am somewhat sorry for the old Union, although he was a noisy old braggart," remarked the British counsel on hand for the jubilation.[10]

Legislatures and secessionist conventions across the Deep South followed South Carolina's lead: Florida, Alabama, Georgia, Louisiana. Jefferson Davis was inaugurated president of the new republic on February 18, calling it the "true meaning" of what had been intended in the American Revolution. "The Constitution formed by our fathers is that of these Confederate States," he said. Vice President Alexander Stephens assured the public that the core elements of the old 1787 constitution would be "preserved and perpetuated." But he acknowledged that "some changes have been made," namely the protection of tariffs to help one state over another; a ban on federal spending for infrastructure; a six-year term for the president; and an eternal guarantee of slavery.[11]

In its own declaration of secession, Mississippi made the reasoning plain:

> Our position is thoroughly identified with the institution of slavery—the greatest material interest of the world. Its labor supplies the product which constitutes by far the largest and most important portions of commerce of the earth. These products are peculiar to the climate verging on the tropical regions, and by an imperious law of nature, none but the black race can bear exposure to the tropical sun. These products have become necessities of the world, and a blow at slavery is a blow at commerce and civilization.[12]

The national unraveling came amid significant opposition in the South. Skeptical planters questioned whether an independent

North might be a greater menace to slavery than a polarized country held together with twine. They pointed to the proslavery language in the Constitution, the unbalanced Congress, and the long success of Southern intimidation as factors in their favor. In the spring of 1861, most Virginians tended to agree their interests lay under the American flag and not with the hotheaded secessionists, whose conduct was frequently embarrassing. But shortly after Texas radicals forced the Unionist governor Sam Houston out of the capital and cast a rushed vote to leave the nation, insisting that "the servitude of the African" should "exist in all future time," the Virginia General Assembly bowed to pressure and called for a convention of its own to determine the destiny of the "First State of the South," the biggest in population and prestige.[13]

The nascent Confederate States of America, with its provisional capital in Montgomery, Alabama, had already taken a hardline stance on the explosive question of U.S. military bases within its boundaries. To whom did they belong? The fire-eaters in South Carolina demanded the surrender of Fort Sumter in Charleston Harbor, which had been built in the same era as Fort Monroe, and with the same grim architectural stylings. Army Major Robert Anderson and 127 men holed up inside the low-slung fort while repeated attempts to resupply them via ocean steamer were repulsed by artillery shots fired by cadets from the Citadel military academy, standing on platforms recently built by enslaved people.

Emissaries from South Carolina had already made a visit to Richmond designed to flatter Virginia politicians. In a four-hour speech before the General Assembly, Christopher Memminger tried to persuade its members to finish the work of their revolutionary forefathers and lead a new Southern republic into independence—a fresh birth of freedom for slave owners under a constitution written right, with all ambiguities removed. Having received a lukewarm response, they refitted a town house on Washington, DC's K Street into their new "embassy," designed a diplomatic seal as elaborate as that of the Court of St. James, and sent a dandified young secretary holding a gold-tipped cane, "a dude of the dudes," to demand Fort Sumter's surrender. Massachusetts congressman Henry Dawes looked on this display as "a huge joke" and "a harmless outcome of the vanity and pride of South Carolina." But the underlying matter was deadly serious. South Carolina epitomized Southern society, as well as its increasing conservative radicalism.[14]

In this moment of high national drama, on February 13, 1861, Virginia delegates packed into Richmond's Mechanics' Institute, at the corner of Ninth and Main. Hampton sent the lawyer and slaveholder Charles King Mallory. Anticipating a crush of spectators, the organizers draped the walls with new upholstery and put up an iron railing to separate onlookers from the tables arranged in a semicircle. A giant portrait of George Washington stared down from the wall, as if to remind Virginians of the sacrality of the federal union, or of the necessity to resist central power—however the viewer chose to interpret it.

As soon as the talking started, a primary crack in Virginia politics became clear: the long-standing sense of victimhood felt by the miners and small farmers of the highlands west of the Blue Ridge Mountains, where slavery had always been sparse and new railroad connections to Cleveland and Pittsburgh had weakened economic ties to the lowland regions. This was hardcore Whig country, where the lodestar politician was Henry Clay, "The Great Compromiser," and loyalty to the Constitution was strong. "We can look to Richmond for taxes and treason, but for little else," complained the *Wheeling Daily Intelligencer.* Future Confederate general Jubal A. Early, a son of the Blue Ridge Mountains, was among those heaping scorn on paranoid slaveholders, and the subversive emissaries up from Montgomery who wanted to split the nation in two. At the start, only about one-sixth of the delegates were in favor of immediate secession. Lincoln let it be known through a back channel that if they adjourned without a decision, he would call off any missions to resupply Fort Sumter and order Anderson to surrender. "If you will guarantee me the state of Virginia I shall remove the troops," he told delegate John B. Baldwin. "A state for a fort is no bad business."[15]

But that trade never happened. Goaded by wealthy slave owners, Virginia's convention staggered on for nearly two months amid lengthy speechmaking and procedural squabbles. John Tyler volunteered to lead a peace conference at Washington's Willard Hotel to head off an armed conflict with a potential compromise on slavery's extension. Elder statesmen gave lofty speeches in the high-ceilinged room at Willard's, making repeated references to the Founding Fathers, but found no consensus. "The thing to be done is to let the South go," muttered Salmon P. Chase on the street one night after the day's pointless discussion was over. The radicals at the *New-York Tribune* ridiculed the "Old Gentlemen's Convention," and a young Henry Adams wrote to a friend, "I suppose they will potter ahead until no one feels any more interest in them, and then they may die." Even Tyler privately confessed his attempt to save the Union was "a poor, rickety, and disconnected affair," and he ended it by trying to convince New Jersey to become a part of the new confederacy of slave states. Down in Virginia, secessionists sharpened their rhetoric and strengthened their position, branding those who wanted to stay in the United States with the supreme insult: they lacked manhood.[16]

Social class played a role in fueling the growing sentitment. Slaveholders had long occupied the upper rungs of the First Families of Virginia and commanded the highest levels of money and social clout. Their rhetoric channeling the spirit of 1776 and the romantic "resistance to tyrants" had a corresponding psychological effect on their lower-status neighbors, a contagion suggested by a *New-York Tribune* correspondent who watched a similar dynamic unfold the same month in neighboring Maryland. He thought "the intense proslaveryism" he saw on the streets of Baltimore was "*simply the sign of a caste*" because "it is aristocratic to be pro-slavery," and those who aspired to higher stations and wanted to curry favor with the elite had to display "an extra amount of Southern ardor and pro-slavery talk."[17]

Among the loudest voices for Virginia secession was none other than Henry Wise, who had done so much to bring acrimony to the halls of Congress when he served as a representative. He had gone on to become Virginia's governor and had interviewed John Brown in his cell for three hours and came away, incredibly, with admiring words for the "cool, collected and indomitable" warrior who impressed him as "the gamest man I ever saw." Then he signed Brown's death warrant. At the convention, he urged the seizure of federal property in Virginia—just as Brown had tried to seize the armory and just as the South Carolina contingent was now trying to seize Fort Sumter. The "car of war" was bearing down on everyone, warned Wise, and the whole of Virginia was "endangered by invasion." The only options were independence or death.[18]

One of Wise's Tidewater allies, Edmund Ruffin, shared a strange admiration for the steadfast radicalism of John Brown, calling him "a brave & able man" and the embodiment of physical courage in the name of a cause. "In this quality he seems to me to have had few equals." Like his friend Wise, Ruffin had a mane of long hair and a dyspeptic temper. Complaining that the Virginia convention took more time electing doorkeepers than South Carolina had spent in deciding to leave the Union, he took a train down to Charleston to tour the battery of cannons surrounding the besieged Fort Sumter, guns only waiting to be fired.[19]

As the Sumter crisis intensified, torch-bearing mobs prowled the streets of Richmond shouting insults at anyone perceived to be on the Unionist side. Those showing hesitation were suspected of being in league with the "Black Republicans," secret abolitionists under their cotton-fiber suits and in love with their own honeyed professions of love for the antislavery Constitution. "The conceited old ghosts who crawled from a hundred damp graves to manacle their State and deliver her up as a hand-maid to the hideous Chimpanzee from Illinois have determined that not one word of their rubbish and gabble will be lost to posterity," wrote the editor of the *Richmond Examiner*, eager for the talking to be over and to prepare for whatever patriotic slaughter would come. It was not clear if they understood that Virginia was condemning itself to become a battleground.[20]

News clattered over the telegraph of Confederate shots fired at Fort Sumter on April 12, the opening of the war everyone knew was coming. Anderson's troops were without proper ammunition, down to their last scraps of hardtack and bacon, and unable to do much but volley a few dozen cold iron balls at their attackers. Edmund Ruffin had been given the honor of lighting the fuse on one of the first shots at Fort Sumter from nearby Morris Island, the formal opening of the Civil War, and he also claimed to have been the first man to have entered the gates after Anderson surrendered.[21]

Lincoln called for the rebellion to be smothered. "Great demonstrations made throughout the day, and hundreds of secession flags are flying in all parts of the city," wrote clerk J.B. Jones. Tyler brought the disquieting news about federal troops now aiming the guns of Fort Monroe at the village of Hampton. For Elizabeth Van Lew, the daughter of a prominent Richmond family, the conversation seemed insane. "Think of a community rushing gladly, unrestrainedly, eagerly into a bloody civil war!" she wrote in her diary. "One day I could speak for my country, the next was threatened with death. Surely madness was upon the people!" A group of University of Virginia students broke down the door to the roof of the Mechanics' Institute and raised up an improvised Confederate banner before they were chased off. They were only a few days too early. A roar of support from boardinghouse windows made downtown Richmond "sound like the Lunatic asylum had been moved farther down the road," said one observer.[22]

Lincoln had just said in his inaugural message, "I have no purpose, directly or indirectly, to interfere with the institution of slavery in the States where it exists." But when he called on Virginia to help supply troops to put down the uprising in the Lower South on April 15, with the added aim of redressing "wrongs already long endured," Governor John Letcher dramatically refused the order. The Unionists lost their advantage. Delegate Jubal Early moved over to the secessionist column, as did Tyler, who confided to his wife that "the God of Battle" was now in charge and the future was "full of peril." And indeed, there was not one day of the Civil War in which Virginia would have territorial integrity; the presence of Fort Monroe was only the tip of the Northern spear. More than 120 significant military engagements would be fought in Virginia in the next four years, and tens of thousands would die violently on its soil.

The final vote for secession came in at 88–55, after Henry Wise took the dais and waved a horse pistol in the air, announcing that local militias would soon be taking control of all federal installations within state boundaries, just as South Carolina had taken over Fort Sumter. He lamented that Virginians couldn't have marched into Washington, DC, and seized it by force "before the

Republican hordes got possession of it." But he promised that Virginia would conquer Fort Monroe, he vowed, even "if it costs ten thousand of her sons."[23]

Wise and John Tyler walked through the Mechanics' Institute arm in arm, to rousing applause and shouts, symbolizing the radical capture of the middle. Most delegates who voted for Unionism left the city as soon as they could, fearing for their safety. And many who cheered in public confessed doubts when they were away from the crowds. "One gentleman who signed the ordinance of secession told me that if he had not done so, the streets of Richmond would have run with blood," wrote Van Lew in a private letter. Charles King Mallory of Hampton had been among those voting in favor of disunion, but—perhaps in reflection of the divided feelings of his neighbors—he had not said a word during the lengthy proceedings.[24]

Robert E. Lee resigned his commission in the U.S. Army and accepted the command of Virginia forces. Volunteer militia units sprung up everywhere. Four of them mustered within sight of the guns of Fort Monroe, including the spit-and-polish 115th Virginia, made up partially of students from the Hampton Military Academy at Pee Dee Point, where the headmaster, John Baytop Cary, had equipped all the desks with an oil rag for keeping the wood shining like mirrors. "Colonel Cary had gotten the reputation for being very strict, and all knew he had to be obeyed, so there was very little of disobedience to his rules or missing of lessons," recalled a student.[25]

Part of Cary's new job was hustling as many enslaved people as could be spared out to strategic points around Hampton for the erection of parapets, redoubts, and other fortifications in expectation of a federal attack. The failed defense of Fort Sumter had been a feeble embarrassment under President James Buchanan, but nobody now expected Abraham Lincoln to surrender a prize like Fort Monroe, though it was deep in Southern territory and could be supplied only by steamship. At the same time, the U.S. War Department ordered several regiments of Massachusetts Volunteers to reinforce the 1st Vermont under the command of Justin Dimick. The race to establish control of the Virginia

Peninsula was on. Both sides rushed to build and secure as many fortified positions as they could before fighting commenced.

Soon after, three enslaved men walked off the job at Sewell's Point. They went to the shore of the water, commandeered a boat, and set off across the long reach of water toward the federal pentagon at Old Point Comfort, the windswept tip of land that John Smith thought would be "fit for a castle" the first time that he saw it.

* * *

That General Benjamin Butler's novel formulation of "contraband" should have been cooked up at the 1619 *White Lion* landing spot was a delightful literary irony for Edward Lillie Pierce, an attorney with degrees from Harvard and Brown. He had joined the 3rd Massachusetts on a whim, and sent dispatches from the fort to the *Boston Traveler*, later compiling his dispatches into a feature article for *The Atlantic*, a prime organ in the church of New England intellectualism.

His article opened with a brief account of the 1619 arrival. "It was fitting that the system which from that slave-ship had been spreading over the continent for nearly two centuries and a half should yield for the first time to the logic of military law upon the spot of its origin," he wrote.[26]

Pierce had reason to curry favor with General Butler, who he must have known was an avid reader of his own press clippings, but he also seemed genuinely impressed with the political stroke of the term "contraband"—a backdoor method of making slave freedom palatable for Northerners squeamish about the implications of Black equality. "Contraband" was like a cooling saucer, a halfway house, a not-quite-there that could be rescinded after the storm of secession had died down.

"There is often great virtue in such technical phrases in shaping public opinion," Pierce wrote. "The venerable gentleman, who wears gold spectacles and reads a conservative daily, prefers confiscation to emancipation. He is reluctant to have slaves declared freeman but has no objection to their being described as contrabands."[27]

Another observer at Fort Monroe with literary ambitions took a slightly different and more direct view. Theodore Winthrop was a Yale-educated abolitionist who, before shipping off to Fort Monroe, told his family: "I go to put an end to slavery." He wrote in his notebook a line from the Roman poet Horace, *Solvuntur risu tabulae* (The legal case is erased with a laugh). Then he added his own interpretation of what had just happened, and what was about to happen. "An epigram abolished slavery in the United States," wrote Winthrop. "'Negroes are contrabands of war.'"[28]

The semantic shift caught on. "I observe that the word 'contraband' has established itself in a new sense as designating a class of biped mamalia. This we owe to General Butler," wrote New York financier George Templeton Strong, using—with some irony—a dehumanizing term for an enslaved person. The lawyer Charles C. Nott noticed that Northern racists inclined to use disparaging terms for Blacks were able to accept the new term with ease, given how it was a new weapon against the rebels. "Those who love to ponder over the changes in language and watch its new uses and unconscious growth, must find in it a rare phenomenon of philological vegetation," he wrote. "Never was a word so speedily adopted by so many people in so short a time."[29]

The financial loss to the Confederacy translated into military advantage. For that reason alone, the contraband policy was gaining favor in the Lincoln administration. On July 1, Lincoln himself told Illinois senator Orville Browning that "the government neither should nor would send back into bondage such as came to our armies." He did not then see it as a step toward abolition, or even a permanent measure, though others in Washington had different ideas. Browning himself had told Lincoln that the time was coming when "it will be necessary for you to march an army into the South and proclaim freedom to the slaves. When it does come, do it. Don't hesitate. You are fighting for national life—for your own individual life. God has raised you up for a great work. Go boldly forward in the course his providence points you."[30]

Another Illinois congressman pressing Lincoln for tougher action was Rep. Owen Lovejoy, whose brother Elijah had been shot to death by a proslavery mob in the town of Alton, Illinois, in 1837 after they threw his printing press in the Mississippi River. Owen Lovejoy shared the abolitionist fervor of his martyred brother and viewed the contraband decision at Fort Monroe as a wedge to force open the broader question of slavery. He introduced a nonbinding resolution on July 8 stating, "It is no part of the duty of the soldiers of the United States to capture and return fugitive slaves." The House was operating only at half-strength, as lawmakers from Confederate states had walked out the month before. The Republican Party dominated. Yet the vote was 93 in favor to 55 against. Lovejoy complained that many who voted yes were "timid and vexed" to appear to be on the side of Blacks but felt they had to make a public show of being tough on the rebels.[31]

Confusion now reigned across the U.S. Army. General Irvin McDowell, soon to lose a humiliating confrontation at Bull Run, ordered fugitives returned to their owners—terms that had stood in the North for more than a decade. George McClellan, who would become Lincoln's top general, promised slaveholders loyal to the Union that not only would he refuse entry to contrabands seeking protection, he would, "with an iron hand, crush any attempt at insurrection on their part." When Joseph K.F. Mansfield's troops captured Alexandria, Virginia, he told his officers they must "respect private property" of the rebels and throw any unaccompanied enslaved person into the city jail. By contrast, other officers showed their support for enslaved people, including Colonel Harvey Brown, who would "not send the negroes back as I shall never be voluntarily instrumental in returning a poor wretch to slavery."[32]

In St. Louis, the impulsive general John Charles Frémont took a different approach than McClellan and released a declaration of martial law that promised a firing squad for armed rebels, confiscation of all their property, and immediate freedom for their enslaved people. "Thank God a beginning has been made," said the *Chicago Tribune*, calling the manumission the "daybreak of the nation," while the *New York Evening Post* said, "Mr. Frémont has done what the Government ought to have done from the beginning. War is war."[33]

Lincoln was less enthusiastic about what he called the "purely political" edict out west. Such a radical measure could push border states into the Confederate column, one of his greatest material fears. "I think to lose Kentucky is nearly the same as to lose the whole game," he confided to Browning. One of Lincoln's oldest friends, Joshua Speed, wrote the president a letter in which he shared that he could not eat or sleep after hearing of Frémont's order, out of the worry that it would inspire a violent uprising across the South. He asked: "Will not such a proclamation read by slaves incline them to assert their freedom?"[34]

The president sent Frémont a dispatch so carefully worded as to seem deferential, informing him the order could "alarm our Southern Union friends" to the point of seceding, or cause a wave of mass executions of loyalists. Within two months, Lincoln relieved the popular general of his command in Missouri, a state crucial to the control of the Mississippi River and the overland route to the Colorado gold fields that could supply the Union with hard currency.[35]

In his annual message to Congress, Lincoln warned against "radical and extreme measures," but abolitionists and now even some wavering antislavery Republicans thought it only proved Lincoln's inability to think creatively. "He would keep things precisely as they are," complained the abolitionist Gerrit Smith. "He would have the fugitive slave sent back to the very spot he came from, and into exactly his former relations. He would not allow one line or letter of the Constitution to be disturbed by the necessities of war."[36]

But Butler's contraband decision had unleashed a powerful idea that could not be called back. News of it spread wherever the U.S. Army made an advance and picked up—as if by gravitational force—a new column made up of dozens or hundreds of self-emancipated people trailing behind the cannons. An officer serving in Alabama in 1862 witnessed a remarkable sight:

> Crying children, hoary age and athletic youth were there. On foot and in wagons, mounted on horses, mules, and jackasses, loaded down with burdens containing all manner of worthless traps and contrivances, being the sum total of their worldly goods; on through the moonlight came the strange procession. In spite of its ludicrous aspect and the irresistible impulse to laugh, there was to me something strangely sublime in the spectacle of these thousands of human beings fleeing from bondage to freedom.[37]

Except for a minority of idealists, mainly New Englanders, abolition had not been a popular cause among Union fighting men.

The fight with the South was supposed to have been about secession. But the migration of enslaved people had begun to foster a shift in consciousness. Officers and privates alike could see the pragmatism behind enticing slaves away from the Confederacy, flipping their enemy's tools against him as a moral and physical weapon. "Public sentiment is undergoing a change," wrote a Virginia man to the *New York Times*, "and there are many now looking forward to the abolition of Slavery who never thought of it before."[38]

Far off on the Kansas frontier, a U.S. Army soldier listened to a twelve-year-old boy tell a harrowing story of running through the woods toward the bluecoats to get away from an abusive master. "Does not this incident show how thoroughly diffused among the slaves is a love of freedom and a knowledge of the present crisis?" the soldier wrote home in a letter. One of his fellow volunteers saw the same basic urge driving the mass exodus into Kansas. "Running away has got to be an epidemic among the negroes of Missouri, or perhaps I should say, a *plague* among their masters. Leavenworth, Lawrence, Ossowottomie, every town, is black with contrabands." He spent extended time in conversation with them, "and while each hour my abhorrence and detestation of the system increased, I, at the same time, found my prejudice against the race giving way."[39]

Whatever their political beliefs, Union soldiers wasted no time in turning some of the refugees into personal servants. "Nearly every staff officer has two or three of these handy genii, and the task of many a mounted trooper or even Aide-de-Camp, is superseded by some bright negro errand boy," wrote the *New-York Tribune*'s correspondent. But there was, of course, no guarantee of a changed mind. Some confided hatreds in rhetoric matching anything that would have been said in a roadside tavern in Alabama. "Nasty, idle, dirty beasts," complained a Union officer. "I wish to Heaven they were all at the bottom of the Chesapeake. The General insists on it that they do work, but they are far more trouble than they are worth."[40]

But in general, the more that U.S. Army soldiers heard and saw in the contraband camps, the more their attitudes shifted. The war, said a soldier with the 3rd Wisconsin Volunteers, was "abolitionizing the whole army" because of the "evils" they had witnessed. "You have no idea of the changes that have taken place in the minds of the soldiers in the last two months," he wrote to the *Wisconsin State Journal* in October 1861. Wherever shadow regiments of freed people trailed behind the U.S. Army, there were shared campfires, shared rations, and shared stories. A New York soldier named Rice C. Bull remarked, as so many others did, on the strange new music they brought. "They sang the plantation hymns and songs and it was as natural for them to dance as to breathe," he wrote. "They often had banjos which they strummed for music; when they had no banjos our boys would beat time on their knees with their hands." Particularly when they took a religious turn, the songs communicated a powerful idea to the frontline soldiers: the surety that a long-prayed-for deliverance was on the way, if it had not already arrived.[41]

A general liberation throughout the United States was "going to come," predicted a Black Methodist deacon at Fort Monroe to a visitor, James Ashley, a congressman from Ohio with a political commission in the military. A gruff abolitionist who had been present at John Brown's execution as an observer, Ashley had a smile, said a friend, "like sunshine playing above a rock."[42]

In the muddy field outside Fort Monroe, a group of refugees stood around Ashley with questions.

"What are you going to do with us?" one asked the congressman.

"We shall not harm you," he assured them.

"We know that, but will you send us back?" another answered. "We want to know because if you don't, our friends will follow."[43]

* * *

One of the fugitives who had found his way to the fort, George Scott, knew how to stay ahead of his enemies.

Long before the war broke out, he had run away from his master—a widely disliked man named A.M. Graves—and found refuge in a cave in the woods. A few enslaved people who lived nearby brought him food under cover of night. When Graves went looking for him with a pistol and a Bowie knife, Scott disarmed him in hand-to-hand combat and kept both weapons. When the heat died down, he would sometimes venture out for paid day labor, keeping a wary eye out for Graves. After he heard of the contraband decision, Scott joined up with Colonel Abram Duryée's regiment and volunteered to scout the woods he knew so well from his time on the run. "I can smell a rebel further than I can a skunk," he told people.[44]

Scott was one of the ex-slaves gathered in the camps around Fort Monroe who would be recruited into the U.S. Army as a spy. No employment paperwork was ever created and no formal acknowledgment of service ever given, but the people who had grown up amid the Virginia Peninsula's forests and fields, learning how to stay unobtrusive and nearly invisible, proved to be a valuable military resource for Butler and other Union field commanders who could see past their own prejudices. To be enslaved was to have known a double existence and a talent for improvisation: the need to appear compliant in front of an owner while doing what was necessary, though forbidden, when punishing eyes were averted.

"They have been spies all their lives," theorized Colonel Thomas W. Higginson, a Unitarian minister. "I should not attempt to give them instructions. They would be better able to teach me." No less an authority than Allan Pinkerton, chief of the U.S. Secret Service, found enslaved people "ever ready to answer questions and to furnish me with every fact which I desired to possess." He had special praise for John Scobell, who conducted several undercover operations in Virginia in which no Confederate suspected the amiable "rollicking negro" with a rich stock of Scottish ballads was actually a "cool-headed, vigilant detective."[45]

Enslaved people knew the countryside around Hampton and the habits of their masters, easily fading into the background of a Southern pastoral scene. "They crawl through the underbrush at night like a portion of the gloom, and if seen lounging about the field in an old plantation dress, seldom arouse suspicion," said the correspondent George Wilkes in a letter to the *New-York Tribune.* One panicked Union scout came rushing into Fort Monroe with news of a Confederate cavalry regiment on the march and their telltale hoofprints in the mud. A freed enslaved man took a look at the same road and corrected the assessment. A few ordinary horses and mules had just passed by.[46]

In George Scott's secret journeys through the woods once inhabited by the Powhatan and coveted by English colonists, he watched between branches as several Confederate companies clustered near an artillery battery about seven miles from Old Point Comfort. Colonel J.B. Magruder had deliberately placed them here in hopes of provoking one of the first infantry fights of the war, knowing that a frontal assault on Fort Monroe would be useless. Scott hid in the bushes for nearly a day, cradling his revolver and counting soldiers, until one of the outpost guards spotted him and squeezed off a shot, nicking the sleeve of his coat. Scott retreated, noting the location near Big Bethel Church, and brought the information back to Colonel Abram Duryée.[47]

The Confederates had built their camp amid the faded earthen mounds shoveled into place by the troops of Lord Cornwallis during the siege of Yorktown eighty years ago. They were also standing in the way of Butler's anticipated road to Richmond and future military glory. The knot of rebels had to be cleared out.

Perhaps Butler was thinking of his recent bloodless march on Baltimore when—based almost entirely on Scott's detailed report—he ordered a column of 3,500 federal soldiers under Duryée's command to head north on the night of June 9 and prepare to attack at dawn. A group of contrabands gathered to cheer on the detachment, which included the 5th New York Infantry Regiment dressed in the distinctive sashes and pantaloons of North African Zouave troops. In a sign of the exodus happening all over the region, their march through the darkness was soon interrupted when a "squad of negroes" approached the blue-clad units asking for directions to the "freedom fortress"—yet more enslaved people who had either slipped away from their bonds or been abandoned by their owners.[48]

Butler had told his men to wear a white cloth tied around their left arms to prevent friendly fire. But it was a disaster. Before they encountered the rebels, the 7th New York Volunteer Infantry mistook the blue uniforms of a fellow New York unit for gray and neglected to yell out the pre-agreed watchword "Boston." They fired at their fellow Union soldiers, killing two. The shame and confusion heightened when Union troops surrounded the related church at Little Bethel, expecting to have trapped a mass of Confederates, only to find the structure empty.

Magruder had told his aides that morning: "God never made a prettier day for men to die on," and he was ready. Assisting him in command was Col. Charles Mallory, perhaps still wondering about the fate of his three wayward men. The firefight at Big Bethel Church dragged on for four hours in a series of unsuccessful flanking maneuvers by the Union. At one point, Theodore Winthrop, the Yale-educated secretary who wanted to see slavery done away with by an epigram, mustered his courage and loaded his weapon. "Come on boys!" he shouted, stepping up on a log, "one charge and the day is ours." A Confederate bullet struck him in the heart.

He was one of eighteen killed that day before Union troops staggered eight miles back to the fort, leaving bloodied coats, canteens, haversacks, and broken carbines scattered and sparkling in the late afternoon sun.[49]

Recriminations began immediately. Northern newspapers ridiculed Butler for not accompanying his own troops in the first major advance of the oncoming war; the *New York Times* made snide reference to the "brace of Massachusetts barristers" who had midwifed the fiasco. Butler blamed Pierce, who in turn cast aspersions on the martyred Winthrop, who some said had been shot by accident by his own comrades.[50]

"The question to be settled among them is not which did the most to prevent defeat—but who were the greatest cowards," wrote a disgusted observer.[51]

"I went over the field after the fight," a Confederate private wrote in a letter. "The sight was sickening. Here lay the body of a Zouave, the blood still gushing from his wound; a little further, the body of one of some other Regiment, with his musket in his clenched hand; and all about lay the dead, with their eyes glazed and fixed."[52]

* * *

Finally tired of Benjamin Butler's military inexperience and hunger for celebrity, Lincoln asked General Winfield Scott to send Butler on a different assignment. He would shortly be on his way to North Carolina, to be replaced by General John Wool. Butler assumed it had something to do with the contraband camp. "What does it mean? Why this?" he complained to Postmaster General Montgomery Blair. "Is this because General Scott has got over his quarrel with Wool, or is it a move on the part of the President, or is it because my views on the Negro question are not acceptable to the government? I suppose the last. Meanwhile I am in the dark."[53]

Butler told his wife Sarah that he suspected he had been removed from Fort Monroe because of his persistence in asking what to do about the freed enslaved people—inquiries he believed were forcing difficult but necessary questions within the Lincoln administration. "The negro will be free," he wrote her. "It is inevitable."[54]

Events were already out of his hands. Congress took a further step toward emancipation with the Confiscation Act of 1861, signed into law the day before Hampton burned. In a confusing

Benjamin Butler. His coinage of the term "contraband of war" to describe escaped enslaved people outraged the Confederacy but won him many Northern admirers in the early days of the war. "A practical joke of stupendous dimensions," said the *New York World.*

tangle of legalistic sentences, it permitted the seizure of property used in the rebellion against the government, including "any person claimed to be held to labor or service" who had been "employed in or upon any fort, navy yard, dock, armory, ship, entrenchment, or in any military or naval service whatsoever, against the Government and lawful authority of the United States." Any rebel must now "forfeit his claim" to any enslaved person who came in contact with the U.S. Army.

The passive voice reigned supreme. If a slave had been property, who now owned that person? Certainly not the government, which was not a slave owner. The forfeiture seemed to pass ownership rights directly to the freed person, without the need for any court case or oversight. Merely touching Union lines would be enough, with the able-bodied individual now presumably a wage laborer for the military. Butler's contraband policy was now federal law.[55]

The bill's primary author, Senator Lyman Trumbull, was also careful not to use the word "slave," but he emphasized the term "insurrection" to make it plain the government was using civil police powers instead of wartime measures. On this crucial point, his intellectual foundation differed from that of Butler, who had "taken Virginia at her word" that she was a sovereign country like France or Mexico. Trumbull, an Illinois lawyer nearly as tall as Lincoln with a nervous disposition, made it clear during his floor speeches that he viewed confiscation not merely as a military tool but as a picklock to force an eventual general emancipation. Wartime measures such as Butler's would likely evaporate at the end of hostilities. A federal law would freeze it in place for good.[56]

An enthusiastic congressman, Thaddeus Stevens of Pennsylvania, said "the time had come when the laws of war were to govern our actions." *Inter arma silent leges*, he said, dramatically quoting Cicero's maxim that "in times of war, the laws are silent." The conflict provided a tremendous opening in the name of emancipation, and the Confederates had only themselves to blame. Stevens held "that if you were in a state of peace you could not confiscate the property of any citizen. You have no right to do it in peace, but in a time of war you have the right to confiscate the property of every rebel."[57]

After the Union defeat at Bull Run on July 16, when it had become apparent the war would not be won easily, an excited Charles Sumner told Lincoln that they should be grateful for it. A fast war would have left slavery intact, he said, and the Union defeat might be seen as the "worst event & the best event in our history; the worst as it was the greatest present calamity & shame,—the best, as it made the extinction of slavery inevitable."[58]

But Lincoln was doubtful about the Confiscation Act. He had been elected on a platform of respecting Southern rights and property, and this signaled an intrusion of federal power into the gates of the plantation. He also remained anxious about keeping the border states of Maryland, Missouri, and Kentucky from seceding. "The severest justice may not be the best policy," he wrote in a statement to Congress, even though he agreed with a strengthening of the contraband policy. "The traitor against the general government forfeits his slave at least as justly as he does any other property; and he forfeits both to the government against which he offends," reasoned Lincoln. A disappointed abolitionist, Maria Weston Chapman, called the measure "an Emancipation bill with clogs on."[59]

In Buffalo, the editors of the *Morning Express* saw it differently: "The confiscation act just passed provides tolerably well for the contraband slave. It distinguishes them from property and recognizes them as men." Congress had essentially made "free men of all negroes." As Republicans pointed out, the wording of the "against the Government" clause could be interpreted to free any enslaved person doing virtually *anything* that could benefit the Confederates: growing cotton, harvesting wheat, or fabricating metal. Applications in the field, however, could turn on the racial attitude, or even the daily mood, of the commanding officer, who had little direct guidance from Washington. "The policy of the Government on this question is as much a riddle and a mystery as the ancient oracles of Egypt," wrote a Wisconsin soldier.[60]

Such was the power of the underground telegraph that some enslaved people, working off smuggled newspapers, took to memorizing passages of the Confiscation Act to cite when they presented themselves to confused Union soldiers. The commanders then had to ascertain the difficult question of whether any given owner was indeed connected to the Confederacy, forcing them to waste time conducting field investigations. The heat of war often got in the way. A bank clerk from Ohio named John Beatty had volunteered for the Union army and was marching with his unit through Tennessee when a young man came rushing toward him from a hiding place in the woods. "Master, I want to go with you!" he pleaded. Beatty had to tell him no, the commander didn't allow it. "The light went out of the poor fellow's eyes in a moment, and, putting on his slouched hat, he went away sorrowful enough," he wrote in his diary. "It seems cruel to turn our backs on these, our only friends." An impatient General Henry Halleck resolved to be done with the whole business, regardless of what Congress had said. He issued General Order No. 3 in November 1861, prohibiting refugees inside his encampments. It was not his job, he reasoned, "to decide upon the relation of master and man."[61]

The argument within the military only reflected the national confusion over the disputed role of slavery as a war aim, and the final legal disposition of those tens of thousands of people trailing behind Union army positions like the trail of a comet. Refusing to "see" slavery was increasingly difficult. Throughout the autumn of 1861 and into the following year, the question kept appearing in the pages of American newspapers and in everyday conversations, a mounting drumbeat. "What shall be done with the negroes?" the *Burlington Weekly Free Press* wondered. Even those who didn't witness the crowds for themselves could not escape hearing about them: the reports of jerry-built villages and tent metropolises lying outside army forts, the shoeless entourages trailing the marching columns of bluecoats, the abandoned cotton fields of Southern aristocrats now cultivated independently by freed people. Under the headline "What Shall We Do with the Slaves?" a correspondent wrote, "This is the question everywhere asked by patriots and traitors."[62]

Slabtown and the other settlements outside Fort Monroe had by then grown to house more than five thousand people. Because the confiscation law applied only to disloyal slave owners, there were almost no camps in the border states. There was only one in

Missouri and none in Maryland. But in the contested ground of the Confederate states where the U.S. Army made incursions, the camps popped up with astonishing frequency, often to the alarm of white neighbors.

When the army went on the move, so too did the bands of freed people. If the commander authorized no rations, the freed people had to forage, risking gunfire from Southern farmers out to protect their crops and property. Those too weak to walk were left behind. "Every soldier had a negro marching in the flanks carrying his knapsack," reported U.S. Army major general Godfrey Weitzel, accompanied through southern Louisiana by "plantation carts, filled with negro women and children, with their effects; and of course compelled to pillage for their subsistence, as I have no rations to issue them." He reported 25,000 refugees trailing behind, outnumbering the strength of his brigades.[63]

"You have no idea of the state of things here," wrote the Presbyterian missionary Thomas Callahan before he launched into a breathless sentence attempting to describe the scope of the refugee problem.

> Go out in any direction and you meet negroes on horses, negroes on mules, negroes with oxen, negroes by the wagon, cart and buggy load, negroes on foot, men, women and children; negroes in uniform, negroes in rags, negroes in frame houses, negroes living in tents, negroes living in rail pens covered with brush, and negroes living under brush piles without any rails, negroes living on the bare ground with the sky for their covering; all hopeful, almost all cheerful, every one pleading to be taught, willing to do anything for learning.[64]

The social crisis reached acute proportions at Cairo, Illinois, a swampy town at the junction of the Ohio and Mississippi Rivers swelling with fugitives from all points, making it the largest camp outside Slabtown. General Ulysses S. Grant had set up an office on the second floor of a bank building, puffing on a pipe as he planned a downstream invasion while his army reserved a row barracks on the west side to house runaway enslaved people. This disgusted the editor of the *Cairo City Gazette*, who complained about federal spending on "feeding vagabond negroes" and the "generally very worthless class of population" living in squalor among them. The Kentucky bounty hunters prowling the streets did not seem to concern him.[65]

Cairo had never been a completely safe place. Every mud walloper and wharf rat in mid-America knew about the tongue of marshy land at the very bottom of Illinois where the clear waters of the Ohio River joined the relentless dirty slog of the Mississippi. The wharves charged predatory docking fees, giving the town a no-go reputation among rivermen, who also risked a knife fight or robbery if they chanced a drink in the taverns. Levee-busting floods had ruined investors who had been sold a vision of a shining metropolis at the confluence of mighty rivers. The name, pronounced CARE-o, instead became a symbol for fraud. Charles Dickens thought it "a hotbed of disease, an ugly sepulchre, a grave uncheered by any gleam of promise" after an 1842 visit to research a novel about American hype and greed. Most Illinois Republicans shared his low opinion, though for different reasons, writing off the downstate region everyone called Little Egypt as a hotbed of proslavery sentiment, closer in geography and culture to Mississippi than Chicago.

Secretary of War Edwin Stanton viewed the Cairo camp as merely a brief stopover for most refugees, urging a program whereby freed people would live "with farmers families" in Iowa, Wisconsin, and other breadbaskets where they could ease a shortage of agricultural labor. "The war has nearly depopulated some townships of able-bodied men, and consequently there is an immense demand for labor to gather the crops," reported the *Chicago Tribune*. "The necessity is so great that people don't stop to cavil about color."[66]

Democrats seized on the problem, looking for an advantage in the 1862 midterm elections. One of its Illinois congressional candidates, J.C. Allen, warned that no "greater curse" threatened the Midwest than the "pouring into it of a flood of free negroes, who are without effort or provision for taking care of themselves." In Iowa, the *Quad-City Times* warned its readers: "A horde of black paupers will take possession of your homes, and you will witness all the horrors which attend the efforts of white men to place the negro on an equality with you." The superintendent of contrabands, John Eaton, called for a halt to the resettlement plan, telling the War Department that freedmen's labor was "obnoxious to the people of Illinois" because most of them were "prejudiced against blacks," even as their unpicked crops rotted in the field.[67]

The mess at Cairo found an echo downstream at Helena, Arkansas, where the U.S. Army, after capturing the town, cleared out a row of brush along Lower Little Rock Road to the south of town, called it "Camp Ethiopia," and made it a temporary home to several hundred people living in ramshackle cabins near the mosquito-infested lowlands—a "terrible hole," in the judgment of one officer, where all manner of diseases thrived. The U.S. Army had set up a hospital, but it was worse than useless. "The negro hospital here has become notorious for filth, neglect, mortality & brutal whipping, so that the contrabands have lost all hope of kind treatment there, & would almost as soon go to their graves as to their hospital," wrote three chaplains.[68]

The rampant illnesses at the Mississippi River camps only played into a Southern trope that slavery was a benevolent institution that ensured a happier life for Black people than any kind of dubious freedom touted by abolitionists. The *Richmond Dispatch* called the contraband camps "little else than pens of idleness, squalor and disease" and chided the "neglect and indifference" of the U.S. Army, which it called a treacherous friend to the enslaved. "During the present war thousands of negroes have been released from servitude to their masters," editorialized the *Dispatch*, "but we say unhesitatingly that in nine cases out of ten, if not in a far greater ratio, the change has been positively injurious to their condition, morally and physically. How many of the contrabands are better provided for than they were in slavery?"[69]

The example set by what was called a "model camp" at Corinth, Mississippi, appeared to refute that argument. In the spring of 1862, General Henry Halleck marched three Union armies toward the strategic junction of the Mobile & Ohio and Memphis & Charleston, a spot called "the vertebrae of the Confederacy" by one of Jefferson Davis's associates. Fierce fighting had left the train depot a smoldering ruin of sticks and the streets littered with empty barrels and "piles of spoiled provisions, sending up an odor which would disgrace a respectable sewer up north." The ruins of Corinth had become a base for expeditionary thrusts into the surrounding territory to disarm rebels, sink flatboats, claim livestock, and burn cotton bushels.[70]

During one of those plundering missions, a woman who guessed herself to be between seventy-five and eighty years of age looked up from milking a cow to see "Yankees heads popping above the fence." She set down the pail and walked up to the captain, who told her he was going to free her and her companions from slavery. "Then we fetched out our old bags and old beds and put in the wagon, and the captain told us to put in provisions to eat," said the woman. "I tell you it was all done mighty quick, and we drove off, some of us riding in the fine carriage and the rest in the wagon." In just a few anticlimactic minutes, their lifetime of forced servitude was over.[71]

Liberating enslaved people was not the point of these missions, but it was the result. "A cavalry raid went out this morning," wrote an approving missionary, "which will break the chains of the captive and bring him into our lines a *free man*." The clashes had sent hill country landowners fleeing for cover, and cleared the way for their enslaved people to seek out Union troops they prayed would be friendly, or at least not hostile. Some hid in blackberry bushes along the roads, trying to judge the shifting temperament of the passing soldiers.[72]

The man tasked with formulating a coherent plan for them in the town of Corinth, James Alexander, had lived with his family in Mississippi before the war and knew hundreds of the antebellum residents, as well as some of the peculiarities of local culture. Their scorn for Northern do-gooders did not bother him. "There were but few friends of the Black man who were willing to undertake the work and endure the reproach then attached to the 'contraband,' the term by which the Freedmen are better known in the South-West than any other," he wrote in a letter.[73]

The army gave him authority over a large meadow owned by Mary Phillips, discreetly separated from town by a low rise called Fort College Hill. Alexander handed out axes to the freed people and encouraged them to chop down sweetgum and pine trees to make cabins, with some supplementary construction help from a pile of lumber liberated from Davenport Mills. Then he laid out a plot for a massive vegetable garden, as well as dirt streets in a grid pattern named for Union generals, both the celebrity fighters and the lesser known: Frémont, Butler, Sweeny, Oglesby, and Lovejoy. Ditches around the village drained the streets when it rained, and sidewalks of planed boards kept down the mud. "Here are your plank roads leading across the bottom," wrote John Duckworth of the 2nd Iowa Infantry. "To our right among the fallen timber we see a few smoking cook pots and around them a few Contraband." Almost immediately, the camp became more populated than the city of Corinth had been before the war.[74]

Alexander insisted on cleanliness and order. A fifty-foot well supplied freshwater and filled a public bathing trough. All the new houses were assigned numbers. A few had porches and gingerbread styling, and residents were expected to provide a general sweeping-out and a morning report each day at 9 a.m. The three-chimney great house of Mary Phillips, described by the wife of a chaplain as a "superb family mansion," was transformed into a hospital, with two attending surgeons regarded as "kind & faithful." A nondenominational congregation called Union Christian Church celebrated its first service with about a hundred in attendance; for some, it was the first time they had been given communion. The Sunday worship could last up to four hours, with earnest prayers for the success of the U.S. Army. The chaplains also sanctified weddings with up to thirty couples present at one time.[75]

The differences in the contraband camps were as distinct as the nation's own idiosyncrasies, with no guarantee that they were an adequate means of preparation for freedom. Edwin Stanton sought to bring some clarity to the "what should be done" question roiling the newspapers in November 1862. He started a fact-finding process by sending the Boston physician LeBaron Russell to Slabtown, which had matured into a community of 7,362 people, some of whom had traveled more than a hundred miles.[76]

Russell rendered his optimistic conclusions in an eighteen-page memorandum of tight cursive. Schools and churches were thriving, he said, as were small businesses. But freed people needed independence more than anything. "Here they live with their families in houses of their own and make a nearer approach to the condition of free northern laborers than is possible when they are crowded together in tents," he wrote. The main problem was the irregular payment of wages, which caused "unnecessary suffering," and cast doubt on the federal commitment to permanent liberty.[77]

And even as the government searched for a more permanent policy, the same insistent question kept coming—asked by thousands of people in essentially the same wording—in taverns, churches, and newspapers all across the North. Democratic papers asked the question most consistently, but mainstream Republican papers picked it up, too.

"What is to be done with the slaves?" asked the *Atlantic Messenger*.[78]

"What is to become of the slaves after this civil war is over?" asked the *Anti-Slavery Standard*.[79]

"What is to be done with them?" asked the *New York Daily Herald*.[80]

"What shall be done with the slaves at Fortress Monroe whose rebel masters have abandoned them?" wondered the *Janesville Daily Gazette* in Wisconsin.[81]

"What is to be done with the slaves?" asked the *Commercial Advertiser* of Baltimore.[82]

"What shall be done with the slaves?" queried the *New York Times*.[83]

"What is to be done with the blacks?" demanded the *Chicago Tribune*.[84]

6

The Riverman

Visitors to the White House often came away frustrated with Abraham Lincoln. He got slippery whenever they tried to nail him down on his long-range plans for confronting the problem of slavery and the related issue of the contraband camps. "My policy is to have no policy," became his default answer to any number of urgent political questions, giving ammunition to his critics who thought him an empty suit or a leaf on the stream, content to drift with the dominant currents of public opinion.

To ease the disappointment when he refused to be cornered, he told mood-lightening stories. One was about a group of Methodist preachers on a journey across Illinois. They argued for two hours about how to ford an upcoming river until an elder grew impatient. "Brethren, this here talk ain't no use," he said. "I never cross a river until I come to it."[1]

Another favorite yarn was about a sawmill owner who decided to open his sluice a little wider, only to have a whole lake come rushing through the mill, destroying it. To another caller who boasted he was willing to "shed the last drop of his blood" for the sake of the Republican claim on the presidency, Lincoln recalled the young Union soldier whose two sisters were embroidering him a belt with the legend "Victory or Death."

"No, no, don't put it quite that strong," Lincoln said he told the women. "Put it, 'Victory, or get hurt pretty bad.'"[2]

These Kentucky-fried anecdotes were part of Lincoln's political brand, and he often took diplomatic visitors aback with a stream of irrelevant anecdotes rendered in light-backwoods patois with pronunciations like *git*, *vittles*, *thar*, and *heered*, and with a full-body performance marked with twinkling eyes, culminating with him bending over in his chair in hilarity, hands fluttering at his sides, gasping like "the neigh of a horse on his native prairie." Although the New York financier George Templeton Strong thought Lincoln had "the laugh of a yahoo" and winced at some of the off-color jokes, he still came away thinking the president was "a most sensible, straightforward, honest old codger."[3]

The jocular tone could obscure the prudence that guided Lincoln. If he was relaxed in his speech, he was studied in his actions. As his personal secretaries John Hay and John Nicolay observed, he kept a "lifelong habit to listen patiently to counsel from all quarters" while "holding his convictions open to the latest moment, and of not irrevocably committing himself to specific acts until the instant of their execution." The cornpone Illinois stories, thought Walt Whitman, were not merely a way to fill the awkward silences and obscure the disappointment of those who wanted more specific commitments from him, but "a weapon which he employ'd with great skill." The perceptive newsman William Russell of the London *Times* had dinner with Lincoln and some of his cabinet expecting to get some exclusive insight on the war and came away hearing nothing but a few horse stories. "Mr. Lincoln raises a laugh by some bold west-country anecdote and moves off in the cloud of merriment produced by his joke," he complained.[4]

The jokes weren't always polite. Lincoln harbored an unpresidential fondness for "a coarse and even nasty story, if it served his purpose," said Henry Villard, who covered the war for the *Chicago Tribune*. While Lincoln's friends were too circumspect—even embarrassed—to repeat most of them for posterity, a few survive. One involved "a man of audacity" about to carve up the poultry for an elegant society supper when he unexpectedly and loudly broke wind, mortifying everyone. "A deep silence reigned," said Lincoln, until the man rolled up his sleeves, picked up the knife, and said: "Now, by God, I'll see if I can't cut up this turkey without farting."[5]

Puzzled listeners searched for crumbs of wisdom, but Lincoln's fables translated poorly to the page, as they often had no point other than to underline the value he placed on flexibility. He used them to explain and even apologize for his frequent "my policy is to have no policy" evasions. The president was often reminded, for example, of the story of the "horse sold at a cross-roads near where I once lived," where a suspicious buyer asked a stable boy if the horse had a splint. The boy didn't know what that word meant but plunged forward: "Well, mister, if it's good for him he has got it, but if it isn't good for him, he hasn't."[6]

Some of the most overwhelming questions of the day came in for this wiggly treatment, even when Lincoln could afford to be candid. Many suspected that he wasn't keeping cards close to his vest so much as he was prepared to invent cards out of thin air when the time came. "I claim not to have controlled events," he wrote to Kentucky newspaper editor Albert Hodges, "but confess plainly that events have controlled me." One visitor to the White House, "whose personal relations entitled him to unreserved confidence," asked him how he planned to handle the reconstruction of the South after the end of the war. Lincoln had no answers for this friend. But he told yet another parable to explain himself. "The pilots on our Western rivers steer from 'point to point' as they call it—setting the course of the boat no farther than they can see, and that is all I propose to myself in this great problem."[7]

In this case, Lincoln was not merely repeating a story he had heard from frontier boatmen. He had experienced those rivers himself. As a young man, he made two trips of more than a thousand miles each on a hand-built watercraft called a flatboat, taking farm goods from the Midwest down the Mississippi into New Orleans. The first journey was in 1828, the other in 1831, and they were formative experiences in shaping the way he thought about slavery and the interconnected nature of the U.S. economy. They also provided him with a lifelong metaphor for how to approach a problem.

The "point to point" theory of Lincoln's leadership style explains much about the administration's overall approach to the contraband problem, from its inception in May 1861 right up to New Year's Day 1863, when the Emancipation Proclamation—itself a provisional and even noncommittal document—took effect. Abolitionist critics howled that his judiciousness on the matter was evidence of cowardice. Lincoln's defenders insisted his gradualist approach came from an unwillingness to subject the nation to shocks greater than it could bear.

A third explanation may be closer to the truth: Lincoln was responding to kinetic events as they emerged, acting on slavery with more passivity than aggression, and leaving its final disposition in the hands of actors down below, offering only a weak proposal that they should be recolonized to Africa or Central America.

Lincoln was the opposite of an impulsive leader. He was not even much of an idealist most of the time. Respect for existing laws should, he once said, "become the political religion of the nation." He had been trained as a lawyer and had tremendous concern for ensuring the durable quality of any new legislation. Lincoln's overriding commitment was not to make slavery illegal but to hold the federal Union together by any means necessary. He searched for what might be possible in the moment. Point to point, indeed.[8]

By the autumn of 1862, America's Black refugee crisis had become unavoidable, even to those who preferred to see it only as a temporary war strategy. It was no longer possible to believe that it might go away of its own accord. There were at least a hundred thousand freed Black people living at the doorsteps of towns and cities across the nation's midsection with no long-range governmental plan for them, even as they showcased a wealth of optical proof that sudden emancipation would not lead to racial violence.

Lincoln devoted no speeches to the contraband question, made almost no remarks about it, and proposed no detailed long-term solutions. He did not have a formal meeting with any freed person who had been a resident in one of the contraband camps until late in 1864. Yet the existence of the camps was a troubling reality that required executive action. A rising tide of voices told him that the camps provided not only a living demonstration project of permanent liberation, but a source of military power. Only then did he choose to act.

"On all questions of expediency, the President maintained not only the right but the frequent necessity of change," concluded James G. Blaine, the Maine congressman to whom Lincoln had told the story about the fluid nature of river navigation. Blaine recalled that Lincoln himself liked to tell people that "principle alone must be inflexible." Everything else, including the application of policy, was open to a constant state of plasticity and improvisation.[9]

The historian Richard Hofstadter has described the Emancipation Proclamation as having "all the moral grandeur of a bill of lading," with all its qualifications and legalisms. It technically freed nobody because it applied only to states in rebellion, which would of course not obey it, and it specifically exempted border states. Lincoln also made it clear it should be seen as "a fit and necessary war measure for suppressing said rebellion," leaving open the possibility that it might be rescinded at the cessation of hostilities.[10]

The wording of the most consequential blow against American slavery up to that point is clearly derivative of the creative legalisms that had allowed the camps to thrive on the edges of U.S. Army positions. Seesawing and erratic federal policy toward the camps begins to make more sense when viewed in this context, as does Lincoln's decision to release the first version of it to the public—timed right after the victory at the Battle of Antietam—but also when the contraband camps were swelling to what seemed like maximum capacity, when the need for a federal vision on "what shall be done with the negroes" had at last become unavoidable.

* * *

The crafting of origin stories has always been a vital ingredient in American politics, and few did it better in the mid-nineteenth century than Richard James Oglesby. An Illinois lawyer and early ally of Abraham Lincoln, Oglesby had a "fine dramatic instinct" and sought "a demonstration which would impress the whole country" prior to the 1860 presidential campaign. Unlike the military heroism or gentlemanly bona fides that had propelled men like Washington, Jefferson, and Jackson into the White House, a western moderate like Lincoln needed to project rough-cut good sense and a connection with the common man to persuade enough wavering antislavery voters to take a chance on him.[11]

Oglesby sought out John Hanks, a relative of Lincoln's who had once taken a flatboat journey with him to New Orleans and had also cut down trees with him to build a cabin and a fence twelve miles west of Decatur, Illinois. The two went riding out to the remote spot in a buggy, and Hanks pointed out the moldering fence of black walnut that he had built with a teenage Lincoln thirty years before. They pried loose two rails, lashed them to the bottom axle of the wagon, and headed to Chicago where Oglesby carried them into the Republican nominating convention. He displayed them with a flourish under a handmade plaque that advertised the Springfield lawyer as the "Rail Candidate." The identity of Lincoln as a "railsplitter" followed him into the general election, making its way into hundreds of newspaper stories, campaign ads, "railsplitter clubs," and editorial cartoons, alongside the complementary image of "Honest Abe," the struggling storekeeper who paid off his debts when he could have easily fled town.[12]

But another of Lincoln's youthful activities could have also served as a potent symbol of his canny frontier instincts and hard-won experience: the trips he took. "Lincoln the Boatman," as historian Richard Campanella has pointed out, might have been an even more accurate political brand than "railsplitter," because the journeys he took down the lower trunk channel of the Mississippi River helped transform his view of the world.

Lincoln was known to use riverine idiom when making a point, telling a Sunday School class, for example, that "the only assurance of successful navigation" in the first riffles on the river of life was launching the flatboat correctly. He described himself in a campaign speech as "a friendless, uneducated, penniless boy, working on a flatboat," amazed to find himself at a rostrum giving a talk to respectable citizens. Just as a modern politician who had once worked as a truck driver might pepper his discourse with road metaphors to establish down-to-earth credibility, Lincoln reached into his Mississippi River days.[13]

That he would join a flatboat crew in the spring of 1828 was less out of a desire for adventure as it was a logical job opportunity for a nineteen-year-old man in Little Pigeon Creek, Indiana. Lincoln's family had moved there when he was seven to clear a place in the woods for a sustenance farm. His mother died of milk sickness from cows that had eaten snakeroot, leaving the family destitute and heartbroken. The surplus flour and smoked ham they could raise fetched much higher prices downriver in Louisiana, where the best farmland was given over to giant cotton fields tended by enslaved people, and the way to profitability was to transport produce there on a cargo vessel made of sawed planks that any decent axman and carpenter could assemble at the side of the Ohio River.

Lincoln and his neighbor Allen Gentry set to building one at Rockport, Indiana, likely made of poplar and oak. When finished, an average flatboat was eighty feet by seventeen feet, slightly less than half the size of a modern basketball court, complete with a steering oar, side oars, a cabin for the crew, a caulked roof to keep the grain dry, and a woodstove for cooking. Lincoln and Gentry likely fronted the money for additional bulk goods like whiskey, tobacco, and hominy to arbitrage in the Southern market. They set off at an unknown date, probably on April 18 or 19, at a place called Gentry's Landing, into the riparian highway that linked the interior North and South in an era before railroads.[14]

The two amateur navigators drifted past sand islands, Indian burial mounds, riverside towns, and glimpses through the trees of Kentucky plantations on the south bank. It would not have been the first time Lincoln had been exposed to the South's peculiar institution; slavery was a household practice near his boyhood home in Hodgenville, Kentucky, though on a small scale, and he had likely seen transport ships on the Ohio in his teenage years. A decade after the second flatboat journey, in 1841, he wrote of sharing deck space on a large riverboat called the *Lebanon* with a group of enslaved people who were "strung together precisely like so many fish upon a trot-line," and were "being separated forever from the scenes of their childhood, their friends, their fathers and mothers, and brothers and sisters."[15]

In a later letter to his friend Joshua Speed, he again emphasized the pathos. "You may remember, as I well do, that from Louisville to the mouth of the Ohio there were, on board, ten or a dozen slaves, shackled together with irons. That sight was a continual torment to me; and I see something like it every time I touch the Ohio, or any other slave border." The 1828 journey was his first intimate experience on that borderline, but he kept no diary of the trip. Whatever he may have thought at that point about the matter that would soon come to dominate national politics went unrecorded, though he made reference to Speed of his habit of avoiding the topic when possible to avoid offending Southern interests. "I bite my lip and keep quiet," he confided.[16]

Lincoln and Gentry passed the tricky confluence where promoters were still a decade away from erecting levees around the swampy point at Cairo, Illinois, where a guidebook called *The Navigator* warned of rough water. The swells "so large and strong that a boat is thrown half around it in passing over them" were known to capsize flatboats whose captains failed to exert powerful rowing. The junction of the Mississippi was one of the only places on the journey where the side oars, called "sweeps," were crucial—the gentle downhill gravity of the river provided the bulk of the momentum, aided by long poles the boatmen used to prod themselves along in the shallows and through the hairpin meanders.[17]

Over the next twelve days, their sixty-six-mile-per-day pace sent them drifting past the rowdy dockside villages under the bluffs at Vicksburg and Natchez, teeming with drunk mariners, fiddle players, gamblers, and coffles of enslaved people waiting for auction, and then deep into the cypress and moss of Louisiana sugar country, where manor houses with double-pitched roofs and broad verandas lined the shores, their wharves on pylons extending from the slimy banks. Below Baton Rouge, Lincoln and Gentry paused to sell some of their goods direct to the slave owners. Here a significant event occurred after dark.

During the presidential campaign of 1860, when he was asked to write an autobiographical sketch that would be printed in a Chicago newspaper, Lincoln worded the whole thing in the third person, beginning with, "Abraham Lincoln was born February 12, 1809, then in Hardin, now in the more recently formed county of La Rue, Kentucky." The narrative of his life included just two sentences about the first New Orleans trip: "The nature of part of the 'cargo-load,' as it was called, made it necessary for them to linger and trade along the sugar-coast; and one night they were attacked by seven negroes with intent to kill and rob them. They were hurt some in the mêlée, but succeeded in driving the negroes from the boat, and then 'cut cable,' 'weighed anchor,' and left."[18]

Whether these were enslaved people desperate for a flatboat on which to make an escape downriver or free Blacks looking for money, Lincoln never said nor speculated. But in telling this story, he may have been trying to signal to white voters that he was a realist about potential enmity between the races. Friends later noticed Lincoln bore a scar on his forehead, a souvenir of the near murder of the future president when he was nineteen. It was a crisis he survived, and he moved on. A flatboat pilot had to respond to circumstances as they arose; some things could not be forecast or planned.

The river grew thicker with flatboats as the pair drew closer to the cotton warehouses, sawmills, church steeples, and factories of New Orleans, the premier international slave port of the South. The American flag had flown over it just a quarter century. Many of the shopkeepers and wholesalers spoke no English. "There is on the globe one single spot, the possessor of which is our natural and habitual enemy," a covetous Thomas Jefferson had written in 1802. "It is New Orleans, through which the produce of three eighths of our territory must pass to market."[19]

The two inexperienced young men from upriver—"Kaintucks" in local parlance, not complimentary—became a tiny part of that commerce in May 1828, looking to get the best deal on the smoked ham and grain they had safely transported to the jammed docks near the Faubourg St. Mary levee, amid the din of what a contemporary traveler called a "great deal of rudeness, and a great deal of swearing" from buyer and seller alike. The chaos extended to fistfights, the dumping of livestock waste, and the occasional spectacular fire breaking out on a flatboat, reaching into wooden barrels and spreading to other boats in a chain reaction because a careless boatman had let a hot coal get loose from his woodstove. The French Creole elite avoided this part of town.[20]

Lincoln didn't talk about what he saw in New Orleans after he and Gentry had dispensed with their cargo and pulled apart their flatboat to sell the lumber. But it was the first big city he had ever seen, and he could not have missed gawking at the crude entertainments, the brothels, taverns, cobblestones, whale-oil streetlamps, and especially the open-air slave markets that generated millions of dollars of revenue each year. One of the most famous among them, Hewlett's Exchange, at the corner of Chartres and St. Louis, featured auctions of Black men, women, and children in scenes of "tumultuous confusion" and bitter crying, where every day within a designated five-hour selling window, families were pulled apart from one another. Cultivated travelers urged first-time visitors to go to Hewlett's to inspect the elegant interiors and see the array of goods, human and otherwise, that made it "the Soul of New Orleans." Campanella estimated that at least thirty-one enslaved people were sold here at this gruesome tourist attraction at the time of Lincoln's first visit. Beyond the cruel spectacle lay Congo Square, where free Blacks were permitted to play drums and dance in a West African style.[21]

Lincoln and Gentry almost certainly made their 1,273-mile journey home by securing an upper deck spot on a steamboat, possibly bartering their labor for a cut-rate ticket, and traveling upriver for nearly two weeks—roughly half the time it had taken them to float downriver. Lincoln's wages for those months totaled $16. But the trip gave him much more, beginning with an exposure to the interconnectedness of American commerce and the vastness of its geography. The Midwest was not a separate country from the Cotton States, and the money flowed upstream just as much as it did downstream. Lincoln and his neighbors benefited from slavery through the cotton in their clothes, the credit in their banks, the rice on their plates, the sugar in their coffee, and even the coffee itself, unloaded by enslaved Louisianans on the New Orleans docks. And it could not have escaped his attention that the farm goods he had poled down the river—especially the high-protein pork—was going to be fed to enslaved people.

How much the trip formed his view of slavery is open for debate. A companion with him on the second voyage, his cousin John Hanks, recalled thirty-five years later to Lincoln's law partner William Herndon that the trip had instilled in Lincoln a severe distaste for the practice. "I Can say Knowingly that it was on this trip he formed his opinions of Slavery; it ran its iron in him then & there," said Hanks, in notes taken by Herndon for a later biography. But Hanks had a flair for exaggeration, as suggested by his later claim that Lincoln, upon watching an enslaved woman being pinched and trotted around on the auction block at New Orleans, grew disgusted and said some version of the line, "If I ever get a chance to hit that institution, I'll hit it hard, John."[22]

Later Lincoln biographers seized on the dramatic phrase and quoted it frequently. But there are multiple problems with the anecdote, not least of which is that Hanks departed the second journey in St. Louis and could not have witnessed the scene as described. However, it is likely that Lincoln did discuss slavery with his relative on the first part of the trip, especially in the environs of Kentucky and Missouri, where the commerce was omnipresent.[23]

Lincoln's own words were certainly more accurate, if not as colorful. Six weeks before his inauguration and at the outbreak of the secession crisis, Lincoln wrote a letter to future Confederate vice president Alexander Stephens, who had just proclaimed slavery and white supremacy the "cornerstone" of the new nation. "God forbid," Lincoln told Stephens, with whom he had been friendly. "When a boy I went to New Orleans on a flat boat and there I saw slavery and slave markets as I have never seen them in Kentucky, and I heard worse of Red River plantations."[24]

His political consciousness on these and other subjects was taking shape as he saw the condition of the nation's rivers and canals unfolding in front of him with each passing mile, and he soon became an ardent Whig in the mold of Henry Clay, whose "American System" called for federal investment in transportation improvements. Lincoln's first big legal client was the Illinois Central Railroad, and as president, he took a keen interest in a transcontinental railroad, signing the 1862 Pacific Railway Act that paved its way. During General U.S. Grant's campaigns to capture the Mississippi Valley and split the Confederacy in two, Lincoln was known to point to military maps and recall his own sighting of faraway places including Vicksburg and Natchez that now held extreme strategic importance. Not for nothing did Lincoln's journalistic antagonist and ultimate admirer Horace Greeley equate the 1828 and 1831 flatboat trips to Lincoln's "freshman year of college."[25]

The year after his second journey to New Orleans, Lincoln enlisted in a local militia to help fight a punitive campaign against a band of Meskwaki Indians, a set of skirmishes called the Black Hawk War. The shy and awkward Lincoln put his name into a spot election for company commander and won, "a success which gave me more pleasure than any I have had since," he later remarked. With no military experience, the twenty-two-year-old Lincoln had no idea what he was doing. But he displayed the same "point to point" approach that became a feature of his governing style. In a self-deprecatory yarn he liked to tell when he was president, he marched his company up to a fence gate but could not remember the formal command to assume single file. So he ordered the company dissolved on the spot, let the men filter through the gate as private citizens, and then reconstituted the company once they were all on the other side. Such creative legalistic maneuvering, or at least Lincoln's enjoyment of it, might be seen as a prefiguration of the contraband decision that would guide Union policy.[26]

The experience convinced Lincoln he could lead, and he ran for the Illinois legislature on a platform of clearing the Sangamon River of debris, making it fit for navigation. He became a regular pilot himself on vessels like the *Talisman*, putting on the sangfroid of a captain, a posture doubtlessly acquired during his flatboating days. While at the helm, he drew into himself, even looking depressed, though the glum visage fell when he threw out wisecracks and stories to put his companions at ease. This oscillation between melancholy and masculine jocundity, refined on the rivers, became a mark of his complex personality. A former crewmate named Stephen W. Garrison, who saw Lincoln in Cincinnati immediately after the 1860 election, remarked: "I could still detect the same expression of sadness on his face that I first saw a quarter of a century previously when we floated down the Illinois together."[27]

The oxbows and meanders of the Mississippi River may also have woven deeper patterns into his mind. Throughout his life from then on, he had a recurring dream of a vague and even ominous image, and it presented itself once again in the White House, shortly after he was inaugurated as president. He later told an associate what it was like: "a vague sense of floating—floating away on some vast and indistinct expanse toward an unknown shore."[28]

* * *

In the early days of his administration, to take the mind off his worries, Lincoln liked to sit in the second-story executive quarters with his feet propped up on the windowsill and a telescope perched between them, aimed at the Potomac River. He liked to watch the boats traversing back and forth and the movements of the Union fleet, many of them moving in an easterly direction, some on their way to supply Fort Monroe. It is possible to imagine him recalling his days as a flatboat pilot in those moments.[29]

"Sitting at the window with a spy-glass in his hand, he would talk with a free-and-easy manner, with whomsoever came—write a note on a card on his knee with a pencil, look through the spy-glass at the distant Virginia hills and down the vista of the Potomac," wrote Henry Whitney. "I recollect once seeing a vessel as far down as we could see near to Alexandria with its masts leaning toward the Virginia shore. Lincoln was puzzled about it; he looked long and earnestly at it. 'I wonder what that *can* mean,' he said half a dozen times."[30]

On April 29, 1861, a few weeks after the bombardment of Fort Sumter, an apparition rose on the Virginia bank beyond the river and the ships: a giant Confederate flag hoisted above Marshall House Hotel, eight miles away in Alexandria, visible with the aid of a spyglass. It was an improvised banner made by a seamstress featuring three broad strips and the clustered stars of the slave states that had seceded, seven of them at that point, Virginia not yet among them. The sight of the treasonous banner fluttering within view of the White House irritated James Lane, the foul-mouthed leader of a brigade of Kansas volunteers awaiting orders. "Let me tell you," he said to the New York general Carl Schurz, peering at the Marshall House through the telescope, "we have got to whip these scoundrels like hell."[31]

Lincoln almost certainly spotted the flag with the same design through the telescope, wondering what it meant. The Constitution that he had just sworn to uphold had included no exit clause. It was far from clear whether the majority vote of a state legislature, or the affirmative results of a statewide referendum, were adequate legal grounds to dissolve a state's covenant with the Union or whether the marriage—once agreed upon—was forever sealed. In the absence of an explicit prohibition, the Confederate states were laying down their own legal planks over the emptiness and calling it a foundation. They understood that in the absence of law there is only force.

The fifteenth president, James Buchanan, had left Lincoln little sense of how to steer forward into such a void, except perhaps to do nothing and let the secession proceed. Buchanan had concluded that, while it might be regretful and even illegal, he had no legal authority to stop it. His attorney general, Jeremiah Black, concurred with him in the ouroboros logic: secession was a crime but it could not be prosecuted. Buchanan told Congress that it was "beyond the power of any president, no matter what may be his own political proclivities, to restore peace and harmony among the states," because such matters were, thanks to the Tenth Amendment, relegated to the states themselves. All of this circular reasoning gave the South time to consolidate power, seat a government, and call up hundreds of local militia groups that would soon coalesce as the Army of the Confederate States.[32]

Buchanan had come into office with decades of government experience and a personality brimming with diplomatic finesse. His childhood in a rural Pennsylvania valley as the son of a Scots-Irish storekeeper had been nearly as humble as Lincoln's, and he also started out as a general practice lawyer who ran for the state legislature and won, climbing upward through skillful navigation of party politics, through the ranks of congressman, senator, ambassador to Russia, ambassador to the United Kingdom, and secretary of state. The girth of his résumé won him the 1856 Democratic Party nomination almost out of inertia. His positions on the sectional controversy were strangely ambiguous, observed his own secretary of state, Lewis Cass, and his speaking style "excited no enthusiasm" and was dull to the point that it would have "ruined any man less eminent." Those who spent time with him noticed a facial quirk: his eyes were misaligned, and he tipped his face forward to fix his good right eye on the listener. For some it was a physical embodiment of never quite knowing where he stood.[33]

Nobody would mistake Buchanan for a charismatic leader. He was instead a living symbol of the permanent civil state, the reliable guest of countless banquets and diplomatic balls who liked to call himself the "Old Public Functionary." To his enemies, who made malicious innuendos about his lifelong bachelorhood and fussy personality, he was "Granny Buck" or "Aunt Fancy." But he was also not hesitant to wield a strong executive hand or send in the military, even to distant theaters. After one of Brigham Young's militias massacred an emigrant party at Mountain Meadows in Utah and the Latter-Day Saints harassed federal officials out of Salt Lake City in 1857, Buchanan sent in the U.S. Army to quell what he called a domestic rebellion and then negotiated a careful détente with Young. The following year, he sent a nineteen-ship naval squadron to threaten the capital of Paraguay in retaliation for an incident involving property seizure and a cannon shot fired at an American vessel. The 2,500 American sailors were away on that frivolous $3 million mission to South America when they might have been reinforcing vulnerable spots like Fort Sumter and Fort Monroe.

But Buchanan had an aversion to confronting the South. He had ridden into office on a wave of support from Southern Democrats who correctly sized him up as a doughface, a Northerner sympathetic to their interests, and his administration's policies ran consistently proslavery, from tacitly approving the farcical slavery constitution of Kansas to backing a provision to write slavery approvingly into the U.S. Constitution and clear up the matter forever. He never visited New England, disliked its antislavery politics, and grew weary of the women in its abolitionist groups, complaining that "their harangues were quite as violent and extreme as those of their fathers, husbands, and brothers."[34]

In his January 8, 1861, message to Congress, with South Carolina's secession threatening to tip a row of dominoes, all he seemed able to do was stall. "Time is a great conservative power," he said.

"Let us pause at this momentous point and afford the people, both North and South, an opportunity for reflection." He took his own advice and vacillated on whether to resupply the starving troops at Fort Sumter. He even made a near-treasonous private assurance to a South Carolina delegation that he would send no ships if they promised not to attack it under his watch. "After all, this is a matter of honor among gentlemen," he told them. "I do not know that any paper or writing is necessary. We understand each other."[35]

Buchanan caved under pressure and sent the steamer *Star of the West* down the coast on a doomed resupply mission. But Major Robert Anderson was, inexplicably, not notified in advance, which meant he had no authority to initiate covering fire should the Confederates on shore launch warning sallies, which they did. The *Star of the West* had to turn back, a huge morale boost to the breakaway South Carolinians, who already enjoyed a wave of self-confidence. Some of Buchanan's own advisers in the State Department, especially William Henry Trescot, had been leaking information to them and even shipping a disproportionate amount of weapons South, later captured, which had perhaps been his intent. For good measure, they suggested low-cost outlets to buy even more armaments—weapons to be used to kill soldiers in the U.S. Army.

By the end of Buchanan's shambolic administration, some were convinced that had he lasted in office, he might have given up and extended diplomatic recognition to the Confederate States of America, acquiescing to a peaceful but permanent fracture. This would have left a rump United States sharing a jagged border with a slave republic. Buchanan was not lazy or naive, and he knew the law in detail. In the White House, he worked sixteen-hour days, agonizing over minor federal correspondence, and made comprehensive rewrites to the point where the overwork and worry made his silvery hair look slovenly and his cheeks twitch like "spirits were pulling at his jaw." When he got nervous, he shredded cigars between his fingers.[36]

Why was he so conciliatory to the South? His most distinguished biographer, Jean Baker, has theorized he had a simple affinity for Southern culture, its sense of gentlemanly honor, and its aesthetics. He named his estate in Pennsylvania "Wheatland" and cultivated it as a Northern version of a Southern plantation, "the beau ideal of a statesman abode," its columns always in the background of his campaign's lithographs.[37]

He had always sought out the companionship of Southerners in Washington, starting with his first mentor in Congress, the Alabama bon vivant William Rufus King, with whom he shared a boardinghouse. "Their grace and courtesy, even their conversational talents, attracted him," wrote Baker. The racial attitudes and the secessionist aggression of the South were only part of the package, and he seemed to have internalized them on a subconscious level. Combined with a rigidity of personality and a tendency to lecture rather than listen, it was a disastrous weakness. "The White House is abandoned to the seceders," complained William Seward to his wife. "They eat, drink, and sleep with him."[38]

In the end, Buchanan made nobody happy. He had gotten elected with an implicit promise to expand the rights of slaveholders. Now his Southern friends were disappointed in his half-hearted Unionism, while antislavery Northerners thought him a stooge. The Democratic Party tore itself apart as a result. "I am like a man on a narrow isthmus; without a friend on either side," he told a visitor, his head drooping to his shoulder.[39]

Buchanan took the customary ride with his successor in a carriage over to the East Portico of the U.S. Capitol for the inaugural address, and the two had said not much to each other on the bumpy ride down Pennsylvania Avenue. "Mr. Buchanan looked old and worn out whilst Mr. Lincoln looked awkward and out of place," thought Charles Francis Adams, who watched the meeting. While they waited in the president's room for the festivities, and for Lincoln to deliver his speech invoking the "mystic chords of memory" that held the nation together, Buchanan took Lincoln aside for what witnesses thought would be an important piece of advice passing from one chief executive to another on the eve of such a crisis. John Hay said he leaned forward in "boyish wonder and credulity" to hear, conscious of having a front seat for a historic transfer of power: "Every word must have its value at such an instant," he wrote.[40]

Buchanan then told Lincoln, "I think you will find the water at the right-hand well at the White-House better than that of the left," and then described "many intimate details of the kitchen and pantry." Lincoln appeared to be paying attention with a morose look on his face but confessed later that he "had not heard a word of it."[41]

For all of Lincoln's willingness to fight secession with blunt force during his presidency, his first year in office carried more than a touch of Buchananism. Both men came at the problem like the lawyers they were. While Buchanan searched the Constitution and couldn't find any presidential power to halt a state from leaving the Union, Lincoln decided the authority indeed existed under the Article II clause, saying the president "shall take care that the laws be faithfully executed." If rebelling states kicked out federal officials and drew up their own laws, even by the will of their legislatures or a popular referendum, the president was compelled to stop it.

But at the same time, Lincoln concluded, the president and Congress had no authority to legally seize property, even human property, from rightful owners. Such confiscation was known as a "bill of attainder," a sullied concept associated with kings and expressly forbidden by the Constitution and every state constitution. Even as he oversaw the biggest expansion of the U.S. military ever seen and approved the doctrine of military emancipation pioneered at Fort Monroe, Lincoln temporized on slavery for the first year and a half of his presidency. To associate the war with Black freedom, he said, would drive the four border states into the pocket of Jefferson Davis.

With all its obstructionist Southern members now gone, a majority Republican Congress became an engine of activity on one single question, to the point that a California senator complained that "hardly a quarter of an hour has passed that has not been occupied by discussing the status of the negroes in the Southern Confederacy." By August 1862, Congress had passed a raft of stalled legislation: a ban on slavery in the western territories; diplomatic recognition of Haiti and Liberia; a prohibition on army officers returning runaways, even to loyal masters; and stepped-up enforcement measures against international slave traders. The burst of productivity was also aimed at rebuilding a better postbellum country: the Pacific Railway Act, which opened the purse strings for a transcontinental railroad; the Morrill Land-Grant Acts, to create state universities; the creation of the Department of Agriculture, to aid farmers; and the Homestead Act, to distribute western lands to loyal citizens of modest means.[42]

The clear pro-emancipation tilt of the new Congress wasn't enough for William Lloyd Garrison, who organized a petition drive calling for "the total abolition of slavery throughout the country," not through any ponderous amendment process but "under the war power." In one day, ten petitions arrived, each bearing thousands of names. Republican representatives dutifully read them into the record.[43]

Antislavery petitions were not a novelty; they had been posted to Congress in periodic waves since the 1830s. "They flowed into the Senate chamber from every portion of the North," observed Alabama's scornful *Montgomery Weekly Mail*. What was different this time was the scale of the effort. The example of the contraband camps gave the petitioners the specific request that Lincoln should now use "war powers" instead of a vague wish that slavery go away. Most were organized by women through churches and antislavery societies. In New Bedford, Massachusetts, 2,007 women signed on to an emancipation plea. Another contained the signatures of 15,000 women and measured seven hundred feet long. Quakers demanded that Lincoln seize "the present golden opportunity" to get rid of slavery once and for all. The stacks of petitions were "flooding the halls of Congress" in 1862 and taking time away from more pressing business, said the disapproving *Freeport Weekly Bulletin*, a Democratic organ in Illinois. The depth of their actual impact is hard to judge, but they were impossible to miss and Lincoln was certainly aware of them.[44]

When a group of preachers from Chicago presented an abolition petition to the White House in September, one said it represented not just public opinion but the will of the "Divine Master." Lincoln answered with a joke that it was strange the only way He could find to deliver this crowning message was a "roundabout route by that awfully wicked city of Chicago."[45]

For his part, Senator Henry Wilson of Massachusetts grew sick of the argument that moving too quickly on slavery was going to anger the South even further and push the border states into rebellion. The time to stop coddling Slave Power was over, he argued, because nothing that Congress had done had generated any of the threatened retaliations from slave owners.

"Every hour of thought and reflection brings me to the conclusion that death to slavery is life to the Republic," he said.[46]

7

Exodus

Though it had been the national capital for more than seventy years, most of the streets in Washington, DC, were dirt thoroughfares where livestock roamed and weeds flourished. The uneven cobblestones on Pennsylvania Avenue jolted those who rode over it in carriages, but it was one of the only paved streets in a rough and swampy town that reached for grandeur beyond its means, exemplified by the beams of the unfinished Capitol dome opened to the sky like a grasping claw. Its architect, William Thornton, had meant it to look like "a large sugar dish between two tea cannisters" but it now seemed as pathetic as the nearby stump of the Washington Monument, less than one-third finished. A diminutive American flag flew from the top like a colored toothpick.

Unfinished ambitions lay scattered everywhere: neoclassical marble buildings set in muddy fields that one South Carolina official likened to a "Sahara of solitude and waste—appropriated as a cow pasture and frog pond, and decorated with a stonecutters yard, a slaughter house, and pig pens." The city was less than one-seventh the size of the more stylish Philadelphia, and several days' journey from the merchant houses of New York. Foreign diplomats held their receptions in the Federalist town houses near Lafayette Square, which served as a small island of good taste set within the malarial swamps and pickpocket-ridden quarters radiating in every direction. The British government classified Washington a hardship post and gave its ambassador bonus pay. During his 1842 visit, Charles Dickens took in the scene from the top of the Capitol: "Spacious avenues that begin in nothing, and lead nowhere; streets, mile long, that only want houses, roads and inhabitants; public buildings that need but a public to be complete."[1]

Washington was at its heart a Southern city, stuffed with Southern clerks enjoying a long heritage of patronage. The Virginia aristocracy had traded enslaved people on the banks of the Potomac since before the Constitution was signed, and the DC laws governing the business had been cribbed directly from the slave codes of Maryland. When he was a young congressman from Illinois, Abraham Lincoln looked out the windows of the Capitol and spotted a notorious slave dealership called the Yellow House at the corner of Seventh and B Streets, immediately to the south of the Smithsonian Institution. He described it as "a sort of Negro livery stable, where droves of negroes were collected, temporarily kept, and finally taken to southern markets, precisely like droves of horses." The Philadelphia doctor Jesse Torrey said he felt nauseated looking at the "solitary, magnificent temple" of the Capitol, located so close to the "blood-smeared chains under its towers."[2]

A free Black man from upstate New York, the professional violinist Solomon Northup, had the nightmarish experience of waking up at the Yellow House on a heavy plank floor after being drugged by kidnappers. The only light came from a "small window, crossed with great iron bars." From the outside, it looked like an ordinary residence, giving away little clue to the suffering inside. Northup would be sold down to Louisiana for twelve years of bondage.[3]

Other firms sold off men and women more openly at the St. Charles Hotel, at Market Square, at McCandless' Tavern, and in a pen within sight of the Smithsonian Institution. Daily parades of enslaved people, chained by the neck and led along in shuffling coffles, were common before Congress ended the capital city's slave trade, but not slavery itself, through the Compromise of 1850. The firms simply moved their pens to the Virginia side of the Potomac or into Maryland. In Baltimore, a sign on a building on Pratt Street read "Hope H. Slatter from Clinton, Georgia," while giving no other clue as to what business was conducted behind the door. Those in the know, however, could recognize the reference as that of a "Georgia trader" dealing in trafficked humans. In the back of Slatter's place, hidden from the street, was a brick jail with barred windows.[4]

No trafficking firm was bigger, though, than the interstate corporation Franklin & Armfield, with headquarters on Alexandria's Duke Street. The managing partner John Armfield sent hundreds of traveling agents out to Chesapeake plantations looking for new human stock and ran newspaper advertisements touting their ability to "pay cash and the highest prices for any number of likely negroes." The destination for most of them was New Orleans, and then a lifetime in the cotton fields. Armfield was known to rape his female captives, whom he called "fancy maids," and proclaimed himself a member of the tribe of "one-eyed men," a reference to his male appendage. But visitors to the velveted front parlor of the Alexandria office saw none of this. They were greeted by "a man of fine personal appearance and of engaging and graceful manners," accustomed to dealing with the richest gentlemen in America. To walk into a place like Franklin & Armfield was to enter a luxury dealership, complete with interior showrooms and financing plans. Buyers could put down cash for one-half the purchase price of a healthy male, and then pay off a twelve-month bond secured by the anticipated future income he would earn for the plantation.[5]

When plantation masters traveled to Washington—be it for government business, to sit for a term in Congress, or simply to buy and sell human beings—they usually came with an entourage of enslaved people. They customarily hid them in one of the city's private jails, like the Yellow House, or sometimes even the municipal lockup in the 400 block of F Street, where the boarding fee ranged from 20¢ per day to a high of 82¢ during the Civil War, when space was at a premium.[6]

In the early days of the Civil War, even a city as accustomed to handling slave traffic as Washington was simply didn't know what to do with the thousands of Black refugees flooding into town. An enslaved man named John Washington was among many who darted north amid the chaos. "I could read the papers and eagerly watched them for tidings of war which had begun in earnest," he recalled, as "almost every day brought news of battles."[7] There was no better alarm bell than cannon fire signaling a chance to leave. Hundreds of laborers raced to Washington, DC, after the Battle of

Second Manassas, some of them wearing clothes liberated from their owners' closets.[8]

Washington city officials reverted to their carceral mindset, as if by instinct, and locked up the refugees from Manassas in the dozens of public and private slave jails that serviced the capital city. A writer for the *Boston Journal* managed to gain entrance to a municipal cell in December 1861 and found twenty men sitting on the brick floor, "silent and sorrowful," having committed no crime. One was wearing only trousers and "tries to keep himself warm by drawing around him a tattered blanket."

Also huddled among them was James Munroe, sixteen, whose owner had deserted him to command one of the rebel batteries on the Potomac River. "He was arrested by the city police because he had no master," and had been shivering there for five months. Charles Jackson saw his wife and children sold off before he was abandoned, then arrested. He could not keep food down and vomited constantly. "I don't expect to live long," he said, "but I don't want to die here."[9]

Those who weren't locked up in places like the Old Capitol Prison were shunted off to a nearby set of five-story tenements called Duff Green's Row, not noted for their cleanliness. Harriet Jacobs, who had once been enslaved herself, made an investigatory visit in the spring of 1862 and wrote a studiously outraged letter to *The Liberator* about what she had seen. "I found men, women and children all huddled together, without any distinction or regard to age or sex," she wrote. "Some of them were in the most pitiable condition. Many were sick with measles, [diphtheria], scarlet and typhoid fever. Some had a few filthy rags to lie on; others had nothing but the bare floor for a couch." Elderly people who had been enslaved all their lives lay shivering and dying.[10]

"What but the love of freedom," she asked, "could bring these old people hither?"[11]

But Jacobs found reasons for hope in the squalor. "Amid all this sadness," she wrote, "we sometimes would hear a shout of joy. Some mother had come in, and found her long-lost child; some husband his wife. Brothers and sisters meet. Some, without knowing it, had lived years within twenty miles of each other."[12]

Camp Barker. President Abraham Lincoln frequently passed by this contraband camp near the corner of Vermont Avenue and S Street in Washington, DC. On at least one occasion, he stopped to sing a hymn with the residents.

These reunions also unfolded within a vacated set of barracks and horse stables on Twelfth Street called Camp Barker, which soon ballooned with tents pitched in all directions and swarmed with both mosquitoes and bounty hunters. U.S. military personnel were forbidden to assist owners in recovering their escaped enslaved people, but the laws didn't stop private agents from prowling the camp in search of people to bind up and kidnap.

The encampment to the northeast of Iowa Circle was "just a mudhole," recalled Anna Harrison Chase, who arrived there as an eighteen-year-old after leaving her plantation in an ox cart following the death of her "young master" in combat. Visitors were sometimes prohibited from entering Camp Barker because of smallpox outbreaks. Those who couldn't find room had to fend for themselves in the traditional slums near Duff Green's Row, tucked in doorways on various city streets or squatting in whatever dwellings they could manage.[13]

Nobody had an accurate population count. At any given time, there were between 15,000 and 25,000 freed people living this way in Washington and in occupied Alexandria, Virginia. Three hundred or more might arrive in a single day, depending on the patterns of the armies to the south and the rate at which they broke up plantations. "We find a great portion of them in what are denominated 'rows' generally made of the cheapest lumber, and covered with felt and tar," reported one observer from Unionist Virginia. Opportunistic landlords could charge up to $15 a month for such hovels.[14]

Charles Harvey Brewster of the 10th Massachusetts Volunteer Regiment watched the stream of new arrivals to Washington and knew in his heart the South was doomed. "This war is playing the dickens with slavery" he wrote, "and if it lasts much longer will clear our country's name of the vile stain and enable us to live in peace hereafter." He encouraged many to flee farther north to evade the slave agents and avoid the unnecessary insurance policy of buying their free papers from their masters back in Virginia. Such an effort would be long and pointless. Take "leg bail," he advised them, by which he meant, "Just keep running."[15]

Romantic love flourished in Camp Barker between people whose lives had been upended by the war, thrown together in uncertain circumstances. To some of the white overseers, natural expressions of attraction seemed distasteful. "In passing among these Freedmen I could but be impressed with the fact that their morals require much care and attention," wrote an offended William J. Wilson. "If we would fit those for usefulness they must be diverted from their life-long examples of licentiousness to habits of virtue and probity."[16]

But most of elevated Washington society took little notice of the refugee problem at the gates—there was a war to fight—so it was up to the city's free people of color to take a leadership role in bringing aid. Foremost among them was Elizabeth Keckly, who had been the property of a Virginia planter and a veteran of the War of 1812. Her father, George Pleasant Hobbs, had been one of the many enslaved men torn from their families and taken southwest. In one of his letters to Keckly's mother, he wrote: "I hope with God's help that I may be able to rejoice with you on the earth and in heaven let's meet when will I am determined to never stop praying, not in this earth and I hope to praise God in glory there we'll meet to part no more forever." He died while still separated from his wife and children.[17]

Keckly had nimble hands and smart taste. She learned the art of dressmaking and grew especially talented in fine detailing. She initially resisted a marriage proposal because she "could not bear the thought of bringing children into slavery—of adding one single recruit to the millions bound to hopeless servitude." But a loan from some white patrons, combined with income from her sewing, let her accumulate the $1,200 necessary to purchase her own freedom in St. Louis. Her newlywed husband succumbed to alcoholism before they could have children, and she migrated to Washington, DC, a young striver looking for work. There she earned a reputation as a master seamstress among well-connected Washington wives. In 1860, she was introduced to Varina Davis, wife of soon-to-be Confederate president Jefferson Davis, then a senator from Mississippi, who had predicted a "harvest-home of death" because of the ascent of the Republican Party, and was already planning his exit from the nation's capital.

The Davises gave her steady work. One night she stayed late in their house to finish a man's dressing gown, a surprise Christmas gift for the senator, and he unexpectedly came down to the parlor near midnight. "That you, Lizzie! why are you here so late? Still at work; I hope that Mrs. Davis is not too exacting!" He peered at the richly embroidered gown in the gaslight, surmised it was a gift for him, then left the room with a curious smile. Keckly later said she had no doubt he wore the formal garment through his turbulent reign as the leader of the slave republic. Despite his repugnant politics, she said, "he always appeared to me as a thoughtful, considerate man in the domestic circle." Varina Davis later tried to convince Keckly to move with the family to the new Confederate States of America, but she politely declined.[18]

Another high-placed woman learned of Keckly's skills and asked her to make a dress double-quick. Though Mary Todd Lincoln had grown up comfortably bourgeoise as the daughter of a Kentucky banker, she felt ostracized by Washington society and was eager to make an impression at her husband's inaugural reception. But the dress she wanted to wear bore a coffee stain. "I cannot afford to be extravagant," Lincoln warned her. "We are just from the West, and are poor. If you do not charge too much, I shall be able to give you all my work." Keckly sewed her a "bright rose-colored moire-antique" that Lincoln loved, commencing a long friendship.[19]

In her off-hours, Keckly took walks around the city, past the contraband camps full of "poor dusky children of slavery," and reflected on the unkindness of Northerners prone to look with contempt on the filth of the settlements rather than see the desperate circumstances of the people fleeing the same oppression that she had lived under just a few years ago. Referring to them directly, she wrote: "The great masses of the North learned to look upon your helplessness with indifference—learned to speak of you as an idle, dependent race. Reason should have prompted kinder thoughts." One of her walks took her past a "brilliantly lighted" house where bands were playing and elegantly dressed people were mingling in the yard; it was a charity event for wounded Union troops.[20]

"If the white people can give festivals to raise funds for the relief of suffering soldiers," thought Keckly, "why should not the well-to-do colored people go to work to do something for the benefit of the suffering blacks?" She pitched the idea to the women in her church. Almost instantly, the Contraband Relief Society had forty members and a small budget. Among the first contributors was Mary Todd Lincoln, who gave $200. British abolitionists sent in donations, as did Frederick Douglass.[21]

Keckly operated within a growing charitable network among Northern free Blacks encouraged to give alms to those just emerging out of slavery. "Let us provide clothing and money to help take care of them," wrote the *Christian Recorder*, the official organ of the African Methodist Episcopal Church. "Let us send them kind teachers, both colored and white; let there be also persons to work with them, and let them till the ground, raise cotton, grain and potatoes, as they understand the ground and climate." From Israel Bethel Church in Washington, Henry Turner put out the call, citing "the extremest suffering" at Old Point Comfort, Hilton Head, and his own city: "We see them in droves every day perambulating the streets of Washington, homeless, shoeless, dressless and moneyless." Contraband associations run by free people of color also popped up in Cincinnati, Brooklyn, Nashville, and Philadelphia, increasing the pressure on the War Department to improve its treatment of the refugees.[22]

Within the ambitious package of lawmaking in the summer of 1862 also came the final abolition of slavery in the District of Columbia. Lincoln signed this bill with a remarkable admission. "I have never doubted the constitutional authority of Congress to abolish slavery in this district; and I have ever desired to see the national capital freed from the institution in some satisfactory way," he wrote. "Hence there has never been in my mind any question upon the subject, *except the one of expediency*, arising in view of all the circumstances."[23]

He was acknowledging the gap between what was morally and legally correct, and what was politically feasible. It could be read, perhaps, as an apology for not acting sooner or as a signal that he was not going to put himself in front of popular sentiment.

An experienced administrator, D.B. Nichols, took over the management of Camp Barker on June 16, 1862. He wrote a revised code of conduct, removed partitions in the crumbling barracks to create airier spaces, and requisitioned more cots so nobody would have to sleep on the ground. An approving Harriet Jacobs spoke with him and said he "seemed to understand what these people most needed." As he phrased it himself in a brief report, "What these people want is regular labor, agricultural if possible, regular sleep and a regular diet." Anyone looking to confirm stereotypes of Black refugees as freeloaders wouldn't find it here. The majority of the 2,500 people who had passed through the abandoned barracks of Camp Barker had already found jobs. Nichols hoped "the mouths of gainsayers may be forever stopped" by this example of unlocked industry. A later investigation confirmed his views: the freed people "support their own poor without almshouse aid, and scarcely a beggar is found among them."[24]

Nichols had another idea: Why not use some of the confiscated plantations just south of the Potomac River as vegetable farms, where the contrabands could work for government wages? The experiment was already underway at Arlington House, the plush estate once owned by the family of Robert E. Lee, now the property of the U.S. government. Union troops had been using it as a bivouacking spot, and they now shared the property with freed enslaved people tending the gardens of the man who was fighting to re-enslave them.

Freedman's Village served as a way for the U.S. government to deliver a symbolic poke in the eye to a prominent Confederate, and as an advertisement of the high costs of disloyalty. Missionaries held public events at the village, using it to showcase that freed people could live well. On a few occasions, they invited congressmen and other distinguished visitors to meet two elderly gentlemen who had been the "trusty servants of Rebel General Lee" and were now living in freedom near a hilltop with commanding views of the U.S. Capitol.[25]

The ironies mounted. Arlington House had always been a showcase, though of a different sort. It had been commissioned in a deliberately ostentatious Greek Revival style by George Washington Parke Custis as a memorial to his step-grandfather, the nation's first president; Custis filled it with furniture and artwork that had belonged to his famous relative, making it a quasi-museum. Enslaved people did the construction work, carefully setting the heavy front columns in place, and nearly two hundred had continued to labor on the property until the outbreak of the war, when Lee's family departed for the South. Visitors often remarked on the poetic circularity of this chain of events. "Looking around this place and remembering what I had heard of the character of the man who owned it before it passed into the hands of its present owner," said Harriet Jacobs, "I was much inclined to say, 'Although the wicked prosper for a season, the way of the transgressor is hard.'"[26]

In her role as president of the relief society, Keckly paid visits to Arlington House, now bearing the name Freedman's Village and conceived as a master-planned community whose ideals of moral progress were embedded in the design. Though she harbored doubts about the suddenness of freedom thrust upon the enslaved people and worried their expectations would be too high, she became heartened by the sight of whitewashed clapboard houses, built in a style mimicking the Lees' mansion, arranged on a quarter-mile avenue curving around a central pond.

Most of the residents had "a fat pig, a dozen or more chickens, and a garden" in front of their dwelling—in essence, "all of these evidences of prosperity and happiness." *Harper's Weekly* concurred, saying the village "presents a clean and prosperous appearance at all times." The government charged the two hundred or so residents $3 a month in rent and offered classes in carpentry, tailoring, shoemaking, and other blue-collar trade skills.[27]

"I trust the Congressmen and others have seen enough of the colored people recently freed to convince them that they can and will take care of themselves—of the many contrabands who have recently been 'turned loose' from time to time," wrote a correspondent from the Black-owned newspaper the *Christian Recorder*. "I venture to say no one has seen them begging or loafing."[28]

Conditions at Camp Barker remained shabby by contrast, but it had one unexpected optical advantage. It lay directly off the road from the White House up to the Soldiers' Home in the cooler and tree-shaded northern reaches of the city, removed from the mugginess and stench of the Potomac marshlands. President Lincoln had relocated his living quarters to the Soldiers' Home in the summer of 1862. His daily three-mile carriage commute to the White House went directly past the camp, giving the president a regular up-close view of what was happening in hundreds of other locations across a wide swatch of the nation's midsection.

"I used to see Mr. Lincoln almost every day riding out to the Soldier's Home that summer," said Anna Harrison Chase, a freedwoman from Virginia. "Of course we did not know what he was doing but he was such a great man."[29]

Her neighbors in the camp included Mary Dines, who had been taught to read and write by her master's children in Charles County, Maryland. After being savagely whipped one day, she determined to escape by following a route toward Washington, DC, described precisely in a local newspaper. Dines caught a lucky ride with a passing hay wagon driven by a Black man that was actually a secret conveyance on the Underground Railroad, and she ended up at the Twelfth Street camp. There she married a spirit preacher named Ben and taught older people how to read through the aid of printed cards bearing Scripture verses. Dines, known throughout the camp for her expert soprano voice, led hymns on Sunday.[30]

She also found sporadic work as a cook at the White House, where some of Lincoln's attendants took to calling her "Aunt Mary" and bought her dresses. Dines recalled to an interviewer nearly six decades later how a U.S. Army sergeant blew a bugle early one Sunday to announce that Abraham Lincoln would be making a visit. The president "wanted to hear them sing and that everything should be apple-pie order," ordering some of the men to decorate an impromptu platform with flags and bunting. The freed people all dressed in the best clothes they had; for some, that involved a cast-off Confederate uniform picked up from a muddy road after a rebel retreat.[31]

When Lincoln arrived, he stepped out of his carriage with a small entourage and came over to an encircled group of senior freed people, where Ben Dines opened the meeting with a prayer and a call for every saint he could recall from the Bible stories to rain down blessings on the president and the first lady. Then Mary, nervous, began to sing a solo first verse of "Nobody Knows the Troubles I've Seen," and her companions joined in on the chorus. As the song concluded, she saw Lincoln "wiping tears off his face with his bare hands."[32]

The sergeant had told them the president and his party could only stay briefly, but he stayed nearly an hour. After the singing of "I Thank God That I'm Free at Last," many in the group, caught up in the spirit, forgot the president was there and began to joyously shout praises in the custom of the old hush harbor. Lincoln "did not laugh at them," as some white observers to this ritual were wont, "but stood like a stone and bowed his head." The last song was the venerable "John Brown's Body," and the president joined in the salty marching tune with a voice as loud as anyone's, though "it sounded so sad."

On a damp evening a few days later, Lincoln surprised the camp with an unannounced visit and asked for Dines. "Well, Mary, what can the people sing for me today?" he asked. "I've been thinking about you all since I left here and am not feeling so well. I just want them to sing some more good old hymns for me again. Tell Uncle Ben to pray a good old-fashioned prayer."[33]

Mary's husband obliged with all the eloquence he could summon, asking for "the Golden Chariot, with its pale white horses, to swing low, and with companies of angels carry him to his Father above." And the president once more joined the freed people in the songs and appeared to grow tearful again when he bid them goodbye.

Dines told this story to a younger family friend, John E. Washington, in the mid-1930s, and most Lincoln historians have treated it with a degree of skepticism, as it is not corroborated with letters or press accounts. For a book called *They Knew Lincoln*, Washington gathered stories from Dines and other elderly Black people who had contact with the sixteenth president. Historians consider the work within the context of the memory faults that come with multiple retellings of cherished stories, and note the generally hagiographic tone of twentieth-century Lincoln scholarship. But it is beyond dispute that Lincoln was familiar with Camp Barker and was known for his openness to chance encounters with civilians around Washington, DC. Dines's account also lines up with multiple other accounts of Lincoln's bouts of melancholia and occasional welling into tears.

The poet Walt Whitman used to see Lincoln frequently on the commute that went past the contraband camp. He wrote his mother about one of these encounters: "I had a good view of the President last evening—he looks more careworn than usual—his face with deep cut lines, seams & his complexion gray, through very dark skin, a curious looking man, very sad—I said to a lady who was looking with me, 'Who can see that man without losing all wish to be sharp upon him personally? Who can say he has not a good soul?'"[34]

* * *

When Lincoln talked vaguely about the "circumstances" that prevented him from issuing a general emancipation, he was not referring to the resistance from Southern slave owners. He was talking about the white racism of the North, what some called "Negrophobia," fueling a panic over a perceived migration of refugees into the cities and the western territories.

Profound racial anxieties clouded the question of Black citizenship. Antislavery and abolitionism may have seemed to align but they were two quite different positions. Northern Democrats and many Republicans, including Lincoln, opposed the westward spread of slavery because forced-labor plantations were seen as unfair competition for free white settlers. Cotton, especially, was held in suspicion: it was most fabulously profitable only in combination with slavery, and its growers tended to claim the most fertile lands, leaving the inferior tracts for small farmers. It was possible, and even common, to dislike both slavery and the enslaved people within a single sentiment.[35]

Postmaster General Montgomery Blair despaired of what he thought was a particular "weakness" among his fellow Americans. "The white people of the United States," he concluded, "will not live side by side with black men as their equals." A resettlement effort into supposedly liberal Boston ended in failure. The new commander of Fort Monroe, General John A. Dix, complained that the Slabtown refugees had "always been and are now a very great source of embarrassment to the troops in this garrison," and would be a severe military liability in case of a Confederate attack. He asked Massachusetts governor John Andrew if two thousand of them might be sent north as a relief measure, and a nervous Andrew, facing a reelection campaign, looked for ways to say no. He knew where public sentiment lay. The *Springfield Republican* observed, with some regret, that most of Massachusetts harbored "a kind feeling toward the negroes who are in bondage, but it is neither a negro loving nor a negro respecting state." A less charitable writer at the *New Bedford Mercury* thought it would be apt punishment for villainous South Carolina to become a colony for freed people everywhere. "Let the experiment be tried on her, and drain into her the surplus negroes of the South and North!"[36]

Governor Andrew took a hasty train trip to Washington to talk Secretary of War Edwin Stanton out of relocating refugees in Massachusetts, stating disingenuously that "motives of humanity" prevented him from accepting the proposal because Black men and women would only wind up as "a swarm of homeless wanderers . . . incapable of self-help" in the chilly streets of Boston. If the freed people were kept in Virginia, he said, they might have a better opportunity to win "a victory over prejudice." The *Boston Post* applauded the rejection, once again stoking fears of highways and railroads "crowded with negroes coming North to depreciate and degrade white labor and fill our almshouses." Democrats had no monopoly on cynicism. Some Republicans wondered if Dix's idea had been a plot to test the limits on emancipation and make them all look bad.[37]

Similar fears plagued Lincoln. He looked for ways to avoid talking about general emancipation. In one attempt, he quietly drafted a set of sample bills that would have offered monetary compensation for Delaware's slaveholders and drawn the process out for thirty years. But nothing captured the president's imagination quite as much as the fantastical notion that freed people would agree to be "recolonized," not anywhere in America but in Africa or Central America. The only way to correct the seventeenth-century error of the Virginia colonists was to reverse the journeys of the *White Lion* and the *Treasurer* and ship the descendants of African captives back to Africa where they belonged, or, lacking that, somewhere or anywhere else.

Lincoln offered special encouragement to the Chiriqui Improvement Company, which sought to move freedmen to a tropical reserve in present-day Panama, a haven that some thought should be named Linconia. Before he became president, he said federal policy should be oriented toward ways to "to transfer the African to his native clime, and we shall find a way to do it, however great the task may be."[38]

The effort to "repatriate" freed enslaved people to Africa was by then a quarter century old, an experiment derided as "moonshine" by its many critics. The American Colonization Society, founded in 1837, took some of its inspiration from the British experiment to resettle poor Black subjects—some of them Colonial Marines from the War of 1812—in the West African colony of Sierra Leone. The ACS settled on a piece of land to the south at Cape Montserrado, renamed it "Liberia," in honor of liberty, and collected donations from churches to found pioneering settlements with names like the Republic of Maryland, Mississippi in Africa, and Kentucky in Africa, which all experienced dizzying mortality rates. Much of the financial support came from Southerners who feared an oncoming race war.

Lincoln's devotion to the general idea of overseas resettlement, however poorly conceived, offered him a reprieve from the far more difficult question of how freedom could be handled on the domestic front. He urged Congress to appropriate $600,000 to pay for the outbound tickets for the people set free by the District of Columbia emancipation, and offered colonization entrepreneurs a $50 bounty for every former slave they could ship away. In explaining himself to a delegation of Black visitors on August 14, 1862, the president displayed astonishing pessimism. "You and we are different races," he told them. "I think your race suffers very greatly, many of them by living among us, while ours suffers greatly by your presence."[39]

After accounts of this embarrassing meeting were published in Northern newspapers, the African American press reacted with contempt. The *Anglo-African* newspaper had already remarked dryly that Lincoln's idea would "stir the hearts of all Confederates." Now Frederick Douglass accused him of white supremacy. "In this address," he wrote, "Mr. Lincoln assumes the language and arguments of an itinerant Colonization lecturer, showing all his inconsistencies, his pride of race and blood, his contempt for negroes and his canting hypocrisy." It would be the moral equivalent, he said, of blaming the horse for the actions of the horse thief. The Philadelphia philanthropist Robert Purvis took Lincoln's words personally. "Don't advise me to leave, and don't add insult to injury by telling me it's for my own good," he said. "Sir, this is our country as much as it is yours and we will not leave it."[40]

A few recolonization schemes ended in disaster. The American Colonization Society shipped only 168 people to Liberia. The onetime Slabtown resident Henry Jarvis disembarked in the capital city Monrovia "and looked about, but I concluded I'd rather come home." A plan to deport several hundred freed people at Fort Monroe to the Haitian island Île-à-Vache likewise failed. The Florida cotton grower Bernard Kock, more a hustler than a philanthropist, had promised them a Caribbean paradise, but then he confiscated all their money and did not provide houses. More than a hundred freed people died of smallpox and other maladies. After the survivors threatened mutiny, Lincoln acknowledged the failure and ordered the experiment halted.[41]

Secretary of War Simon Cameron, the patronage-happy "Czar of Pennsylvania," had circulated a proposal at the end of 1861 to arm the freed people and let them fight the Confederacy under the colors of the U.S. Army. "It is as clearly the right of the government to arm slaves, when it may become necessary, as it is to use gunpowder taken from the enemy," went one sentence in a version that appeared in several newspapers. Though Lincoln would adopt a version of this same policy within six months, the leak infuriated him. "This will never do! General Cameron must take no such responsibility. This is a question that belongs exclusively to me."[42]

Cameron's majordomo style and fondness for sweetheart deals had already become an embarrassment. The genial champagne drinker had climbed upward through Pennsylvania's grubby political culture by becoming "the greatest of wire pullers" and had helped secure Lincoln's nomination at the 1860 Republican convention. But his critics thought him as "corrupt as a dunghill." On January 13, 1862, Lincoln effectively fired Cameron with a new appointment to become the ambassador to Russia. His Pennsylvania rival Thaddeus Stevens had once joked about Cameron's sticky fingers; when confronted about the insult by an angry Cameron, he issued a retraction that made Lincoln shake with laughter: "I apologize. I said Cameron would not steal a red hot stove. I withdraw that statement." Now Stevens joked that Czar Alexander II would be well advised to lock up the silverware. Lincoln found a new secretary of war in the hard-driving lawyer Edwin Stanton, who also happened to be an Ohio Democrat, lending more partisan balance to the cabinet.[43]

Stanton got to work immediately, seeking clarity on the "what should be done" question through a fact-gathering process. He appointed a three-man group of reformers called the American Freedmen's Inquiry Commission (AFIC) to investigate the "great and constantly increasing colored population thrown upon the care of this Department in the progress of the war." The committee, led by Samuel Gridley Howe, sent out questionnaires to camp superintendents and visited camps themselves to prepare a lengthy report for the president asking some of the pressing questions of the hour. "The negro does best when let alone," concluded Howe after sifting through all the replies and the accumulated data. "The white man has tried taking care of the negro, by slavery, by apprenticeship, by colonization, and has failed disastrously in all; now let the negro try to take care of himself."[44]

Here was a federally sanctioned echo of what Frederick Douglass had said on many prior occasions. The incessant question of "what is to be done with the negro?" was not only patronizing but moot. "Our answer is, do nothing with them; mind your business and let them mind theirs," Douglass wrote. "Your *doing* with them is their greatest misfortune."[45]

The preliminary report from the AFIC did not embrace such a laissez-faire policy but nevertheless retained a ringing summary centered on land grants, emancipation, and civil rights for the 4 million enslaved people, more than 12 percent of whom would be a resident of a contraband camp before the war was over. "His personal rights as a freedman once recognized in law and assured in practice," wrote Howe and his associates, "there is little reason to doubt that he will become a useful member of the great industrial family of nations."[46]

The assembled facts and the conclusion of the AFIC were in line with what the *Anglo-African* newspaper had been saying since the opening of the war—that the entire point of Union efforts should be to "make way for liberty, universal and complete" lest the American experiment fail.[47]

8

In the Cipher Room

The most prestigious place to hear a lecture in Washington was the brick castle at the Smithsonian Institution, which had made a name for itself in the lyceum movement of the 1850s, when Americans of all backgrounds considered two-hour speeches the highest form of entertainment, far more respectable than the theater. Public oratory was more than just a learning opportunity; it was a social event to which ladies wore embroidered dresses and men wore high-collared suits. On scheduled lecture nights, a powerful oil lamp under red-stained glass glowed in the Smithsonian Castle's north tower, a beacon that could be seen from the White House balcony all the way to Capitol Hill.

Anyone wanting to lecture in the stuffy auditorium had to impress its gatekeeper, secretary of the Smithsonian Joseph Henry, who thought abolitionists were responsible for the war and let it be known that he did not care for "the avalanche of strong minded women and weak minded men" with "peculiar doctrines" who had come to Washington since the election of 1860. But Republicans now had control of the institution's board of regents. Representative Owen Lovejoy told abolitionists Henry was an "old traitor" whom he would compel to relent.[1]

Though his daughter said he was "troubled" at the ultimatum put before him, Henry had no choice but to approve a series of dangerously freedom-minded speakers including Horace Greeley, the editor of the most widely circulated newspaper in the country, the *New-York Tribune*, which was said to be the second most-read publication in Western states behind only the Bible. Greeley was one of the nation's first big media moguls, with a show business personality to match. "His very look and bearing were cast in part: his moon-faced stare, his flopping trousers, his squeaky slang, his sputtering profanities, his unpredictable oddities, and his general air of an owlish, rustic sage all helped make a popular legend of him in his lifetime," wrote one of his biographers. Greeley had taken a keen interest in the contraband camps. The *Tribune* had been on the Fort Monroe story from the start, with its lengthy dispatches about Slabtown's swelling numbers extensively reprinted in other newspapers.[2]

Two thousand well-dressed people jammed into the auditorium on January 3, 1862, to hear Greeley. The audience included Treasury Secretary Salmon P. Chase, ten Republican congressmen, and President Abraham Lincoln, whose relationship with Greeley was so complicated that he kept a special drawer in his desk to hold his correspondence with the mercurial editor. Staying on the right side of public sentiment was key to Lincoln's war aims, and Greeley had a keen sense of what the country was thinking.

Lincoln must have winced as Greeley launched into his speech. "The greatest evil that can befall us is compromise," he warned. Then he turned dramatically to face the president—with whom he had served in Congress in the 1840s—and told him that ending slavery must be "the one sole purpose of the fight" and that "slavery is the aggressor and has earned a rebel's doom."[3]

The audience kept interrupting Greeley with applause, ascending at one point to a "wild and prolonged cheer." The warm reception proved the abolitionist message was growing—even "as far South as Washington," thought the *Chicago Tribune*. Lincoln only sat with a stony expression. It would be the last Smithsonian lecture he attended. To a radical Indiana congressman by his side, he said diplomatically, "That address is full of good thoughts, and I would like to take the manuscript home with me and carefully read it over some Sunday."[4]

Lincoln could not ignore Greeley's power to define reality for millions of readers, even though the *Tribune* was hardly consistent in its views, praising the administration one day then savaging it the next. "What in the world is the matter with Uncle Horace?" Lincoln asked after reading yet another broadside. "Why can't he restrain himself and wait a little?"[5]

But impatience also came from within his cabinet and from some of his generals. Edwin Stanton kept the president updated on the growth of the contraband camps throughout the late spring of 1862 as the newspapers kept hammering on the question of what was to be done with 4 million men, women, and children. "Gradual emancipation is going on," concluded the *Christian Banner* in Fredericksburg, Virginia, at the end of a story about the burgeoning refugee camp on its border. "They continue to keep rolling in from every Southern point of the compass." In May, General David Hunter caused a stir in occupied South Carolina by declaring the enslaved residents of that state free under martial law—including Georgia and Florida for good measure—and proposing to arm a battalion of contraband camp residents against the Confederates. "Slavery and martial law in a free country are altogether incompatible," he said. Lincoln quickly remanded Hunter for fear of offending the border states.

For those uncomfortable with abolition as a goal of the war, the idea of hitting back at the South by stripping it of a valuable manpower resource proved a more salable tack. Giving enslaved people their freedom, even notionally, would be like bombing factories or setting food supplies on fire. "The very stomach of this rebellion is the negro in the form of a slave," Frederick Douglass had argued in July 1861, shortly after Benjamin Butler's contraband decision. "Arrest that hoe in the hands of the negro, and you smite the rebellion in the very seat of its life." U.S. Army commanders tended to agree. General Ulysses S. Grant stayed neutral on the abolition question but knew a logistical advantage when he saw one. "I am using them as teamsters, hospital attendants, company cooks, and so forth, thus saving soldiers to carry the musket. I don't know what is to become of these poor people in the end, but it weakens the enemy to take them from them."[6]

Republicans in Congress took a giant step forward in July, further cementing the contraband doctrine into the federal code in the Second Confiscation Act, which allowed the government to seize the assets of all disloyal citizens and made it explicit that those freed during the war "shall be forever free of their servitude, and not again held as slaves," prohibiting the military from returning them. "Who, then, is injured by this provision?" asked the *New York Times*. "Not the rebel master, for he deserves his loss. Not the slave, for he receives a boon. Not the Government, for it has lost nothing and has gained a free citizen."[7]

But it presented a quandary. How could the government physically take an enslaved person as property from an American citizen without violating Article III, Section 3, Clause 2 of the Constitution, which prohibited any "Attainder of Treason"—in other words, a confiscation of property from a disloyal citizen—that lasted beyond that person's life, denying the property to any of their heirs? Was the government supposed to send enslaved people back to the sons and daughters of Confederates after the war ended? A matter of national financial health also loomed. The South had invested up to $4 billion in its enslaved assets, more than twice the annual output of all the factories of the North. All that sunk cost would be annihilated, lost not just to a region but to the whole reunited nation.

Lincoln signed the measure, though with a noteworthy legal explanation. Liberated enslaved people did not become the "property" of the U.S. Army or a state but instead ceased to be considered property the moment they reached Union lines. "I perceive no objection to Congress deciding in advance that they shall be free," he wrote in a draft message that asked for a slight revision in wording to clarify that the forfeiture would not apply to heirs. And then came a logistical argument that came directly from the contraband camp experience. The freed enslaved people were now in such a powerful numerical position that it wouldn't even be feasible to send them back. Freedom once gained could not be revoked, lest the U.S. Army be forced into armed combat with runaways from slavery as well as the rebels.[8]

"Indeed," Lincoln wrote, "I do not believe it would be physically possible for the general government to return persons so circumstanced to actual slavery. I believe there would be physical resistance to it, which could neither be turned aside by argument nor driven away by force." The new law never would have made it past a congressional committee and probably would have been laughed out of the building had it not been for Benjamin Butler's original snap decision made on horseback at Fort Monroe. "All hail to this latest born child of progress toward universal freedom," said the *Cleveland Daily Leader*.[9]

Slavery was not imploding in a single stroke but through the tens of thousands of individual escapes to Union lines, and the consequent legal capitulations to this reality. They were incremental but relentless. In March, Lincoln had signed on to a congressional resolution to support the "gradual abolishment of slavery" within loyal states. "You cannot, if you would, be blind to the signs of the times," he wrote.[10]

The most radical abolitionists saw Lincoln's acknowledgment of potential "physical resistance" on the part of freed people as a dodge of moral responsibility, but also as a sign their pressure campaign was working. They sharpened their attacks. In a *New-York Tribune* editorial titled "Prayer for the Twenty Million," a reference to the whole population of the North, Horace Greeley took aim at Lincoln's "mistaken deference to rebel slavery," arguing that a cautious approach had done nothing but pave the way for secession. It was a dubious charge, impossible to prove, but the *Tribune*'s voice was loud enough that Lincoln felt compelled to reply with an open letter to Greeley in the pages of the *National Intelligencer*. There may have been no better window into his point-to-point philosophy of wartime governance:

> My paramount object in this struggle is to save the Union, and is not either to save or to destroy slavery. If I could save the Union without freeing any slave I would do it, and if I could save it by freeing all the slaves I would do it; and if I could save it by freeing some and leaving others alone, I would also do that.[11]

The question weighed on Lincoln. He acknowledged to Illinois senator Orville Browning that escaped enslaved people were coming into Union lines "faster than we can provide for them and are becoming an embarrassment to the government." Further setbacks for the army added to the gloom. The head of the Army of the Potomac, George McClellan, had kept his troops sitting in Washington all winter, professing a state of unreadiness. Even after he agreed to land several divisions at Fort Monroe and attempt a march on Richmond up the Virginia Peninsula, he moved with extreme caution, reluctant to make a head-on challenge even against inferior Confederate forces.[12]

Wherever McClellan's columns traveled, they unlocked even more refugees. The egotistical railroad executive had never agreed with the contraband decision, but he was bound to follow the president's executive order, noting that Black freedom seekers "have always understood that that after being received into the military service of the United States in any capacity they could never be reclaimed by their former holders." McClellan's Peninsula Campaign ended in retreat and failure, amid dwindling Northern morale. He left thousands of new refugees at Slabtown before leaving for home.[13]

Lincoln seemed to have recognized the drift of the river currents in the summer of 1862, and accepted the inevitability of a general abolition. As he once told the radical Republican Charles Sumner, "The only difference between you and me on this subject is a difference of a month or six weeks in time." Even so, Lincoln often spoke of himself as a passive actor doing his best to respond to fast-moving events. Just before the congressional adjournment and after it became clear that McClellan's bid to capture Richmond would end as an expensive boondoggle, the president invited a group of senators and representatives of the four border states to the White House and urged them to adopt a plan for gradual and compensated abolition.[14]

"The incidents of the war can not be avoided," he told them, in language that conveyed an oblique threat, as the lament of a caudillo who wishes he could do more to stop a calamity from befalling a reluctant visitor. Lincoln disavowed personal responsibility, saying instead that slavery "will be extinguished by mere friction and abrasion—by the mere incidents of the war. It will be gone, and you will have nothing valuable in lieu of it."[15]

He had been able to get ahead of David Hunter's order to turn contraband camp residents into Union warriors, he said, but he warned there were no guarantees for the future. "The pressure, in this direction, is still upon me, and is increasing," he wrote. It is difficult to miss the clear reference to the refugee camps—now practically a refugee civilization—in his warning to the congressmen.[16]

Lincoln had a reason to trust the judgment of his Navy secretary Gideon Welles, who had designed an extraordinarily successful blockade of Southern ports and starved the Confederacy of export income. He was also among the first to grasp the military potential of refugee enslaved people, and, just weeks into the war, he had authorized the enlistment of a group of Fort Monroe freedmen onto Union vessels at the lowest rank available, a formal status called "boy" at a pay rate of $10 per month. The men were usually tasked with shoveling coal into boilers: hot, relentless, hand-scarring work. Eight such sailors were on board during the successful invasion of Cape Hatteras, North Carolina, on August 28, 1861.

Lincoln told Welles, whom he had nicknamed "Father Neptune," that he thought a proclamation freeing the enslaved might be "absolutely essential for the salvation of the Union." During this conversation, which happened to be in a carriage to a funeral, Welles watched the president dwell "earnestly on the gravity, importance and earnestness of the movement." But Lincoln was never one to show his whole self to anyone. His former law partner William Herndon had called him "the most secretive—reticent—shut-mouthed man that ever existed," and he was never more so when it came to the most consequential decision of his presidency—perhaps the most consequential decision faced by any president of the nineteenth century. To a delegation of Christian ministers from Illinois, Lincoln confessed himself powerless to answer the burning question of the age: "What should we do with them? How can we feed and care for such a multitude?" None other than General Benjamin Butler, the original architect of the contraband decision that had started the whole refugee crisis, had just told him that freed people were eating more rations than white soldiers in New Orleans, laying the ground for a potential famine. But Lincoln assured the ministers he was trying to "know the will of Providence" on the question that had been bothering him "for weeks past, and I may even say months."[17]

He asked a lawyer friend to come for a visit. The experienced fixer Leonard Swett had helped orchestrate Lincoln's nomination at the 1860 Chicago Republican convention and had earned respect as one who knew how to interpret public sentiment. Lincoln then subjected Swett to what amounted to a lawyer's lecture, going over the arguments for and against emancipation and trying to find flaws in either side while trying to stay scrupulously neutral. Swett got the feeling that Lincoln didn't want a reply as much as he did a silent listener so he could hear himself talk it through. But Swett also perceived a distinct lean in the president's thinking through his choice of words. "He will issue no proclamation emancipating negroes," Swett wrote his wife.[18]

Lincoln spent a lot of time in the summer of 1862 in the cipher room of the War Department, not far from the telegraph office, receiving coded dispatches from the war's multiple fronts every minute. The tense atmosphere, paradoxically, had a calming effect. He told Major Thomas T. Eckert, whose desk he borrowed, that in the cipher room he could work "more quietly and command his thoughts better than at the White House, where he was frequently interrupted." Eckert let him alone at the desk next to the iron safe and sat nearby, monitoring the sounder for news. He had worked in a gold mine and possessed enormous biceps. Once, to prove the shoddy quality of the fireplace pokers in the office, he broke five of them over his left arm.[19]

Lincoln wrote with a small barrel pen as the telegraph chattered, pausing frequently to look out the window, crossing out lines, adding other words. As his old Springfield law partner William Herndon always said, Lincoln was a slow writer, mentally testing every phrase for solidity before moving on to the next. He dotted the margins with question marks for himself to be answered later.

At the end of each day, he handed over the well-worn papers and asked them to be locked in a desk drawer. Only after several weeks did he confide in Eckert that he had been working on a proclamation "giving freedom to the slaves in the South."[20]

* * *

Whether Lincoln had his usual dream of the ship drifting through the mist on the night of September 21, 1862, went unrecorded. Members of his cabinet were not notified of the purpose of the meeting he called them to at the White House the next day at noon.

He began by displaying a book that had been posted to him by Artemus Ward, the pen name of a comedian named Charles Farrar Browne, who delighted audiences by playing a country bumpkin and telling outrageous yarns. The following year, Ward would travel to Virginia City, Nevada, and befriend a young newspaper writer calling himself Mark Twain; the two went drunkenly jumping from rooftop to rooftop until the constable threatened to pepper them with rock salt from a shotgun. At the time of the cabinet meeting, Ward had a short book out with a story called "High-Handed Outrage in Utica" that appealed to Lincoln's sense of rustic ridiculousness. He proceeded to read it out loud.

"In the Faul of 1856," he began, "I showed my show in Uticky, a trooly grate sitty in the State of New York. The people gave me a cordyal recepshun." It was a shaggy dog story, not Ward's best work, about a prominent Utica citizen, an "egrejus ass," thrashing a wax statue of Judas Iscariot out of pious ignorance. Edwin Stanton looked mildly irritated and stood up as if to leave. "Gentlemen, why don't you laugh?" Lincoln asked. "With the fearful strain that is upon me night and day, if I did not laugh I should die and you need this medicine as much as I do."[21]

But then "the president took a graver tone," said Salmon P. Chase. He told the assembled cabinet that he had "thought a great deal about the relation of this war to slavery," but that he had held off acting until the rebel army was driven out of Maryland, a feat accomplished four days ago at Antietam. "I think the time has now come," Lincoln announced.[22]

He acknowledged respect for his department heads but cautioned, "I do not wish your advice on the main matter, for that I have determined myself." But he invited commentary on the grammar or "any minor matter." Before he read the paper that had been in the locked drawer of his desk, the preliminary version of the Emancipation Proclamation, he closed with a gnomic thought. "I must do the best I can and bear the responsibility of taking the course which I feel I ought to take."[23]

A close look at the document shows the marked influence of the contraband camps on Lincoln's thought process. The edict granted permanent freedom to enslaved people "taking refuge within the lines of the army," the only people to whom it immediately applied. This was an implicit but clear reference to the contraband settlements fanned out across the Upper South and the Mississippi Valley. If the rebelling states did not lay down their arms by January 1, 1863, their enslaved people would be "thenceforward and forever free," and the U.S. military would be directed to "recognize and maintain the freedom of such persons." Here he was only restating and certifying the reality of what had been happening in contraband camps since May 1861.

In seeking justification for what he was doing, Lincoln did not point to the Constitution or Congress. He instead used a strange passive-voice phrase: "attention is hereby called" to the Second Confiscation Act and an order prohibiting military officers from returning enslaved people to their owners. Both these measures had grown directly out of the initial Fort Monroe decision and the inarguable crisis created by the swelling contraband camps. The unusual precedent Lincoln was citing left his own role ambiguous, almost constitutionally invisible. He instead, indirectly, pointed to the authority of the facts on the ground that the freed people had created, speaking of them as though they were an impersonal force of nature that changed the direction of the war.[24]

The preliminary Emancipation Proclamation was not Lincoln's finest piece of writing. It had no grandeur or memorable phrases that could be turned into inspiring quotes. The poetic Lincoln of "mystic chords of memory" and "let us now highly resolve" could also be the lawyerly Lincoln prone to tangle up a point within the gnarls of eye-crossing sentences. It came in for withering criticism. The British foreign minister, among many others, noted that it contained "no declaration of a principle adverse to slavery" and did not free anyone in loyal states. "Could anything be more feebly put, or more ineffectually written?" complained Charles Eliot Norton after reading Lincoln's initial statement to Congress. Governor John Andrew of Massachusetts read it as "a poor document, but a mighty act," while his cross-town radical friend William Lloyd Garrison thought the prose bore "the same marks of crudeness, incongruity, feebleness and lack of method" characterizing most of Lincoln's writings on slavery, and wished somebody in the White House would take away his pen. The onetime London bureau chief of the *New-York Tribune* Karl Marx thought the preliminary Emancipation Proclamation was "aesthetically repulsive, logically inadequate, farcical in form" and likened it to the dispatch of one backwoods country lawyer to another. But he also called it "the most important document in American history since the establishment of the Union, tantamount to the tearing up of the old American Constitution."[25]

Careful readers saw through the paradox. They understood exactly what it would do in the short term, which was to guarantee the establishment of dozens of additional contraband camps within areas formerly belonging to the Confederacy throughout 1863. Even the impatient Horace Greeley agreed. "The very hesitation of the President to take the decisive step gives weight to his ultimate decision," he wrote. The proclamation was an "immense fact" that acknowledged the "emphatic conviction" that had come over the nation. And if there was any doubt as to the guarantee, Lincoln himself had given it in his signing statement on the Second Confiscation Act that cited the physical impossibility of ever returning the hundreds of thousands of contraband camp residents to their masters. He could not retract the edict if he wanted to; it would be like shouting back the sea.[26]

The news spread fast through the plantation telegraph. Refugees flocked to the U.S. Army in unprecedented numbers and they would indeed, as Edwin Stanton put it, "turn against the rebels the productive power that upholds the insurrection." Slavery would die as a casualty of war. Benjamin Butler had grasped the link between military emancipation and universal freedom as far back as the previous August. "The negro will be free," he wrote his wife. "It is inevitable."[27]

Some saw a conspiracy. In faraway Santa Cruz, California, the conservative *Weekly Sentinel* complained of "long closeted contraband, confiscation, colonization, emancipation, and Abolition schemes." Lincoln himself had warned a delegation of border state representatives on March 10, 1862, that the contraband matter pushed him toward emancipation because "slaves would come to the camps and continual irritation was kept up." He tried in vain to get them to accept a buyout plan that would have the federal government issuing cash bonds of at least $300 per enslaved person. But events were outpacing any plan for compensated emancipation. Before long, there would be more than 52,000 refugees living in Virginia alone.[28]

This thought could be traced directly to Butler's strategy at Fort Monroe: the treatment of enslaved people as valuable enemy assets to be neutralized. For some, the clothing of the measure in an army uniform was a telling bit of evasion. As scholar Douglas L. Wilson observed, the insipid language was a masterstroke because it lacked a value statement that could be twisted or weaponized. Its aim was not to convince but to be a high wall covered in butter on which no opponent could get a legal toehold. "It succeeded not by eloquence," wrote Wilson, "but by inexquisite language exquisitely suited to the occasion."[29]

After Congress received a preview of the proclamation, Samuel Gridley Howe remarked sarcastically, "The President has been long on the anxious seat, but has at last a change of heart, and has set his face steadily Zionward, though he is as yet rather ashamed of his Lord." But this sentiment missed the ancestry of the proclamation living within the contraband camps. Attributing it only to one man's "change of heart" was to ignore the enslaved people and the massive shift of public opinion that pushed Lincoln from behind.[30]

Robert Hamilton at the *Anglo-African* didn't want to see emancipation walked in through the back door as a war measure. "It is an instrument for crushing, hurting, injuring and crippling the enemy. It is per se no more humanitarian than a hundred pounder rifled cannon." But he agreed with other African American commentators that there was no going backward from this point. "Abraham Lincoln may be slow," wrote Frederick Douglass. "Abraham Lincoln may desire peace even at the price of leaving our terrible national sore untouched, to fester on for generations, but Abraham Lincoln is not the man to reconsider, retract and contradict words and purposes solemnly proclaimed over his official signature. The careful, and we think, the slothful deliberation which he has observed in reaching this obvious policy, is a guarantee against retraction."[31]

Without the eighteen-month pilot program of the contraband camps, an emancipation order would have been too frightening for most Northerners to accept. Even with its tangled wording, the preliminary Emancipation Proclamation is even more remarkable for recognizing those efforts of the freed people, which in practical terms meant chancy midnight escapes and potentially fatal disobedience to their masters. Without these uncounted and largely unapplauded efforts, emancipation would never have happened on an accelerated timetable. In June, the influential philanthropist John Murray Forbes visited the refugee camp in Port Royal, South Carolina, and saw its orderly nature. He came away convinced that "Old Abe would be pushed up to the use of military powers of emancipation."[32]

As Forbes put it in another letter to Charles Sumner: "I used to think emancipation only another name for murder, fire, and rape, but mature reflection and considerable personal observation have since convinced me that emancipation may be, at any time, declared without disorder." This could be done, he insisted, without "infringing on the Constitution." Sumner had Lincoln's ear and he—along with many others—passed along the favorable reports and the legal recommendations.[33]

In a statement to Congress in December, Lincoln amplified the wartime abolition message, calling for a plan of gradual and compensated abolition, just as Britain had done thirty years prior. Once again, he made indirect reference to the enormous population of the contraband camps—in effect, the reality on the ground that was making any of this politically possible. He urged Congress to make it explicit that "all slaves who shall have enjoyed actual freedom by the chances of the war, at any time before the end of the rebellion, will be forever free."[34]

Unable to get a decisive vote, the proposal died in Congress. But Lincoln had given voice to an idea that would soon play a role in debates over how to ease the transition to freedom for 4 million enslaved people. He made a remarkable admission in explaining why the federal government should pay off slaveholders, urging Northern lawmakers to remember "how unhesitatingly we all use cotton and sugar, and share in the profits of dealing in them," a commercial interconnectedness he had witnessed up close in New Orleans. It would not be right, he thought, for anyone to conclude the South had been more guilty than the North for the continuance of slavery.[35]

A few white philanthropists who had been in the contraband camps echoed Lincoln's thoughts about collective guilt. Austa French of Xenia, Ohio, had been along for the Forbes mission to Port Royal, South Carolina, to report on the conditions of the freed people and experienced "strange feelings" as her boat approached the humid coast.

"Slavery is written upon the shore, the trees, the sky, the air," she wrote. "There steals over you the feeling that you are passing under a great cloud of accumulated wrongs in which you are mysteriously implicated, the vague feeling that you yourself have done something awful, somewhere in the dim past."[36]

9

Let My People Go

Lincoln's "fit and necessary war measure" opened the way toward a dangerous idea that had been percolating since the beginning of the rebellion. Frederick Douglass thought ten thousand Black soldiers should be impressed into duty, arguing that anything less would be like fighting an enemy with one hand tied behind the back. Enlisting former enslaved people, especially, would have a force-multiplying effect against a demoralized Confederacy. "One black regiment alone would be, in such a war, the full equal of two white ones," Douglass wrote at the start of the war. "The very fact of color in this case would be more terrible than powder or balls."[1]

But with the exception of the New England abolitionists in the officer corps, most Union commanders resisted Black enrollment for fear of cowardice in the field, or lack of discipline, or even of seeing Union carbines turned against white soldiers in revolt. Lincoln dreaded the prospect of "fifty thousand bayonets" dropped on the battlefield, only to be picked up by Confederates. "I do not think much of the Negro," confided Henry Halleck, whose victory at Corinth had cleared the way for the most successful of contraband camps. Benjamin Butler himself had said the conflict was "a white man's war," in which enslaved Blacks were expected to be bystanders or, at the very best, low-paid construction workers. But small steps in this monumental shift in direction had been taken even before the preliminary emancipation proclamation in September 1862 made the arming of freed people inevitable. The idea found its first expression in the contraband camps.[2]

The refugees in the converted meadow north of Corinth, Mississippi, organized themselves into police-like units to keep order and watch for Confederate raids. And Colonel Thomas

Wentworth Higginson had organized a group of Black men at Port Royal on martial lines that would soon become the 1st South Carolina Volunteer Infantry (Colored). "They had more to fight for than the whites," he reasoned.[3]

A few from Port Royal became scouts and spies. Before the outbreak of war, an enslaved woman in Savannah named Susie King Taylor had taken clandestine reading lessons and become proficient in forging passes for those who dared slip out onto the streets after dark. After Union forces captured the South Carolina Sea Islands, she sought safety behind their lines and eventually taught members of the Black militia how to read. They, in turn, taught her how to load and fire a weapon. She cleaned guns, packed cartridge boxes, and prepared them for missions. "I learned how to handle a musket very well while in the regiment, and could shoot straight and often hit the target," Taylor said. "I assisted in cleaning the guns and used to fire them off, to see if the cartridges were dry, before cleaning and reloading, each day. I thought this great fun."[4]

One of the first genuine heroes of the conflict was a Black man named William Tillman, who was serving as a cook on the schooner *S.J. Waring* in June 1861 when it was hijacked by Confederates. Informed by the rebels he would be sold into slavery once they arrived in Charleston, Tillman responded by waiting until after midnight before sneaking to the bridge, where he clubbed the captain and threw him overboard, put the rest of the rebels in chains, and took command of the vessel, sailing it back to a Union port to widespread acclaim. Even the *New York Herald*, usually derisive of Blacks, felt compelled to praise him as "a courageous man" with "high mettle." The newspapers made much of the detail, possibly exaggerated, that after Tillman hacked the rebel commanders with a knife, they tried to bind their wounds with an American flag they had cut up to make an improvised rebel battle standard.[5]

Black activists seized on the example. In San Francisco, the writer J. Madison Bell published a poem in the *Pacific Appeal* titled with the perennial question: "What Shall We Do with the Contrabands?" He answered the question speedily. "Shall we arm them? Yes, arm them!"[6]

Just such a policy had been urged, and the same motives suggested, by Northern radicals since the opening days of the war, to the consternation of doughfaces who warned that elevating an enslaved person to a uniformed soldier with insignia on his shoulder would mean not only universal emancipation but the dreaded outcome of racial equality. "If you make him the instrument by which your battles are fought, the means by which your victories are won," warned a Democratic congressman from Ohio, "you must treat him as a victor is entitled to be treated, with all decent and becoming respect." This was a frightening prospect to many. As another congressional critic, Benjamin Thomas, put it, "No man who has ever served under our flag, whether for a day or for an hour, can ever again be made a slave. Where, then, shall they go?" Journalists had no trouble finding Union enlisted men and officers who thought it degrading to fight alongside a Black man. The war measure was not a sign of resourcefulness to them but a sign of weakness.[7]

But Lincoln's proclamation had opened the door. The discipline that freed combat engineers had already demonstrated in the contraband camps—they were essentially soldiers without uniform or rank—had laid down a foundation of credibility. In January 1863, the 1st South Carolina went marching through Beaufort in a display that scandalized white onlookers, a scene soon to be repeated in hundreds of surrendered Southern cities. "There's my Tom," said one horrified planter, recognizing one of his former field hands, wishing to cut his throat. Within four months, Black troops helped assault Port Hudson on the Mississippi River and bravely repulsed a Confederate attack at Milliken's Bend. "You have no idea how my prejudices with regard to negro troops have been dispelled by the battle," wrote a white officer. "They are far superior in discipline to the white troops, and just as brave."[8]

Regiments popped up everywhere freed people were gathered. Brigadier General Lorenzo Thomas came down to Corinth to make what amounted to a recruitment speech in the front yard of the Verandah House, the headquarters of General Grenville Dodge. Hundreds signed up on the spot. "Slavery is dead," concluded a white Mississippian, loyal to the Union. "It has committed suicide. We are now making the best possible disposition of these people."[9]

Within weeks of Thomas's speech, more than four hundred freed men had been arranged in multiple companies of the U.S. Colored Troops (USCT), clothed in blue uniforms, bearing Enfield rifles imported from Britain, and learning the basic maneuvers of presenting arms and standing at attention. "They are a stalwart-looking set of men," wrote James Redfield of the 39th Iowa Infantry. "If they fight as well as they look, woe be unto the rebels. I have faith in them." By August 1863, they were out in the field repairing roads and bridges for General William Rosecrans near Iuka, Mississippi, an extension of the engineering work they had been doing around Corinth. But this time it was in uniform. "It is understood that the organization is strictly based upon military rule, and is subjected to the same rigid discipline of the white soldier," reported a correspondent from the *Cincinnati Gazette* invited to watch. "And it is remarkable that this class of persons bear the discipline with as much ease as the most patriotic of whites."[10]

The 1st Alabama Infantry of African Descent was certified as combat ready in late June 1863 in a flag ceremony. A middle-aged soldier named Rufus Campbell received the national colors on behalf of the regiment. "Having felt through a long life the evils of slavery, I rejoice at the opportunity of rescuing my children from such a fate," said Campbell. "Why there's not much blood in a man anyhow, and if he is not willing to give it for the freedom of children and friends, he does not deserve to be called a man." One of his comrades, a corporal named Sullivan with a reputation as an amiable jokester, followed up with a mordant observation about the scars that many of them bore on their backs from multiple whippings in slavery. "We today for the first time have had given to us the stars, but many of us have received *stripes* before."[11]

Only white officers were permitted to command Black privates, and the man selected to lead the 1st Alabama was one who had known them well: James Alexander, the no-nonsense superintendent of the Corinth camp who insisted on sharp appearances. "When formed, their line was as good as it could be," said an observer, and the men "evinced a better knowledge" of infantry basics than most white companies. Once the call for enlistments had arrived, no force seemed able to stem the enthusiasm among Black men to take up arms against the Confederates. Approximately one-eighth of the total population of the Corinth camp enlisted in the USCT, a rate matched by reports from other camps, where it was not uncommon to see a man in a blue uniform drilling with a rifle the day after he ran away from a plantation. "Recruits are pouring in every day, and often I am not in my office for ten minutes during the day," reported one overwhelmed officer in Virginia. "Last night ninety recruits came into camp, eighty-five of whom had masters day before yesterday. This morning forty more have come in, and thirty of these were slaves yesterday."[12]

A twenty-five-year-old man named Jerry Sutton, the eventual stepfather to the great-great-grandmother of future U.S. first lady Michelle Obama, ran away from slavery in Tennessee and found his way to Corinth, where he joined the regiment. In the summer of 1863, he was thrown into combat. General William T. Sherman had commenced his march toward Atlanta and needed to protect his railroad supply line to Nashville, so he ordered General Samuel Sturgis from Memphis into northern Mississippi to harass Confederate cavalry under the command of Nathan Bedford Forrest.[13]

Sturgis picked up the 1st Alabama—by then renamed the 55th U.S. Colored Infantry Regiment—at Corinth and marched south with them toward Tupelo. At 9:30 a.m. on June 10, an advance party of federal cavalry met Forrest's horsemen at a rural junction called Brices Cross Roads. Operating with half as many men on a day that grew oppressively hot, Forrest successfully flanked the Union lines and captured a bridge over Tishomingo Creek to their rear, forcing a retreat. But the 55th and 59th U.S. Colored regiments, who had been assigned to guard the wagon trains in the rear, laid down covering fire and protected the federal forces from almost certain capture. The sight of Black men shooting at them doubtlessly came as a psychological shock to the rebel soldiers.

In hand-to-hand combat, Private Claiborne Merriweather of the 59th Colored Regiment beat a rebel soldier to death with the butt of his empty Enfield rifle, then took the dead man's loaded carbine and began shooting more rebels with it. Union teamsters turned over some of the wagons and set them on fire as distractions, adding to the general confusion. "I would turn & shoot & then retreat," recalled a Black private named George Jenkins. When a bullet caught him in the hip, "I fell like a dead man & fainted away, I reckon." He was taken prisoner. His comrade Andrew Jackson, shot in the leg, was also captured but avoided a trip to the horrific prisoner of war camp at Andersonville, Georgia, only by agreeing to be re-enslaved by a Confederate officer.[14]

In their retreat, white troops from the Union front dropped their ammunition boxes and bolted down the road toward safety, clawing their way past each other and over a wagon that had capsized on the narrow bridge over Tishomingo Creek. A mortified Sturgis described the scene thusly in his report: "The road became crowded and jammed with troops, wagons and artillery sank into the deep mud and became inextricable. No power could check the panic-stricken mass as it swept toward the rear." Some waded across the creek, where they were gunned down in the water by Confederates on the high banks.[15]

Brices Cross Roads went down as a Union catastrophe, and Sturgis asked to be relieved of command once he got back to Memphis. But most observers acknowledged that the USCT regiments had fought with distinction. Union soldier Abner Olds wrote home to Ohio: "With one accord, the white troops that were in the expedition complimented the colored soldiers for their valor and determined bravery." Though it was their first experience of combat, "they behaved, under very trying circumstances, with a coolness and confidence worthy of old troops," verified a lieutenant from Illinois, who was amazed at their general stoicism and ability to take punishment. He watched "numbers shot in the arms, hands, legs, their clothing soaked with blood, marching along with the rest, without a sign of pain."[16]

The recorded injuries of a formerly enslaved soldier in Company B, nineteen-year-old private Sandy Sledge, are one indication of the ferocity of the rearguard engagement: three buckshot wounds in the left leg; a bullet lodged in his right leg; two bullets in the broken right arm; a broken right middle finger; a shot in the head that fractured his skull and cost him the hearing in his left ear. After taking these hits, Sledge was left behind by the retreating U.S. troops. He and another private crawled off into the woods and remained there for two weeks before flagging down a passing squad of the 3rd Michigan Cavalry, who took him to a Memphis hospital. Sledge survived his wounds, though his friends later testified his personality was never the same.[17]

Reports of gallantry from the U.S. Colored Troops kept coming in from every theater of the war. The 1st South Carolina Volunteer Infantry fought an engagement on the St. Mary's River with "fiery energy," shouting to one another "Never give it up!" as Confederate bullets rained down on them. The 54th Massachusetts had marched through a crowd of twenty thousand cheering white Bostonians on their way to the wharves as they prepared to mobilize on the batteries outside Charleston. Meanwhile, the 2nd South Carolina Volunteer Infantry, accompanied by Harriet Tubman, came ashore at a rice plantation on the Combahee River, freeing 750 enslaved people and putting the torch to barns and crops. A secessionist planter named Cuthbert was taken prisoner and rowed out to a navy ship, while his enslaved people made up a mocking song about it on the spot: "All our old masters ran away, Hallelujah. Master's going to prison now, Hallelujah." The gunboats departed the area with Cuthbert in chains, their decks packed with refugees, many of them asking to be put into immediate military service.[18]

"I've never seen such a sight," recalled Tubman after the war. "I laughed and laughed and laughed."[19]

Six weeks later, the 54th Massachusetts took astounding casualties in its assault on Fort Wagner outside Charleston, but the bravery of the regiment elicited nearly universal admiration, even from Confederates. And it did nothing to quell recruitment in the Lowcountry; Fort Wagner became a rallying cry like the Alamo or Bunker Hill had been for an earlier generation of whites. "It seems that pretty nearly all the refugees join the army," said an official from South Carolina. Advertisements for runaways packed Southern newspapers like never before, and food production plummeted as fields went unharvested. By the middle of 1863, more than seven-tenths of the male enslaved population of Charles City County, Virginia, had run away to join the federal troops. "There is not one negro in all the South, who will remain faithful . . . not one," lamented a Tidewater planter.[20]

One of thousands of examples came from Samuel Ballton, who had married a woman named Rebecca at the outbreak of the war but his master placed him on a work detail on the Virginia Central Railroad. On the holiday called Whitsun, the seventh Sunday after Easter, he and several other men stole some bacon and flour and headed for the Yankee lines near Spotsylvania Court House. Ballton became a cook for the 6th Wisconsin Regiment, but worried constantly about his wife. He made an incursion back into rebel territory and found her. "Rebecca, I'm going to take you to freedom," he said. He would think of it for years as the proudest moment of his life. The couple made their way to New England, where he enlisted in the 5th Massachusetts Cavalry and fought with them as a corporal until the collapse of the Confederacy, when he was among the first Black soldiers to enter Richmond.[21]

Another example of raw courage came from Henry Jarvis, the man who sailed to Fort Monroe by night across Chesapeake Bay. He had joined the merchant marine during the Civil War and traveled to Cuba and Africa, but then landed in Boston in 1863 in time for the general call for the U.S. Colored Troops.[22]

Jarvis had told Benjamin Butler that the secessionist conflict "had got to be a black man's war for sure," and now he was finally able to become a soldier in it. Colonel Robert Shaw's famous 54th Massachusetts regiment was already full. But he enlisted in the Massachusetts 55th in the suburb of Belmont, listing his occupation as "laborer" and signing his affirmation with an X under the declaration, "I will observe and obey the orders of the President of the United States, and the orders of the officers appointed above me, according to the Rules and Articles of War."[23]

He answered to an abolitionist Quaker from Pennsylvania, Norwood Hallowell, who defied his church's pacifist teachings to command the 55th Massachusetts. They had a streak of derring-do, running a string of successful attacks against Confederate forces along the shore of South Carolina. As an enthusiastic member of Company K, Jarvis impressed his fellow soldiers with his bravery. At times, his fighting spirit bordered on the foolhardy. During a skirmish on James Island, south of Charleston, in July 1864, he jumped up on a wooden parapet in a hail of enemy fire and returned fire.

"O God, I've got you," he hollered at the rebels.

"Get down from there, corporal," a captain told him, after giving a ceasefire order. "They will shoot you." Jarvis was lucky that day.[24]

Then came November 30, 1864, when the regiment tried to take out a Confederate fortress called Honey Hill that overlooked a crucial rail link between Charleston and Savannah. The only way to approach it through the swamp was along a path on which seven artillery pieces were precisely trained, and "it was like rushing into the very mouth of death going up this road," reported an officer. The 55th Massachusetts nevertheless made the attempt, charging down the road "cheering and yelling" but suffering heavy casualties. Jarvis was one of them.[25]

"There I was wounded three times; first in the arm, but I kept on fighting until a ball struck my leg and I fell," he recalled. "I was struck once more in the same leg, and I lay on the field all night. I should have bled to death if all our men hadn't been drilled in using a tourniquet and supplied with bandages. I just had time to stick my knife in the knot and twist it tight before I fainted."[26]

A childhood friend named Peter Drummond helped drag him off the field. When Jarvis was brought to the medics, they considered amputating his leg but, after concluding he would soon die of blood poisoning, figured it wouldn't be worth the extra pain. He did not die. He spent six months in a U.S. Army hospital, where pieces of bone kept protruding from his wounded leg. When he went back to Hampton, the stitches opened again. Doctors had to saw the leg off after all.[27]

Lincoln had been skeptical about the abilities of the U.S. Colored Troops. But his thinking changed as reports of their gallantry flooded the telegraph wires. "The colored population is the great *available* and yet *unavailed of* force for restoring the Union," he wrote to the military governor of Tennessee, Andrew Johnson, urging him to raise several battalions. Panicking Southerners redoubled their slave patrols and tried to foil runaways by hiding their shoes. When federal armies drew near, they moved their enslaved people away en masse, sometimes in coffles. "Every sound black male left for the enemy becomes a soldier we have afterward to fight," lamented General Edmund Kirby Smith.[28]

Homegrown resistance against slaveholders had always been present in the South and manifested itself in countless hostilities—the malingering in the fields, the running away, the periodic uprisings, the occasional beatings of masters. Now that antislavery power could be channeled in the form of military might. "Lincoln and the Republicans expected that slaves would run for their freedom if given the chance, and they constructed their antislavery policies on that expectation," writes the historian James Oakes. "They realized they could not destroy slavery if they did not win the war, and they eventually concluded they could not win the war unless they reversed decades of federal policy and enlisted tens of thousands of African Americans in the U.S. Army."[29]

The president also took a White House meeting with Abraham Galloway, the ex-slave from North Carolina who spied out Confederate vulnerabilities at Vicksburg, and then managed to recruit hundreds of recently liberated men into the 1st North Carolina Colored Volunteers. Galloway came as part of a delegation of five Southern Black men, four of them ex-slaves. At that meeting on April 29, they pressed Lincoln on the question of voting rights for the freed people of the Confederacy, which would, their letter said, "finish the noble work you have begun."[30]

Robert Hamilton, the editor of the *Anglo-African*, was not present but reported that Lincoln had been cordial and "their interview was a pleasant one," with the president giving "assurances of his sympathy and earnest cooperation." This was the first time the president had sat for a meeting with former contraband camp residents. It was also his first reception of a delegation of Black Southerners. This time, there was no clumsy talk of "separate races" or colonization plans.[31]

In New York City later that summer, Galloway met with fellow contraband soldier William Benjamin Gould, who had also escaped from slavery in Wilmington, North Carolina, though not by slipping onboard a vessel but outright stealing one and hailing the USS *Cambridge* as it was standing in a blockading position. Gould was welcomed aboard and almost immediately recruited into service for the U.S. Navy. He then began a diary that made explicit mention of his desire to avenge the wrongs committed by the First Families of Virginia in the seventeenth century when they received the first shipment of kidnapped Africans at Old Point Comfort.[32]

"Was it an act of friendship that that caused the F.F.V.'s to buy those misfortunate ones and make them Hewers of Wood and Drawers of Water to clear thair land, to Build their Cittys and feed their Mouths?" he wrote acidly, echoing the Book of Genesis. "And from the doings of that eventful day spring all of the evils of slavery in that country."[33]

Lincoln's change of heart mirrored that of thousands of white soldiers who fought alongside Black regiments. It wasn't solely their bravery in battle that paved the way; simple day-to-day contact also had a humanizing effect. Lyman Ayer of the 2nd Minnesota Battery thought "the prejudice in the army against them is fast giving way." Many admitted they had doubted the proclamation's wisdom. One of them was Herman Lorenzo White of the 22nd Massachusetts, who initially had peppered his letters home with racist epithets, but eased up as the integration progressed and the soldiers experienced one of the enduring aspects of war: bonding under fire. "It is astonishing to see the harmony that exists between them and the white troops," he wrote from Petersburg in 1864. "They fight, work & eat together without regard to color &c, set and chat together about the war and such like old chums, such is war, every black soldier killed in battle is an equivalent for one white man."[34]

Equality was not that simple. Once in the armed services, Black soldiers had to accept lower wages than their white counterparts, could not be promoted higher than sergeant, fought disease, and faced a gruesome possibility if they were captured. In addition to the perceived moral offense at having to fight Black men with guns, Confederate officers quailed at the idea of keeping separate prisoner of war camps for white and Black. The solution was often to execute Black captives where they stood. After a battle at Marks' Mill, Arkansas, "they were piled in great heaps about the wagons in the tangled brushwood, and upon the muddy and trampled road." Most notoriously, at Fort Pillow, Tennessee, on April 12, 1864, up to five hundred Black soldiers were massacred after they held their hands up in surrender. The commander who ordered it, Nathan Bedford Forrest, was the same cavalry wizard who had forced the retreat at Brices Cross Roads, and he reported with evident glee that the Mississippi River "was dyed with the blood of the slaughtered."[35]

If he was trying to create a deterrent through the message that Black prisoners would be killed rather than given quarter, he miscalculated. "Remember Fort Pillow!" became a rallying cry among regiments determined to fight to the death and take as many rebels as possible along with them in the belief that capture would be fatal. Some made an oath on their knees never to give up and "give no quarter, take no prisoners, make it dangerous to take the life of a black soldier by these barbarians." The Confederates knew what the Fort Pillow cry meant when it was aimed at them, and a soldier from a regiment in Virginia surmised "that piece of infernal brutality enforced by them there has cost the enemy already two men for every one they so inhumanely murdered."[36]

Black soldiers also faced hazards from their own side. Some commanders ordered them into the most dangerous positions to spare white troops. If one got shot, said an officer, "all you have to do is send out and get another one." Plenty of recruitment agents aimed to do just that—they trawled liberated areas for enough bodies to fill the demand from wealthy young men out to hire a substitute, as well as state governors trying to meet their regimental quotas. Some agents bribed provost marshals for access to the latest incoming waves of enslaved refugees. A Massachusetts soldier deplored "this traffic of New England towns in the bodies of wretched negroes, bidding against each other for these miserable beings."[37]

For many, though, the experience of wearing a Union coat and fighting slave owners immediately after arriving at a contraband camp was a feeling beyond description. After liberating plantations and watching enslaved people drop their hoes, said one Black recruit, "we could then truly see what we had been fighting for." Whenever white planters beheld such a sight and saw the Black faces of those liberators in uniform, thought Henry Mc-

Neal Turner, the Black chaplain of the 1st U.S. Colored Troops, they seemed in a daze, "musing as to whether they are actually in another world, or whether this one is turned wrong side out."[38]

The crowning irony of it all did not escape George W. Hatton of the 1st USCT, who was posted to Wilson's Landing near Jamestown, Virginia, the place where he noted "the first sons of Africa" had been sent to labor in the tobacco fields 245 years earlier, thereafter "looked upon as an inferior race by all civilized nations."[39]

In a scene by then repeated in various ways thousands of times all over the South, a group of enslaved women heard about the colored Yankees in their midst, took a chance, and ran away to them. Hatton had been born free in Maryland, and although he had heard terrifying stories of slavery, this was the first time he had seen its brutalities up close. He and his comrades looked with disgust at the scars on the women's backs and listened to their stories with mounting anger.[40]

In the following days, Union soldiers captured the owner, an aristocratic planter named William Henry Clopton, and lashed him to a tree. One of his former enslaved people, William Harris, then took a whip, administered twenty lashes, and then invited the women to do likewise and "remind the gentleman of days gone by" as all watched, including the white commander, Brigadier General Edward Wild, who referred to Clopton as a "sniveling saint" and felt no pity for him. "I wish that his back had been as deeply scarred as those of the women," he commented, "but I abstained and left it to them."[41]

But such events were uncommon. Despite some exceptions, units were generally known for their restraint against slaveholding planters they captured. The exceptions, however, were memorable affairs. Upon liberating portions of the South, some habitually inquired as to the identity of the cruelest master in town, then went to his house to pay "respectable compliments" that included a ransacking of the house, after which they tied the owner to a horse backward and carried him along in the column as a trophy.

Turner, an African Methodist Episcopal pastor, was present on one of these missions in North Carolina when formerly enslaved

Henry McNeal Turner of Israel Bethel Church was present when the Emancipation Proclamation was read aloud from the front of the White House. "Men squealed, women fainted, dogs barked, white and colored people shook hands, songs were sung," he reported. "Nothing like it will ever be seen again in this life."

troops learned of "one infamous old rebel" who kept a woman in irons. When they learned of this and other outrages, "the boys grew incensed and utterly destroyed every thing in the place," turning a piano into splinters with an ax, cutting up the master's imported carpets, and distributing whatever valuable items they could salvage to the man's stunned enslaved people as a form of reparations. After the owner protested, speaking "saucily" to the troops, one of them put him on the floor with a punch to the face. The house was later burned to the ground. Though Turner was a preacher, he seemed unable to repress a smile at these and other acts of rough justice. "I have seen numbers of the finest houses turned to ashes," he said.[42]

General William T. Sherman ordered the 1st Alabama Colored, now renamed the 49th and 55th USCT, transferred to occupied Memphis. Civil society there had broken down to the point that a Union general warned "it is impossible for any one to say whether the state of slavery exists or not." Courts hadn't convened in months, sheriffs were nowhere to be found, and nearby fields were picked clean from constant foraging. The Black troops arrived shouting and stomping, taking gratification at the plantation owners' stunned reaction to "what they had never before seen and had never expected to see—their own slaves powerfully and lawfully armed for their overthrow, and led and commanded by those whom they considered their invaders," reported Robert Cowden, who had been wounded at Brices Cross Roads. When a unit called to duty at Natchez, Mississippi, received orders to dismantle slave pens at a place called Forks of the Road, they picked up sledgehammers with "the wildest enthusiasm" and worked all night long to dismantle the onetime market for human beings with "a terrible earnestness." Not a few of them had once been imprisoned there.[43]

By the end of the war, the USCT had swelled to 186,000 enlisted men, representing 10 percent of the total Union fighting force. Their abilities in the field not only hastened the end of the war but made a deep impression on those who witnessed them in action. Twenty-three of them would be awarded the Congressional Medal of Honor. Although racial equality was a long way off, it had become evident that freed people would not rise in vengeful rebellion against Northern supporters of slavery.

Seeking to get as many Northern free Blacks as possible to join up, Frederick Douglass traveled throughout the country giving a speech called "Men of Color, To Arms!" He began each address with an appeal to "brothers and fathers" and closed by leading a rendition of "John Brown's Body." Among those who enlisted were two of his sons. Douglass famously told an audience in Philadelphia: "Once let the black man get upon his person the brass letter, U.S., let him get an eagle on his button, and a musket on his shoulder and bullets in his pocket, there is no power on earth that can deny that he has earned the right to citizenship."[44]

Though he made his appeal to Northern audiences, the overwhelming majority of recruits were residents of Southern contraband camps prior to 1863 or came from places liberated by the advances of the U.S. Army. Their journey from slave to soldier went remarkably fast. George Hatton called it a "shocking reverse," echoing the thoughts of a Black sergeant at Milford Station, Virginia, who marveled at what he saw in his journey south in pursuit of Robert E. Lee's army.

"The very people who, three years ago, crouched at their master's feet, on the accursed soil of Virginia, now march in a victorious column of freedmen, over the same land."[45]

* * *

Lincoln had trouble sleeping on December 31, 1862, just hours before he finalized the Emancipation Proclamation. The South had not surrendered, the grace period was over, and the moment was imminent.

"Well, what do you intend doing?" asked his wife, Mary Todd, who thought going forward was a mistake.

"I am a man under orders," he told her, looking upward. "I cannot do otherwise."[46]

When the proclamation arrived damp from the Government Printing Office at 10:45 a.m., Lincoln noticed a minor error—it failed to include the closing ceremonial flourish, "In testimony whereof I have set my hand"—and he asked for a corrected version. While everyone was waiting, the president went to greet people at the traditional New Year's Day reception at the White House, shaking hands and exchanging palaver with a stream of well-wishers. A reporter from the *Sacramento Daily Union*, Noah Brooks, watched as visitors were announced, to whom the president, "his heavy eyes brightening, says 'I am glad to see you, Mr. Snifkins—you come from a noble State—God bless her.'"[47]

Lincoln did this for three hours until he could peel away to his study to pick up a steel-tipped pen. His right hand was quivering from the morning's exertion of shaking hundreds of hands.

To a curious William Seward standing next to him, Lincoln assured, "I never in my life felt more certain than I was doing right than I do in signing this paper." Then he forced himself, with some difficulty, to write his entire name with bold and steady strokes, signing it as "Abraham Lincoln" instead of his customary "A. Lincoln." "If my hand trembles when I sign the Proclamation, all who examine the document hereafter will say, 'He hesitated.'"[48]

The order he signed was essentially the same as the September document, except with a few key deletions. It eliminated any mention of colonization schemes or compensation schemes for slaveholders. It changed the wording of "forever free" to the simpler and perhaps more equivocal "free." And it also did not cite Congress, arrogating the authority to the presidency. The wording recalled Lincoln's executive decision of May 1861 to put down the secession movement with military force and avoid a congressional declaration of war. That would have been tantamount to recognizing the Confederacy as a foreign government and not an internal rebellion. That convenience of presidential power had then been an asset; it now worked against Lincoln because it left him exposed and subject to claims of tyranny.

Lincoln's executive reach—even overreach—on January 1, 1863, to make emergency repairs to what scholar Noah Feldman has called "the broken Constitution" would not have passed a judicial test in peacetime. It also would not have passed the crucial test of public opinion had it not been for the experiment that began at Fort Monroe on May 22, 1861, which had since grown to include at least a hundred thousand people. Lincoln would later acknowledge the limitations of what he was doing and give yet another oblique nod to the contraband camps. "It might be added that it only aided those who came into our lines and that it was inoperative as to those who did not give themselves up," he said.[49]

Yet another irony of the war: General Butler's original trick of reasoning was born out of the idea that the Confederacy was indeed a sovereign power outside of the United States. "I am under no constitutional obligation to a foreign country, which Virginia now claims to be," he had told John Baytop Cary. And out of that idea grew two Confiscation Acts and the Emancipation Proclamation, aided by Lincoln's determination to make a war measure stick in peacetime. Legality was key to everything; Butler and Lincoln had both been raised up in the law. And the president was especially conscious that wartime measures could be eviscerated by Supreme Court rulings once the hostilities had concluded.[50]

Some newspapers in the North grumbled that the proclamation freed nobody because it exempted the border states, plus the rule of U.S. law did not and could not apply to the seceded states. But it did immediately grant freedom to those in hiding along the coasts of South Carolina and Georgia, as well as those in areas occupied by the U.S. Army in sections of Arkansas, Florida, Mississippi, and North Carolina. New Year's Day in those places represented a permanent removal of the ambiguity that had hung over the contraband camps for nineteen months. And Lincoln signaled it would apply everywhere in nonexempted areas into which the U.S. Army would advance in the coming days. As he put it in a letter to a skeptical general, "To use a coarse, but an expressive figure, 'broken eggs cannot be mended.' I have issued the emancipation proclamation and I cannot retract it."[51]

What he was doing represented a reversal of everything he had said about slavery through his thirty years of public life: that he would never interfere with bondage where it existed, and moreover that neither Congress nor the president had any authority to tamper with the institution's supposed constitutional guarantees. While he may have called himself "naturally anti-slavery," he always said it was the president's job to faithfully execute the laws, not make them up. Herein lay the legal root of Lincoln's fabled wishy-washiness, a doctrine that mirrored the hands-off principles of James Buchanan in form, if not specifics. But that reading of the U.S. Constitution had led to a protracted civil war, which is, of all possible outcomes, perhaps the most vivid expression of any constitution's failure.

A key fact about a point-to-point riverman is that he is not free to go anywhere he likes on the water's surface. He is instead drawn along by the current, swelling with powerful force behind him, and he may operate only within the channels of that flow. He cannot go upstream for long. He can only do his best to keep the craft safely going in the inexplicable direction that had been carved out for him. "I claim not to have controlled events, but confess plainly that events have controlled me," Lincoln said later. "Now, at the end of three years' struggle, the nation's condition is not what either party or any man devised or expected."[52]

The bondage of 4 million people, a question that Lincoln would ultimately come to acknowledge was "somehow the cause of the war," came to an end through a series of stopgap measures remarkable for their short-range vision, devoid of grandeur or poetry until the very end, and in their own way as shambolic and utilitarian as the seventeenth-century Virginia Colony's acceptance of slavery had been. War blows down social orders once thought inviolable, exposing the latent absurdities within what was once considered proper. The residents of the contraband camps had laid the groundwork for federal action—through their insistent presence; their willingness to join the Union cause; to put on blue uniforms and fight for the United States and its flawed Constitution; and their adamant refusal to return to their previous lives or submit to a recolonization scheme. All these were powerful forms of advocacy. They ultimately pushed Abraham Lincoln from one point to another. The tandem forces of enslaved resistance and executive power, when combined with congressional action and the mailed fist of the U.S. Army, destroyed the South's signature institution.[53]

The night before Lincoln signed the final proclamation, hundreds of churches around the North observed the old Methodist tradition of the Watch Night service, praying for hours on New Year's Eve for divine will to be manifest. This is how their British coreligionists, both Black and white, had celebrated the night before August 1, 1838, when slavery was officially abolished throughout their empire, counting down the old beast's dying hours until its smothering at midnight, and they were now seeing the fruits of decades-long activism in their own country. Lincoln had certified a genuine revolution in American life—one that the enslaved people had set in motion themselves.[54]

Crowds gathered outside the White House to hear the proclamation for the first time in public, read from the pages of the *Evening Star* and grabbed by eager hands. "Men squealed, women fainted, dogs barked, white and colored people shook hands, songs were sung," reported Henry McNeal Turner of the Israel Bethel Church. "It was indeed a time of times and a half time. Nothing like it will ever be seen again in this life. Our entrance into Heaven itself will only form a counterpart." Lincoln appeared briefly at an upstairs window but did not emerge to say anything. Over at the Smithsonian Institution, the daughter of the Southern-sympathizing secretary felt differently. "The prospects of the country are very dark," wrote Mary Henry in her diary.[55]

Black communities celebrated across the country. Even those who had been skeptical of Lincoln now hailed him. In Chicago, the sole Black survivor of the Harpers Ferry raid, Osborne Perry Anderson, told a gathering at Quinn's Chapel that the event was "God's vindicating the principles" of the old long-bearded radical John Brown, "who fought and died for the right." In New York City, the abolitionist pastor Henry Highland Garnet, born a slave, presided over a Watch Night service at Shiloh Presbyterian Church that featured a funeral dirge on the organ for the victims of slavery, followed by "tumultuous cheers" and "shouting, praying and rejoicing." A few days later, in a more secular event, Garnet held what he called an "intellectual jubilee" at Cooper Union, where Lincoln had given his famous "House Divided" speech. At Ohio's Oberlin College, the co-ed multiracial evangelical institution that sent dozens of missionaries and teachers to the contraband camps, president and founder Charles Finney reflected on the sense of mission of its graduates: "Every man and woman felt that his, or her, best efforts should be given to the freed people."[56]

The day's exuberance had special meaning in the contraband camps. At Port Royal, the teacher Charlotte Forten watched the procession of the 1st South Carolina Volunteers, a "fine, soldierly set of men" looking smart in their blue coats and red pantaloons before an "eager wondering crowd of freed people in their holiday-attire, with the gayest of head-handkerchiefs, the whitest of aprons, and the happiest of faces." The cooks barbecued ten oxen next to a grove of live oak trees, as a reformed former slaveholder read the proclamation out loud. As he finished, "a strong male voice (but rather cracked and elderly)" rose up and began to sing, as others joined in: *My country 'tis of thee / Sweet land of liberty . . .*

"Just think of it!" wrote Thomas Wentworth Higginson of that moment. "The first day they ever had a country, the first flag they had ever seen which promised anything to their people . . . I never saw anything so electric. It made all other words cheap; it seemed the choked voice of a race at last unloosed."[57]

U.S. Army brigadier general Rufus Saxton then made an emotional appeal to the assembled free people, sounding more like a preacher than a military man. "It is your duty to carry this good news to your brethren that are still in slavery," he said. "Let all your voices, like merry bells, join loud and clear in the grand chorus of liberty—'we are free, we are free'—until, listening, you shall hear its echoes coming back from every cabin in the land, 'we are free, we are free.'"[58]

He needn't have worried. That same day, Confederate general Joseph Finegan lamented that news of the proclamation had induced many enslaved people to bolt from their plantations, despite official attempts to suppress it. The message had been "conducted through swamps and under cover of the night, and could not be prevented." The censorship meant that the majority of Southern enslaved people heard about it before their masters did. One secessionist questioned by a U.S. provost marshal in Virginia said that "his negroes had told him of the proclamation five days before he heard it in any other way." A Unitarian minister named Moncure Conway, who had seventeen relatives in the rebellion, had no doubt about the power of the slave grapevine, especially on this most important of subjects. "If [the president] were on the upper Mississippi and proclaimed emancipation, it would be told in New Orleans before the telegraph could carry the news there," he wrote. In case that wasn't enough, the railroad investor John Murray Forbes printed up 1 million copies of the proclamation on small slips and then handed them out in bunches of fifty to Union troops, who were instructed to scatter them like seeds wherever they traveled. Shortly thereafter, the Lincoln administration rescinded its restriction on enticing enslaved people away from their plantations, allowing the army to spread further discord and chaos throughout the South.[59]

The atmosphere was more subdued on New Year's Day in Slabtown outside Fort Monroe, which was on the list of exempted places. Local tradition in Hampton holds that the proclamation was read aloud under the branches of an oak tree that grew outside the school Mary S. Peake had founded. But no contemporary documentation of this event exists. The cloudiness is perhaps reflective of the ambiguous legal status still occupied by the 2,500 residents of Slabtown: freed by the U.S. Army, but still not emancipated by the federal government.

Much of the celebration that day seems to have erupted in the secessionist hotbed of Norfolk across the bay, where the presence of federal soldiers made it possible for up to four thousand Black people to parade through the city with fifes, drums, and brass. "They carried several Union flags and cheered loudly for the downfall of American slavery," wrote an observer. The Black teacher John Oliver, looking on at the spectacle, reported that slaveholders in the nearby countryside began to treat their enslaved people even worse, telling them "no one on earth has the power to free them."[60]

At the Twelfth Street camp in Washington, DC, superintendent Nichols ordered the entire document to be read aloud, slowly, before the assembled crowd. Then various residents were invited to stand on the platform and say a few words, if they wished. "They can't sell my wife and child anymore, bless the Lord," said one man. "No more of that. No more of that, now."[61]

A refugee named William Beverly also testified to the trouble he had seen. "Handcuffs, beatings, all done away. Never part

Coming into camp. News of the Emancipation Proclamation spread fast through the plantation information networks, and refugees flocked to the Union army in unprecedented numbers. As War Secretary Edwin Stanton put it, this was "the productive power that upholds the insurrection."

from children again and don't know if ever meet again. . . . I trusted in the Lord and believed that the U.S. Army would prevail." A Black minister had future-looking advice for all those assembled. "Don't lean on our master," he said, pointing to camp superintendent Nichols. "You must depend on yourselves."[62]

The entire camp, two thousand strong, then joined an unnamed elderly woman in singing a now-familiar hymn together with such fervor and energy that a reporter from the *Evening Star* concluded that the revolutionary legend around it was true—"that this piece is the negro *Marseillaise*," a kind of national hymn turned proclamation.[63]

Go down, Moses
Way down in Egypt land
Tell old Pharaoh
Let my people **GO**.

10

Who Shall We Trust?

Peter Bruner succeeded in reaching freedom on his fourth attempt. His prior bids to get away from an abusive Kentucky master and into a Northern free state had all ended after suspicious bounty hunters clapped him in jail after he could not produce his free papers, though one of those times, he had gotten tantalizingly close to the Ohio River. But at 5 a.m. one morning in the summer of 1864, he started walking southwest from his master's farm in Winchester and didn't stop.

This journey was different. The U.S. Army had opened a supply depot and contraband village at Camp Nelson, just upriver from Frankfort near a set of limestone palisades. And a general exodus of enslaved people was on, even though the camp didn't precisely offer freedom but rather unpaid labor chopping timber for military roads.[1]

"I came upon sixteen colored fellows who were on their way to Camp Nelson and of course I did not get lonesome," Bruner recalled to his daughter years later. "I had plenty of company. Just a half hour before sun down we arrived at Camp Nelson and had come forty-one miles in that day." In his previous interactions with Union troops, Bruner had been told it was a "white man's war." But within the week, he enrolled in Company C in the 12th Heavy Artillery and was ordered to duty on "recruiting" missions to liberate any enslaved people he could find for service, even though Kentucky was a loyal state not covered by the Emancipation Proclamation. This was quasi-legal at best, and potentially hazardous to the recruiter. "Masters hold onto their slaves as Pharaoh did to his bondsman," wrote missionary John Fee.[2]

The aggressive policy to break up plantations had been concocted by Kentucky military governor John McAuley Palmer, whom

Abraham Lincoln had appointed with a simple directive: "Go to Kentucky, keep your temper, do as you please, and I will sustain you." Palmer took it as a license to rid the state of slavery by fair means or foul, resolving to "drive the last nail in the coffin" of the institution by bringing the hard edge of war to deadender guerrillas and bulking up the ranks of the USCT to top capacity, even with freed people who said they were not willing to fight. Kidnappings became common. Peter Bruner reported holding some enslaved people at gunpoint. "They cried, some of them, like babies and we had to let them go." Through these and other methods, Palmer succeeded in enlisting up to 57 percent of the enslaved male population.[3]

Palmer went to the White House on a visit in 1865 and found Lincoln getting a shave and a haircut. After the two exchanged pleasantries, Palmer sought to make a joke by saying that if he had known a national crisis was on the way when he was a boss of the Illinois Republican Party, "I would not have consented to go to a one-horse town like Springfield and take a one-horse lawyer and make him president."

Lincoln only smiled and said he wouldn't have done that either. "If we had a great man for the presidency," he said from the barber's chair, "one who had an inflexible policy and stuck to it, this rebellion would have succeeded and the Southern Confederacy would have been established. All I have done is that I have striven to do my duty today, with the hope that when tomorrow comes, I will be ready for it."[4]

He kept improvising for the remainder of his presidency, moving from point to point in accordance with events, though he made it clear the Emancipation Proclamation would not be revoked. "The promise must be kept and I shall never recall one word," he said. A report from the American Freedmen's Inquiry Commission arrived on Edwin Stanton's desk on June 30, 1863, concluding that the contraband camps had been a successful experiment in the freedom of enslaved people, placing them on a seeming trajectory to become full American citizens. One of the greatest threats, however, came from a lack of confidence in federal guarantees. "They must have tangible proof of the reality and unchangeable character of their emancipation," wrote Samuel Gridley Howe.[5]

The best way to seal the question forever, Lincoln thought, would be through molding the flawed Constitution into an antislavery document. But he also thought it too soon to act, even though one of his top commanders, Ulysses S. Grant, had concluded from the Mississippi Valley in August 1863 that "slavery is already dead and cannot be resurrected" because of the flood of refugees unlocked from all the abandoned plantations. "I do not agree with those who say that slavery is dead," Lincoln told Governor Edwin Morgan of New York. "We are like whalers who have been long on a chase—we have at last got the harpoon into the monster, but we must now look how we steer, or with one 'flop' of his tail, he will yet send us all into eternity." As ever, the careful mariner steering through unknown waters.[6]

When critics complained that Union forces weren't moving fast enough to smother the leviathan of rebellion, or that the haziness of the Emancipation Proclamation was making the transition from slavery too difficult, Lincoln brushed it off with a smile. "Oh, there is no alternative but to keep pegging away," became his customary response to anxious inquiries in 1864, another way of saying that his policy was to have no policy. "Prudence was the very essence of President Lincoln's statesmanship," wrote his secretaries John Hay and John Nicolay, "and he doubtless felt it was not safe for the Executive to venture farther at that time."[7]

When it came time to dedicate the Soldiers' National Cemetery with brief remarks at Gettysburg, Pennsylvania, on November 13, 1863, he extended the meaning of what he already said and gave new shape to the war. The railroad tycoon and philanthropist John Murray Forbes had urged him to clarify the essential nature of the war and "teach your great audience of plain people that the war is not the North against the South, but the People against the Aristocrats." Lincoln may also have been influenced by a printed sermon by the Boston abolitionist Theodore Parker, who, himself borrowing from a line of Daniel Webster's with a similar thrust and tempo, defined American democracy as "a government of all the people, by all the people, for all the people."[8]

Lincoln's 272-word Gettysburg Address brought a biblical grandeur to what had been done with reluctance and as the culmination of logistical policies cobbled together at the squalid edges of military camps. He framed the war as a test of the values of the Declaration of Independence—"that all men are created equal"—and not of the stained Constitution. His sentences were short and interlocked; tapped out, repetitive, and nearly staccato—"we cannot dedicate, we cannot consecrate, we cannot hallow"—like the sounds of the telegraph office in which he composed the far more turgid statement that set the nation on its course of an expanded definition of liberty.[9]

As scholars have observed, the only legal action taken at Gettysburg that day was the opening of a twenty-two-acre cemetery at the edge of a small Pennsylvania city. But Lincoln put a new civic theology into simple words, one that reached into New Testament concepts for his mainly Christian audience. A "new birth of freedom" pointed to the new birth experience of Christ's sacrifice, just as Lincoln pointed to the sacrifice of Union soldiers for a country soon to be cleansed of its original constitutional sin and dedicated to the unalloyed principles of equality, no longer strangulated in law.[10]

Liberty now carried a broader and more expansive meaning. And the war, years underway, had found its great purpose. By the end of 1864, Secretary of State William Seward told the U.S. ambassador to Great Britain that "the course of events has been such as to justify the assumption that, in point of fact, the war is a principal force in a popular revolution against African slavery." His choice of words is telling: the "course of events" had been the prime driver of emancipation. When the activist Sojourner Truth went to the White House to thank Lincoln for all he had done for the abolitionist cause, he brushed off the compliment with more accuracy than modesty. "Had our friends in the South behaved themselves," he told her, "I could have done nothing whatever."[11]

Slavery in the United States died in sputters over the next twelve months. In January 1865, the House narrowly passed the Thirteenth Amendment over Democratic objections. It stated: "Neither slavery nor involuntary servitude, except as a punishment for crime whereof the party shall have been duly convicted, shall exist within the United States, or any place subject to their jurisdiction." The final clause was a lawyer's last yank of the wrench, putting to rest the fear that the accumulated weight of federal policy could one day be subsumed in the name of states' rights.

Lincoln put his signature on it under the word "Approved" before it went to the states for ratification. The president's authorization was mainly a symbolic gesture; the law didn't require it. Still, Lincoln felt it important, given all the ambiguities clustered around the emancipation measures up to that point. But now it would be in the Constitution, beyond all future challenge. There were twenty-seven free states and nine slave states in the Union, just enough to ensure ratification. Lincoln called the amendment "a King's cure for all the evils. It winds the whole thing up."[12]

Lincoln made the intent behind his actions even more plain in his Second Inaugural Address on March 4, 1865. "One eighth of the whole population were colored slaves not distributed generally over the union but localized in the southern part of it," he said. "These slaves constituted a peculiar and powerful interest. All knew that this interest was somehow the cause of the war."

Then came a reference to the long sin of the Virginia Colony, whose redemption had come in the form of terrible carnage. "Yet, if God wills that it continue until all the wealth piled by the bondsman's two hundred and fifty years of unrequited toil shall be sunk and until every drop of blood drawn with the lash shall be paid by another drawn with the sword as was said three thousand years ago so still it must be said 'the judgments of the Lord are true and righteous altogether.'" In his deferral to the Almighty, one can perhaps hear a muted explanation of Lincoln's caution as he let the trailing force of law catch up with the leading edge of reality in the contraband camps. Or, as he said the year before to the editor of the Frankfort, Kentucky, *Commonwealth*, "I claim not to have controlled events, but confess plainly that events have controlled me."[13]

Through the spring, federal armies inched through northern Virginia. On April 3, 1865, a telegraph came through in the same

War Department office where Lincoln had composed the Emancipation Proclamation:

> HON. EDWIN M. STANTON, Secretary of War, Washington, D. C.:
> We took Richmond at 8:15 this morning . . . The city is on fire in two places . . .
> G. WEITZEL, Brig.-Gen'l Comd'g.[14]

Lincoln told his aides he wanted to visit the rebel capital and boarded the gunboat USS *Malvern* for a journey that took him down the Potomac into Chesapeake Bay; around the corner of Old Point Comfort and the flourishing village of Slabtown; up the James River by tugboat past the ruins of Jamestown; and finally by rowboat to the docks at Richmond. Crowds swarmed him immediately as he walked hand in hand with his twelve-year-old son Tad. The city's jailers, mindful of their new federal overseers, had opened the cell doors for hundreds of imprisoned enslaved people, and some professed friendship and good wishes in hopes their captives would not take vengeance. Nobody did.

"The colored population went wild with enthusiasm," wrote T. Morris Chester of the *Philadelphia Press*, one of the few Black reporters on the staff of a white newspaper at that time. "Old men thanked God in a very boisterous manner, and old women shouted upon the pavement as high as they had ever done at a religious revival."[15]

Lincoln and his son trudged up the hill to the Confederate White House, where the elder Lincoln sat in an easy chair in Jefferson Davis's office for a few minutes. He offered no words of triumph but only asked for a glass of water. The audacity of the visit worried Admiral David Porter, who posted a guard at the president's cabin door on the ride home. Lincoln seemed totally unconcerned. So many written death threats had poured into the White House mail room that he kept a special drawer for them, occasionally pulling out the collection to show visitors. "I cannot bring myself to believe that any human being lives who would want to do me harm," he said. But there had been at least one prior attempted assassination. On his nightly ride from the White

House past the contraband camp in August 1864, somebody had fired a single shot at him from the darkness as he neared the gates of the Soldiers' Home. Private John W. Nichols went down the road to investigate and found Lincoln's eight-dollar silk hat lying on the road with a bullet hole in it.

"The next day I gave Mr. Lincoln his hat and called his attention to the bullet hole," wrote Nichols, years later. "He remarked rather unconcernedly, that it was put there by some foolish gunner and was not intended for him. He said, however, that he wanted the matter kept quiet, and admonished us to say nothing about it. We felt confident that it was an attempt to kill him, and a well nigh successful one, too." Lincoln himself told the story to his bodyguard Ward Hill Lamon, but laughed it off as an amateurish act by a "disloyal bushwhacker," who didn't put him in as much danger as had the frightened and runaway horse. The caution he always displayed in his political choices did not extend to his personal safety.[16]

Four days after Lincoln's walk around Richmond, Robert E. Lee surrendered the Army of Northern Virginia, signifying the military collapse of the Confederacy. As he watched Lee leave the conference in the living room of a borrowed house in the tiny town of Appomattox Court House, General Ulysses Grant felt a strange depression fall over him. He later wrote, "I felt like anything rather than rejoicing at the downfall of a foe who had fought so long and valiantly, and had suffered so much for a cause, though that cause was, I believe, the worst for which a people ever fought, and one for which there was the least excuse." Pockets of armed resistance persisted for months afterward. The last organized clash between armies took place eleven weeks after Lee's surrender on a desolate salt plain called Palmito Ranch in far southern Texas. Hotheaded commanders on both sides, knowing the war was over, made a last reach for battlefield glory. This "final, lonely, meaningless little spatter of a fight" ended as a Confederate victory.[17]

On April 11, Lincoln made a speech from a north window of the White House about the reconstituted government of Louisiana, which had just extended the franchise to educated freed people and those who had served in the U.S. Colored Troops. He urged the nation to accept the terms and welcome Louisiana and other states into the Union as though they had never left. "The colored man too, in seeing all united for him, is inspired with vigilance, and energy, and daring, to the same end," he said to the assembled crowd, finishing with a classic Lincoln equivocation: that he would make no "exclusive and inflexible" plan for Southern reconstruction and await the emergence of new events before saying anything else. "In the present situation, as the phrase goes, it may be my duty to make some new announcement to the people of the South," he said. "I am considering, and shall not fail to act when satisfied that action will be proper." And that was it.[18]

Lincoln's speech had been lawyerly and boring, so much so that a few people had begun to wander away, but it contained the seed argument for extending voting rights to every freed person in the South. In that sense, it was like the Emancipation Proclamation: dull, confusing, and utterly transformative. Noah Brooks of the *Sacramento Daily Union*, who had been standing to the right of the president and holding a candle aloft so Lincoln could read his speech, looked out on the north lawn at "a vast sea of faces, illuminated by the lights that burned in the festal array of the White House, and stretching far out into the misty darkness. It was a silent, intent, and perhaps surprised, multitude."

Within that crowd, the twenty-six-year-old actor John Wilkes Booth turned to a friend named Lewis Powell and observed that Lincoln intended to extend full citizenship to Black people. "That is the last speech he will ever make," he assured Powell.

On the night of April 13, Lincoln had his recurring dream again, the one of floating on the water that may have been an embedded memory from his flatboat days on the Indiana frontier, preparing for a voyage deep into the unknown country of the South. He mentioned it that morning to a bodyguard named William Crook. "In the dream a ship under full sail bore down on him," recalled Crook years later. "At the time he spoke of it he felt that some good fortune was on the way to him."[19]

That night, Lincoln went to the theater with his wife to see a performance of *Our American Cousin*, a comedy that played on the old trope of coarse country folk getting the advantage on wealthy elites: one of the president's favorite genres. The main character of the play, Asa Trenchard, was a classic bumpkin in the mold of Artemus Ward. About midway through the play came one of its biggest laugh lines, an insult directed by the protagonist at a stuffy Englishwoman: "Don't know the manners of good society, eh? Well, I guess I know enough to turn you inside out, old gal, you sockdologizing old man-trap!"

As Ford's Theatre erupted in laughter, Booth stepped into the presidential box, fired a single shot, and then leaped onto the stage hollering, "Sic semper tyrannis!" (Thus always to tyrants!), the state motto of Virginia.

* * *

One by one, the contraband camps shut down. Their churches were closed, their houses dismantled, their schools broken up, and their cemeteries left abandoned, their locations grown over and forgotten. No ceremonies marked their passing.

The physical remnants of the camps, in many cases, went into the rebuilding of the South. Wooden beams and joists that had once held up the roofs of freed enslaved people became a part of the new homes and fences of returning white landowners. The *Nashville Daily Union* advertised an auction of "old lumber" near the corner of Church and Broad Streets, the spot "known as the Contraband Camp," where thirteen large barracks were to be broken down and sold.[20]

The dispersals varied in character from the harsh to the relatively humane, usually depending on the attitude of the officer in charge. In the squalid camp at Helena, Arkansas, the remnants of the settlement along Little Rock Road not already swept away by spring flooding were torn apart in less than a week after a city ordinance called for the removal of "all buildings or other obstructions in the public streets." The residents had no choice but to return to the cotton fields, seeking work from their old masters, though a new Unionist city government invited some to help patch up levees blown apart during the war. Those freed people who refused a work contract would be treated as "common vagrants," authorities warned. The superintendent Henry Sweeney spent more time hectoring them than assisting them.[21]

"You have many defects, many faults to overcome," he told a gathering of them, "and as it be for your own interest, I shall try, as far as this is in my power, to point them out to you so that you may avoid them, because if you do not strive with all your might and energy to avoid these faults, you will never come to anything. If I speak very plain to you, believe me, it is for your own good."[22]

An easier closure took effect in Wilmington, North Carolina, when J.L. Rhoads of the 37th Colored Infantry ordered a gradual dismantling of the settlements with an emphasis on sanitation. "When he first took command, the negroes were living in a state of the most shocking filth and squalor, and the rate of mortality among them was fearful," reported the *Philadelphia Inquirer.* "Their barracks are now faultlessly clean and orderly, the ground adjacent carefully policed and a state of comparative health restored." Rhoads reduced the population from 1,500 to 180 within three months without having to make forced evictions.[23]

Brigadier General Clinton Fisk, by contrast, went on a mission to get rid of the dozens of settlements in eastern Tennessee as quickly as possible, immediately prying the houses apart for lumber and shooing off the residents to find agricultural work on nearby farms and plantations. "He states he has made a constant effort to break up all contraband camps in his district," reported the *Louisville Daily Journal*, "and encourage freed men to seek labor in the country and not congregate in cities." By the fall of 1865, less than a hundred people, almost all sick and elderly, were still taking rations. Now that the wartime emergency was over, the camps were seen not just as eyesores but as breeding grounds for the long-feared uprising of Black people against their former masters. As one official in Louisiana put it, "The good of the community and the freedmen requires that such congregating should be prohibited & broken up."[24]

At Camp Nelson in Kentucky, Fisk ordered a colonel to do "*everything* to break up the camp and not entail *suffering*." But he recognized the inevitable outcome. "There will be some suffering do the best you can," he added. The U.S. Army emptied out almost as fast as the camps, as state regiments demobilized and went home, leaving the freed people under a shaky civilian authority. Shrugged Captain T.E. Hall: "There have always been more here than could be cared for."[25]

Without anywhere else to go, and despite admonitions from Fisk not to do this, many of the evicted refugees staggered into Louisville in hopes of finding a job, or at least a means of survival that the countryside could not provide. Kentucky was the last American state to give up slavery—it did not legally end here until the Thirteenth Amendment was ratified over its objections in December 1865—and the threat of being sold back into bondage was quite real in the months after the war. Staying away from kidnappers and bounty hunters added to the evicted refugee's troubles.

"This morning, about daylight, I saw hundreds of these poor creatures, women and children, laying along the pavement in a drenching rain," reported a visitor to Louisville. "They told me they were unable to find either work or a mouthful to eat, and that they had wandered about the city a week picking up mouthfuls of offal—the only food they could get—and sleeping on the sidewalks without shelter. Where is our superintendent of freedman's affairs in this department?"[26]

He posed an excellent question. The Bureau of Refugees, Freedmen, and Abandoned Lands, usually called by the simpler name the Freedmen's Bureau, had been formed in March 1865 as a direct result of the data gathered by Samuel Gridley Howe's commission of inquiry. It held the distinction of being the very first government agency dedicated explicitly to social welfare, with the paradoxical status of being housed within the War Department—yet another legacy of the militarized character of American emancipation. It faced a nearly impossible task from the start: the uplift of 4 million people into citizenship amid bombed-out infrastructure and weed-choked fields in regions that had seen fighting, and a defeated white power structure seething with resentment against both freed slaves and occupying Yankees.[27]

"Decatur, Alabama, once a pleasant town, has experienced the fate of so many Southern cities and is a mass of ruins and rubbish," went one widely distributed press item in the summer of 1865. "Two miles North is a contraband camp containing over six hundred negroes, who have under cultivation about one thousand acres of corn and cotton."[28]

Many of Howe's respondents from the contraband camps had thought the ideal—and poetic—solution was to punish the

Confederate overlords by handing over their estates to their own enslaved people to be run as collective farms. Such land reform projects had been successfully demonstrated at high-profile freedmen's villages at Arlington House and Davis Bend, as well as dozens of other camps. As the historian Bennett Parten has observed, the federal government was already in the business of giving away land through the Homestead Act of 1862, which offered a free tract of Western property seized from Native Americans to anyone willing to settle on it for five years and add improvements. The homesteading spirit carried over into William T. Sherman's famous Special Field Order No. 15, which sought to break up four hundred thousand acres of coastal property for freed people to farm—a proposition that took on the nickname "forty acres and a mule."

Sherman underwent a small evolution in thought as he made his famous march from the ruins of Atlanta down to Savannah near the Atlantic Ocean, saying at first he had little use for the "crowds of these people coming to us through roads and across the fields," as one of his officers put it. He looked for a way to "clear the army of surplus negroes, mules, and horses," a typical objectification among U.S. Army generals, even as he ordered his army to "forage liberally" on the farms of wealthy slaveholders. Such loose standards of judgment were often ignored by enlisted men who stole food from poor Georgia whites and even from enslaved people. When Sherman happened upon a soldier quaffing a cup of purloined molasses, the soldier turned up a guilty face and shouted "forage liberally!" as a feeble defense. Everyone laughed but Sherman.[29]

Mindful of how capricious U.S. Army officials could be at any given moment, enslaved people often hid in the brush as the columns trudged by. They used trails that snaked between plantations that their owners knew nothing about: a parallel world of the South that had concealed secret rendezvous spots and hush harbors, and now offered a chance at liberation. As the historian Stephanie Camp concluded: "The rival geography created by the enslaved over generations offered, in wartime, the literal roads to freedom."[30]

Sherman arrived in Savannah trailing an entourage of approximately twenty thousand freed people, a number more than twice the population of antebellum Atlanta. But he did not let them roam the graceful squares and town house rows of Georgia's colonial-era port city; they were camped in a penumbra on the rural coastal plain where they were left vulnerable to rebel kidnappers. At the direction of Edwin Stanton, Sherman convened an evening meeting of twenty freed people on January 12, 1865, to solicit their opinions on what should be done for freed Blacks. He meant it not so much as a humanitarian gesture as a way to quickly rid himself of the bothersome entourage of liberated people trailing his army. "The way we can best take care of ourselves is to have land, and turn it and till it by our own labor," said the leader of the delegation, a pastor named Garrison Frazier.[31]

Sherman's order to resettle the freed people on confiscated plantations at Port Royal and neighboring areas was firmly in the firefighting approach to emancipation formulated by General Benjamin Butler at Fort Monroe. It was also another example of the alliance of convenience between the U.S. Army and freed enslaved people. But Sherman appears to have been a reluctant patron; his friend General Henry Halleck had warned him that men who had Lincoln's ear were complaining that Sherman had not done enough to "open outlets by which the slaves can escape into our lines" so as to drain the life out of the Confederacy. "I believe that a manifestation on your part of a desire to bring the slaves within our lines will do much to silence your opponents," he suggested. A resentful Sherman later complained that federal resettlement policy was done "not of pure humanity, but of politics." As it ever was in the Civil War, short-term strategy had a way of creating lasting social realities.[32]

The most successful refugee camp of them all, at Corinth, Mississippi, was already a casualty of military whim. The railroad junction, once esteemed as a prize worth the spilled blood of thousands, had become an afterthought in the autumn of 1863, and the contraband camp had barely registered in Sherman's thinking. On January 11, 1864, he ordered the whole town vacated. "Abandon Corinth and Fort Pillow absolutely, removing all public property to Cairo or Memphis," he wrote.[33]

That meant the end of the freedmen's village, where more than three thousand people just emerged from a lifetime of slavery had established a sophisticated community and offered one of the best-regarded units of U.S. Colored Troops to the army. "The order fell like a bomb-shell among our contented people," said the Oberlin missionary George Carruthers. "But military orders are preemptory, and without a reason why, and must be obeyed."[34]

Sherman's lieutenants marched them away from their hand-built wooden cabins and clean streets to a freezing orchard on the Mississippi River two miles south of Memphis, where they once again had to live in tents. "Their gardens and farms"—including the cotton fields that had netted the government at least $30,000 in harvests—"were abandoned to the rebels," said the Quaker philanthropist Levi Coffin. The rapid shutdown of Corinth also portended the demise of the collective farming enterprise in which freed people made profitable use of the fields abandoned by fleeing slave owners. But these settlements had fast become targets for Confederate deadenders, as well as returning landowners ready to use both lawsuits and harassment to reclaim their property. The anger ran deep and wide. "We are ridden of power to cultivate our fields, we cannot be represented in the markets, the country is gone to ruins and weeds, our country towns are changed to contraband camps," complained a group of whites in Marshall, Texas.[35]

The Freedmen's Bureau struggled to meet its objective of protecting Black property and taking over the hundreds of schoolhouses established by the American Missionary Association and other charitable groups during the fighting. While land titles lay in a state of confusion, most agents took the safe route of not giving away confiscated lands to freed Blacks but leasing them out to wealthy white cotton growers, who in turn paid field wages to local Blacks willing to do the work. Complaints about stiffed payment, whippings, and overwork were supposed to be directed to the Freedmen's Bureau, which made halfhearted gestures at enforcement. Some U.S. Army officers who had employed freed Blacks as cooks and manservants encouraged them to give up on the South and settle in the officers' hometowns, in more frigid winter climates. One man named Gus who fled toward Sherman's marauding columns in Georgia accepted the suggestion from Captain J.G. Randall to move to the unheard-of place Mukwonago, Wisconsin. There he changed his name to August.[36]

William T. Sherman's observation that politics was driving the question of land redistribution was proving all too accurate. His Special Field Order No. 15 did not last for long after the war. Under pressure from displaced white landowners who still held the deeds to confiscated lands, President Andrew Johnson asked Sherman to justify the radical action. "I know of course we could not convey title to land and merely provided 'possessory' titles to be good so long as war and military power lasted," wrote Sherman defensively. "At that time, January 1865, it will be remembered, the tone of the people of the South was very defiant, and no one could foretell when the period of war would cease. Therefore, I did not contemplate that event as being so near at hand." The revolutionary "forty acres and a mule" order was soon countermanded in the name of restoring national harmony among whites, leaving freed people to fend for themselves.[37]

At Slabtown outside Fort Monroe, camp superintendent Charles Wilder made an emergency fundraising effort among Northern philanthropists to buy most of the town out from under the former owners to provide to the freed people "undisturbed occupation of their huts and gardens." But the fort's commander ordered the village dismantled, to Wilder's extreme displeasure. He said he hated to see slavery's wealthy offenders rewarded and the victims punished further. Perhaps the inventive dislocation of the war was not as lasting as it had seemed. "The most bitter ringleaders and fermenters of treason before, during and since the war are restored to all the rights of citizenship with all their property real or personal, while thousands of true loyal men are left out in the cold," he wrote.[38]

That cold was both figurative and literal. When some resisted giving over the first homes they had known in freedom, the commander sent detachments of soldiers to kick them out and tear the roofs off the cabins, making them unlivable shells. Over at Norfolk, meanwhile, those who had learned to read from pictures of animals and letters in John Oliver's schools were told they "must prepare to leave this or any other government farm in this district" within thirty days. Those at Yorktown were granted only a little more time. After the gardens were torn up, a resident named Bayley Wyat wondered if he would have to sleep in the woods after having expended so much of his life's energy first for his master, and then for the U.S. Army.[39]

"Our cabins are threatened to be turned down over our heads if we do not go, and we must be drove about from place to place, and chased as hounds chase rabbits," he said at a public meeting. "And we must go; and I ask again, where shall we go, and who shall we trust?"[40]

Epilogue

The contraband camps dissolved into the fabric of the land. Their presence faded from the collective memory of America. However, those who lived within their makeshift boundaries and those who visited or served in the forts nearby carried their stories forward. The stories endured through the trials of Reconstruction well into the twentieth century, bearing witness to a part of history often overlooked yet deeply transformative. Most of the individual stories of struggle and victories were not preserved in documents and have been irrecoverably lost. But a few are known.

Elizabeth Keckly, who raised thousands of dollars for the refugees of Washington's Camp Barker, accompanied her friend Mary Todd Lincoln back to Springfield, Illinois, in 1865. She helped Lincoln sell some of the dresses and jewelry she wore at White House functions, a move that exposed Keckly to criticism from those who presumed she was cashing in on a martyred presidency. She then published *Behind the Scenes*, a generally respectful memoir about being a servant to the Lincolns that enraged Washington society elders for what they felt was a violation of household privacy and the standards of confidentiality expected of African American servants. "She would have much better stuck to her needle," said a disdainful reviewer from the *New York Times*. "As mere gossip, the book is mainly a failure."

Having lost many of her clients after the scandal, Keckly took up teaching home economics to freed Black women at Wilberforce University. She died in 1907 as a resident of the National Home for Destitute Colored Women and Children, an institution that her charity efforts in wartime had helped to found.[1]

After his discharge in Charleston, South Carolina, on August 29, 1865, the war hero Henry Jarvis went back to Fort Monroe, the place where he first claimed his freedom. There he found work as a maintenance man at the Freedmen's School founded by Mary S. Peake, the place with the big oak tree where the teachers said the Emancipation Proclamation had first been read out loud.[2]

Henry Jarvis would talk freely about his wartime experiences, if he was asked, and even talked about his miserable time as a slave. But he would draw the line if asked to repeat any of the work songs from the Eastern Shore the enslaved people would chant when shucking corn. "Them's wicked songs," he would explain.[3]

His wife Nellie, whom he had married at Fort Monroe at the pronouncement of Lewis Lockwood, had grown tired of waiting for him during the war. When he contacted her to tell her he had returned to the United States from his attempt to migrate to Liberia, she told him "she thought she'd marry another man." That was as good as a divorce. He married a second wife, Loisa, and they had several children together in a low-ceilinged cabin outside Hampton. Loisa tried to teach him how to read, even though he thought it wasn't biblical for a man to be taught by his wife. She only laughed at him.

Jarvis hadn't thought much about religion or the concept of sin until right after the Civil War, when he learned some Bible verses at the Hampton Institute and was convinced of his need for salvation. He felt so weak at this conviction that he could barely stand. Then, feeling a divine spirit rising inside him, he began praying loudly. People thought him crazy, but he understood it differently.

"When you've got the glory in your soul," he explained, "you can't help hollering and shouting." From then on, he saw his entire life as a long journey away from evil.[4]

His old war injury gave him stabbing pains as the years wore on. Prosthetic legs never worked; they hurt his stump too bad. He was declared invalid and given a pension of $15 a month on the recommendation of his old commanding officer, Charles C. Soule, who called him a "very faithful soldier." Jarvis would go on to have two more children with a third wife, Mary Jane, who eventually had to care for him full time. Rheumatism had invaded his joints, his shoulders had stiffened, and he could barely turn over in bed. "He needs the continual attention of a nurse to dress and undress him," wrote a doctor.[5]

One night in 1872, at his hand-built cabin in Virginia, Jarvis told the story of his escape to two Black teachers from the Hampton Institute, M.F. Armstrong and Helen W. Ludlow. A single gas lantern sputtered on a shelf. Jarvis spoke resolutely and openly in a thick Tidewater accent. Near the end of the conversation, the teachers asked him if he forgave his enslaver, the meanest man on the Eastern Shore, who had whipped him and tried to murder him with a rifle all those years ago.

The question took Jarvis off guard.

"The glow died out of his face, and his head dropped," wrote the teachers. "There was, evidently, a mental struggle. Then he straightened himself, his features set for an inevitable conclusion. 'I'd forgive him, Lord knows I'd forgive him, but'—his eyes kindled again as the human nature burst forth—'but I'd give my other leg to meet him in battle!'"[6]

Benjamin Butler, the lawyer general who formulated the contraband theory, kept going back and forth on racial questions.

After he was appointed the military governor of New Orleans in 1862, he ordered his troops to return freed enslaved people to their owners, which contravened not only his Fort Monroe doctrine but also the Confiscation Act that his action had inspired. But he made liberal use of the same law to claim bales of cotton from traders thought to be disloyal. In one case, he ordered the seizure of a set of family silverware from a woman trying to cross a Union checkpoint, an incident that lent him the unflattering nickname "Spoons Butler." His tenure in Louisiana was marked by other erratic conduct, including a general order that any female showing contempt for one of his soldiers would be arrested on charges of "a woman of the town plying her avocation," or a prostitute.[7]

After he was reassigned to Norfolk, and eventually a repeat command of Fort Monroe, he claimed he had an epiphany on slavery while stationed in the Deep South. "When I saw the utter demoralization of the people, resulting from slavery, it struck me that it was an institution that should be thrust out of the Union," he said in a speech.[8]

Butler left the army under a cloud of suspicion for questionable business dealings in Norfolk. He spent the postbellum decades managing a thriving law practice, serving four terms in Congress as a Republican, overseeing his textile mills, and investing in mineral claims in the West. He died in 1893, still an active attorney. The inscription on his grave marker in Lowell reads: "The true touchstone of civil liberty is not that all men are equal but that every man has the right to be the equal of every other man—if he can."[9]

Emma Whitehurst and her husband Edward managed their grocery store in Slabtown up until August 15, 1862, when two detachments of white soldiers returning from George McClellan's failed Peninsula Campaign rolled up in wagons.

They cleaned out the Whitehursts' entire inventory that afternoon, with officers standing by in apparent approval. All of them were tired and frustrated from the retreat from the gates of Richmond, yet they helped themselves like locusts to the Whitehursts' carefully tended store: corn, flour, potatoes, butter, ginger cakes—all of it gone.

"Hurry up," yelled one Yankee soldier, "and put [it] in the wagon." His companions slaughtered six hogs from the yard in front of a furious Edward Whitehurst, who tried to complain to a provost marshal.

"You can't do anything," the official told Whitehurst, warning the couple "not to make any resistance, as the soldiers were hungry and would get something to eat." Their entire investment, painstakingly saved up during slavery from the original $500 nest egg, vanished in a single afternoon.[10]

There is some evidence they managed to reacquire at least a little capital. The year after the war's conclusion, Edward Whitehurst testified in a court case over the disputed ownership of a horse. He swore in an affidavit that he had sold Albert Jones a certain black horse with a white star on its forehead. More than a decade later, still married, the Whitehursts sought compensation for their lost inventory from the Southern Claims Commission, a federal agency dedicated to reimbursing loyal citizens who felt themselves victimized by overzealous interpretations of the Confiscation Acts during the war. The commission agreed they had been wronged but paid them only $115, a fraction of what their goods had been worth. By that time, the couple had bought land on a tract near Hampton from a man named Frank Dennis. In the 1870 census, Edward listed himself as a "farmer" and Emma listed herself as "keeping house."[11]

They had joined nearly seventy thousand veterans of the contraband camps of the Virginia Peninsula—from Hampton, Newport News, Yorktown, and Norfolk—living dispersed throughout a region scarred by the environmental changes of war. "A good many of the houses gone, the fields uncultivated and covered with shrubbery, fences burned, orchards destroyed, and everything laid waste," reported George West, an alum of the spit-and-polish Hampton Academy whose family farm had been confiscated by General Butler's troops and was now occupied by freed people who saw the land as theirs.[12]

West and others sought to reclaim both their old homes and their place in the white social order after the end of the war, aided by Andrew Johnson's policies in Reconstruction that emphasized official pardons and the restoration of abandoned plantations to those who had joined the rebellion. West had spent most of the conflict hiding out in Richmond, but returned to Hampton with the aim of establishing himself as a new man of the reborn South.

He began by confronting thirty Black men occupying a farm his family had deserted in 1861, which had since been reassigned to the Freedmen's Bureau. He ordered them to stop cutting down trees, and they walked away, frightened. He told his father, who filed a lawsuit for the possession of the farm and won it back. By that point, almost all the Tidewater land under the jurisdiction of the Freedmen's Bureau was scheduled to be returned to former owners by December 31, 1866, putting an end to the widespread dream of "forty acres and a mule." By the end of the following year, the bureau's land and labor agents would be gone from Virginia entirely.[13]

Not content with the return of his land, George West also shot and killed the horse of a freed man he found grazing on his oat field. He also tried to harass a former slave named Joe Wilson for taking lumber from a forest of disputed ownership. In the initial wave of Reconstruction, Wilson "rode about with a calvary sable and two revolvers around his waist," and was also elected magistrate. The judicial title didn't matter to West.

"I warned Joe and all others if I caught them stealing from me, that I would shoot to kill them," he said.[14]

After traveling from Hampton to the churches of the North to raise money, William Roscoe Davis returned to his home at Wood's Mill, a former plantation building near the Emancipation Oak. He was devoted to campaigning for the property rights of those who had taken shelter outside Fort Monroe, insisting that "the colored people did not expect any lands to be given to them," just rented or sold at a fair price.[15]

Davis was willing to fight hard for what was his, but he could also be forgiving to those who had wronged him. He had taken the audacious step of filing a lawsuit against a white slave owner named Banks for his wife's freedom before the war broke out. Now, given Hampton's small-town atmosphere, it was impossible to avoid crossing paths with Banks. So he arranged a meeting with his former rival, but warned his children beforehand, "If you call him master, I'll whale you good."

When the former slave owner arrived, he put out a hand to shake. "Well, William, I guess we can bury the hatchet now," he said.

"Yes, Mr. Banks," replied Davis, "let bygones be bygones; we are all men now!"

His daughter said nothing, only looked downward. Arthur P. Davis, one of Davis's grandsons, later said there was "quiet but real drama" in the exchange.[16]

Known as a masterful orator, Davis took over the pastorate of the Baptist church on Lincoln Street in Slabtown, where his "essentially puritanical" style was not for everyone. "He brooked no backsliding in his members," said his grandson, and "tended to run them away with his rigid and uncompromising attitude." He permitted no dancing or theatergoing, but most of those just out of slavery were not inclined to heed him. Still, he was progressive in one important respect: having been whipped so many times himself, he hated the idea of corporal punishment and was appalled to learn that a white schoolteacher was using the rod on Black children at the new school downtown, especially when it happened to one of his nieces. The parallels to slavery were too strong.

Davis urged the American Missionary Association to found a more humane institution, to which it responded by appointing a former commander of U.S. Colored Troops named Samuel Chapman Armstrong to start a school at Wood's Mill. The two initially clashed over the curriculum—Armstrong wanted to teach blue-collar trades, while Davis wanted to emphasize Latin and Greek—but they came to a compromise and co-founded Hampton Institute, where Henry Jarvis went to work after the war.

Davis kept a gadfly interest in public affairs and served as a doorkeeper to the Virginia Constitutional Convention in 1867. But he steadfastly refused to run for any of the Reconstruction offices then open to Black candidates, aware of his own limitations. "I think my grandfather's attitude towards the Negro and politics was of the you-must-crawl-before-you-can-walk kind," wrote Arthur Davis. He wielded a sharp tongue against politicians, however, and often chided them in public meetings just as he once lectured his congregants who had fallen into sin. Within the family, this tough treatment from Father Davis was known as "getting jacked up."

In spite of his blunt personality, or perhaps because of it, he maintained a friendship with the white congressman Joseph Segar, whose family had donated the land for the first contraband camp outside Fort Monroe. Davis made sure Segar got votes, and the connection secured him a federal job as the lighthouse keeper at Old Point Comfort, where enslaved people had first touched Virginia soil in 1619. He kept night watches there in the tower, where a revolving gas-powered light spun around and around, casting its beams out to the dark bay.

The beaches over at Segar's Hygeia Hotel were reserved for whites only, so the spread in front of the lighthouse Davis managed became a de facto beach for people of color, and he sometimes opened his cabin at the base of the lighthouse as a place for travelers to stay.

Lighthouses were then under the jurisdiction of the Treasury Department, subject to annual inspections. A retired U.S. Navy admiral came down for a look one year. Without introducing himself or even removing his hat indoors, a violation of Victorian-era manners, he spoke to Davis in harsh terms, throwing out various orders for putting things shipshape.

"Just a minute, Admiral," Davis told him. "This may be a government lighthouse, but it is also my home and you must respect it as such."

There was a long pause.

"The admiral looked at this ex-slave with amazement," reported Arthur Davis. "He then slowly removed his hat and apologized."[17]

Samuel Ballton, the cook who traveled back into Virginia with the 6th Wisconsin Regiment to rescue his wife Rebecca, moved with her to Brooklyn after the war, and then out to the small Long Island hamlet of Greenlawn, where he worked as a tenant farmer in the cabbage fields and squirreled away what money he could to make small investments in real estate along the railroad tracks. His lots ascended in value as more settlers arrived, seeking suburban relief from New York City but also wanting access to the Long Island Rail Road.

Ballton transferred some of those earnings into cucumber fields, and his timing was once again prescient, as factories in nearby Huntington started to use mass production techniques to send jarred food around the country. He also served as a wholesale agent for Boston companies. During the 1899 growing season, Ballton's fields produced 1.5 million cucumbers, earning him the nickname "The Pickle King of Greenlawn." Many of the tenders in his fields and construction workers on his houses had been sharecroppers recruited from the South who became permanent residents of New York.

He and Rebecca built a comfortable five-room house near the center of town, where they celebrated their fiftieth anniversary in 1911. They were active in Republican politics, pillars of the Greenlawn Presbyterian Church, ran a lunchroom, and gave money to indigent residents.

"What do we think of Samuel Ballton of this village?" a neighbor said in 1910. "Well, I'll tell you. We consider him as being a man who has a real faith in Greenlawn, a man who really is doing things here."[18]

Susie King Taylor, who taught members of the 1st South Carolina Volunteers how to read, moved to nearby Savannah when the Port Royal camp started to empty out. "A new life was before us now, all the old life left behind," she said hopefully. Taylor opened the city's first school for Black children. Though her husband was a veteran and a skilled carpenter, "the prejudice against his race" barred him from working in construction, so he instead took contracts for loading cotton bales onto ships at the docks. He died two years later, and Taylor was obliged to quit teaching after the opening of the public Beach Institute school took all her students.[19]

She found work as a cook and laundress for a wealthy white woman, who took her to Boston, where she remained into old age, devoting time to the Woman's Relief Corps, an organization for female veterans of the Civil War. She had no interest in returning to Georgia; her heart had been broken by the widespread lynching, discrimination, and failed promises made to the freedmen during Reconstruction.

"I wonder if our white fellow men realize the true sense or meaning of brotherhood?" she wrote in 1902. "For two hundred years we had toiled for them; the war of 1861 came and was ended, and we thought our race was forever freed from bondage, and that the two races could live in unity with each other, but when we read almost every day of what is being done to my race by some whites in the South, I sometimes ask, 'Was the war in vain? Has it brought freedom, in the full sense of the word, or has it not made our condition more hopeless?'"[20]

Abraham Galloway, who had spied on the rebels throughout the Confederacy, created "a great sensation" when he spoke at a political meeting in New Bern, North Carolina, in 1865. His message was an extension of what he and a delegation of four others had told Abraham Lincoln in person at the White House the previous year—that Black voting rights were the key to a restored nation.

"I believe the negro ought to be allowed to vote; I am sure we would not abuse it," he told the crowd, which gave him repeated rounds of loud applause. "If the negro knows how to use the cartridge box, he knows how to use the ballot box."[21]

He was talking about the approximately 180,000 U.S. Colored Troops who had fought for the Union cause. Galloway had personally helped raise nearly five thousand of them on recruiting trips to North Carolina. His preternatural ability to blend into many backgrounds, so useful during the war, became a formidable asset in the art of postbellum racial politics. He then moved to Wilmington, where he had made his brazen escape from slavery, and started a campaign against white supremacy and the Ku Klux Klan, which had just formed a local chapter. The state, like others in the South, attempted to put a check on freed people by passing Black Codes, which allowed local authorities to jail suspects on vague charges of "vagrancy" or "loitering" and put them to work on county farms.

Galloway tried to set an example for others by refusing to get out of the way for white people on the sidewalk; challenging them directly when he felt patronized; and openly carrying a revolver to back up his words, which were rhetorically formidable. "His power of sarcasm and brutal invective, and the personal influence given him by his fearlessness and his audacity, always secured him a hearing," wrote John Richard Dennett, a New York reporter who spent time with him.[22]

Galloway pushed for Black voting rights for the rest of his life—in speeches to North Carolina's constitutional convention, through his service as a state representative, and in open confrontation with the local Ku Klux Klan, against whom he organized a volunteer Black militia. The *Wilmington Sun* said, with some alarm, that his posse patrolled the streets with torches and "hooting and yelling and firing pistols and guns." This show of resistance, occurring immediately before an April election, led to a decisive vote approving a new state constitution that ensured a universal male franchise with no requirement to own property.[23]

When Galloway died unexpectedly at the age of thirty-three on September 1, 1870, possibly of a fever or a heart condition, at least two-thirds of the Black population of Wilmington came out for his funeral.

Robert Hamilton, the editor who accompanied Galloway on a tour of Slabtown, returned to New York City with high hopes after the Emancipation Proclamation. But personal disaster intervened. His brother Thomas, the financial guru who held the

Anglo-African together, died of typhoid fever shortly after the war ended. Feeling ill himself, and without a strong business collaborator, Robert Hamilton did his best to keep the family enterprise going, but it published its final issue on December 23, 1865. He gave singing lessons and did manual labor to keep himself out of poverty.[24]

Peter Bruner, who escaped slavery to Camp Nelson and became a recruiter for the U.S. Colored Troops, found work as a janitor at Miami University of Ohio, where he learned to read and write. The university president asked him to be a ceremonial greeter for special events, and he always did so in a top hat and a tuxedo.

Bruner got married to Fannie Procton, the daughter of a local farmer, and joined the Bethel African Methodist Episcopal Church. Both his marriage and his church membership lasted more than fifty years. In his old age, one of his daughters persuaded him to dictate a memoir of his time in slavery and his escape. He closed the book with this sentence: "Though my life has been one of many hardships, I feel there awaits for me a crown of righteousness, and I shall have rest forever more."[25]

Jefferson Davis, the president of the Confederate States of America, fled Richmond on April 2, 1865, after being passed a telegram as he sat in his pew alone at St. Paul's Church. The message from Robert E. Lee read: "I think it is absolutely necessary that we should abandon our position tonight." His lines had broken at Petersburg, and there was nothing now that could stop the U.S. Army from entering the Confederate capital.

He and his wife Varina took a train loaded with $13 million in gold bars from the Confederate treasury to Danville, North Carolina, where he issued a proclamation urging the continuance of the fight. "We have now entered upon a new phase of the struggle," he wrote. The slave nation might be reconstituted out west, he thought, or perhaps in Mexico, where it could "have the world from which to choose a location." In any event, he feared being hanged as a traitor and resolved to stay ahead of his pursuers.

Some of the remaining troops with him threw away their uniforms and sold their rifles after they heard news of Joseph E.

Johnston's surrender of the Army of the Tennessee. He attempted to steal through Georgia unobserved with a retinue of ten men, including Postmaster General John Reagan. In the predawn hours of May 9, two cavalry units found the party sleeping in tents outside the tiny town of Irwinville. Varina Davis was wearing a formal dress sewed for her by Elizabeth Keckly. A legend spread that Jefferson Davis had been captured wearing his wife's clothes. She may have draped a cloak around him in his last effort to escape the federal cavalry, but the point of the story was to humiliate the rebel president with an unmasculine image. "Jeff Davis was never a good looking man, but it appears his wife's dress made him *captivating*," chortled a Pennsylvania newspaper.[26]

Federal officials imprisoned the rebel president in expectation of an upcoming trial in the most secure location they could find, which happened to be an artillery chamber at Fort Monroe in Virginia, where it all began and where it all started to end. They pinned a wall-length American flag in his cell for him to stare at, to contemplate what he had betrayed, and posted two sentries to march back and forth in front of him at all hours of the day. He stayed there two years, "musing over the past, with glimpse of landscape and the poetry of passing clouds to alleviate his sorrows."[27]

Legal arguments dragged on. The judge in the District of Virginia wouldn't sign on to a treason case because Davis was being held by the military, over which the district had no authority. But no precedent could be found to hold a tribunal, either. *New-York Tribune* editor Horace Greeley, who had urged an all-out march on Richmond in May 1861, now insisted, along with millions of Northern Democrats, that putting the rebel president on trial would be counterproductive and divisive at a time when reconciliation was needed most. Davis was finally taken before a federal court in Richmond, where his bond was set at $100,000. Greeley stepped forward to personally sign the note, and thousands of angry *Tribune* readers canceled their subscriptions in response.[28]

Davis's attorneys had argued that the passage of the Fourteenth Amendment, which stripped the right to vote from high officials of the Confederacy, was a punishment that nullified his indictment. It was an extraordinarily weak argument, but the Johnson administration had no appetite for a show trial. Acquittal was conceivable, given the likelihood of the jury being stacked with sympathetic Virginians already beginning to talk nostalgically about the "lost cause," a phrase coined by Davis himself. Such a result would be politically disastrous, suggesting the rebellion had been legitimate after all. On February 15, 1869, prosecutors laid aside indictments against Davis and thirty-eight other former Confederate officials in the name of healing the country.

Davis went free. He traveled to Britain and France, seeking work to keep himself solvent, but eventually returned to Mississippi, where he lived out his days in a donated seaside estate in Biloxi, working on a book called *The Rise and Fall of the Confederate Government* that made little mention of slavery but went into detail on troop movements and legislative arcana. Years earlier, when manacled to a bed at Fort Monroe, he had been more philosophical. An army doctor named John Craven had been assigned to look after his health. The two shared a pipe of tobacco and talked about the reasons for the war.

"Should I die, repeat this for the sake of my people, my dear wife, and my poor darling children," Davis told the doctor. "Tell the world I only loved America, and that in following my State I was only carrying out doctrines received from reverenced lips in my early youth and adapted by my judgement as the conviction of riper years."[29]

General Ulysses S. Grant, whose campaigns in Tennessee and Mississippi had sent tens of thousands of people toward the contraband camps, was elected president three years after the end of the war. He pursued vigorous Reconstruction policies during his first term, appointed Black officials to federal office, supported the election of freedmen to Congress, and tried to suppress the new terror group called the Ku Klux Klan. But corruption scandals marred his second term in office, and his administration's commitment to racial parity went into decline, thanks to fierce resistance in the South and growing apathy among Northern Republicans.

After he left office in 1877, he went on a tour of Africa, Asia, and Europe, paying courtesy calls on various monarchs and becoming the first former U.S. president to circumnavigate the globe. While in Berlin that June, he met with Chancellor Otto von Bismarck, in an office in Radziwill Palace with high ceilings and Turkish rugs on the floor. The master diplomat who had corralled twenty-five regional principalities, duchies, and kingdoms into a German Empire seven years prior appeared resplendent in a high-collar Prussian military uniform with brass buttons and epaulets.

Grant accepted an invitation to review German troops in the morning, but with some reluctance. "The truth is I am more of a farmer than a soldier," he said, adding that he joined the military with some regret and retired in happiness.

"What always seemed so sad to me about your last great war was that you were fighting your own people," said Bismarck. "That is always so terrible in wars, so very hard."

"But it had to be done," replied Grant.

"Yes, you had to save the Union just as we had to save Germany."

"Not only to save the Union but destroy slavery."

"I suppose, however, that the Union was the real sentiment, the dominant sentiment," said the chancellor.

"In the beginning, yes," said Grant, "but as soon as slavery fired upon the flag it was felt, we all felt, even those who did not object to slaves, that slavery must be destroyed. We felt it was a stain to the Union that men should be bought and sold like cattle."

The two chatted about military strategy for a few minutes before Grant brought the conversation around once more to his realization, after two years of fighting, that the war had a moral purpose.

"There had to be an end of slavery," he said. "Then we were fighting an enemy with whom we could not make a peace. We had to destroy him. No convention, no treaty was possible—only destruction."

"It was a long war and a great work well done," noted Bismarck, "and I suppose it means a long peace."

"I believe so," said Grant.[30]

The swampy town of Cairo at the southernmost point of Illinois where Grant had planned his Tennessee campaigns became a permanent home for about 1,800 of the refugees who had no place else to go. They took jobs on the riverfront, built institutions like Ward Chapel AME Church, opened small businesses, and tried to live stoically in the face of routine slurs from their white neighbors. The capital of Little Egypt never outgrew its reputation as the meanest town in the state, a place sodden with levee leakage, cheap liquor, and racial anger.

Rules of hard segregation modeled after the Deep South took hold. Police became notorious for their aggression: an estimated 15 percent of the town was said to have done time in jail by 1917. The federal government built a public housing project named Pyramid Court on the site of the old contraband camp west of downtown. Black residents had asterisks printed next to their names in the phone directory. When the city built a swimming pool with municipal funds, it tried to ban Black citizens from using it by deeming it a "private club." When state officials ordered its integration, the city responded by filling the pool with concrete.[31]

After a Black soldier died suspiciously in the city jail in 1969, backlash protests erupted. A vigilante group called the White Hats ran "patrols" with dogs and rifles in Black neighborhoods that turned into shooting missions. A young NAACP leader named Preston Ewing Jr. organized a boycott of white-owned businesses. The governor sent in the National Guard. The main drag, Commercial Street, became a burnt-out husk. Cairo lost 90 percent of its population and turned into a ghost town, a casualty of its own racism. Though still a county seat, it lacks a gas station or a grocery store. The U.S. Department of Housing and Urban Development demolished Pyramid Court in 2019, leaving an empty spot where the contraband camp had been. Nearby are the ruins of a nursing home with a tar-paper roof falling in.[32]

Ewing was one of the few who never left. In retirement, he became the town's historian, with an office in the city's Queen Anne redbrick public library. On a summer afternoon, he showed a visitor the empty spot near the Mississippi River levee where freed people had clustered in U.S. Army barracks one hundred and sixty years ago.

"They had a belief that life would be better," he said.[33]

Slabtown was never closed in a formal sense. It only faded away.

The permanence of Fort Monroe afforded it a greater protection than almost every other contraband camp in the days immediately after the war and during the rocky transition from military to civilian authority. Five thousand residents mostly paid their own way through a combination of oystering, farming, unloading ships for the quartermaster, and taking in laundry. D.B. White started a paper for the freed people called, with a note of defiance, the *True Southerner*. The new town featured restaurants, shoe shops, makeshift beer bars, a sash factory, a blacksmith's forge, and hundreds of vegetable gardens. Government rations were handed out only to the sick or elderly.[34]

"Here lives the freed negro, undisturbed and unmolested," wrote the *Philadelphia Inquirer* in the summer of 1865. "And *mirabile dictum* to our Southern friends, they earn their own subsistence." The correspondent noted that schools and churches enjoyed high attendance, and literacy rates were rapidly climbing. "Sending their children to school is considered a sacred privilege by these people just emerging from bondage, and they will forego anything but this."[35]

But the demobilization of the army was about to put hundreds of cooks, laundresses, nurses, and valets out of a job, as well as end the soldier's pay for U.S. Colored Troops stationed at Fort Monroe. The Freedmen's Bureau had only half-rations to give the malnourished, and no firewood was provided to those freezing during the unusually cold winter of 1865. Some free people desperate for wages humbled themselves by venturing back to their old plantations, only to be run off with shotguns by resentful ex-masters.[36]

Further trouble emerged when two of the owners of the underlying land, Joseph Segar and Jefferson Bonaparte Sinclair, gave notice they intended to start evictions unless they were paid rent. Like many white Southerners, the war had bankrupted them. All their paper records had gone up in flames during the burning of Hampton, and nobody was sure who owed how much to whom. The assessed value of Slabtown came to $51,000, not enough for them to squeeze out to pay off creditors. A visitor writing for *Harper's Weekly* described the village's essential modesty: "The houses are of one story, without attic or basement. Shoe-shops and restaurants are built on the same plan, a few feet reduced. Residences of the higher class of people are marked by a blanket partition and illustrated newspaper hanging on the walls."[37]

Freed people called a meeting to protest their eviction from a place they had tended so carefully. "Those who assert we are not capable of maintaining ourselves, either wickedly misrepresent and malign us or are grossly ignorant of our capabilities," they said in a collective statement, pointing out that the ground had yielded nothing but clover before they arrived and made it far more productive. With Segar's and Sinclair's finances in a hopeless tangle, the evictions did not occur for another six years. The land went into receivership and the courts subdivided the land north of King and Queen Streets into narrow lots to be sold at auction, sometimes as cheap as $85.[38]

Among those who moved away from the camp in those years was Robert Langley Brooks, the man who had run away from his master in Mathews County and found his way to a job as an officer's valet at Fort Monroe. According to family legend, he served dinner to Abraham Lincoln and shook his hand when the president stayed at the fort from May 6 through May 12 in 1862 to review the troop buildup and preparations for the Peninsula Campaign. After the war, Brooks found a job working for Albert Howe, the head of the agricultural department at Hampton Institute, and helped plant magnolia and elm trees along Victoria Boulevard as part of a beautification project. He lived with his wife in a two-story house they both owned at 3812 Shell Road.

The hand-built cabins of Slabtown began to disappear as residents erected permanent structures. Many freed people became homeowners in this way, but it created a distinct pattern of segregation, as whites made it clear they had no intention "of swimming and wallowing in the water of the same bath-house with the gentlemen from Africa." Some who experienced their first taste of freedom in Slabtown moved away permanently, in pursuit of jobs advertised in Washington or Boston.[39]

Some of the genteel patterns of old Hampton persisted, though, and just as its residents liked to assure Northern visitors that only "a mild form of slavery" had been practiced there, so too did they look past the residential patterns and separate public accommodations to claim racial harmony. Blacks and whites had a lengthy entwined history in Hampton. Shepard Mallory had been one of the three men who rowed away from the rebel fortifications at Sewell's Point to seek protection at Fort Monroe, the very first "contrabands." In January 1889 he married Ann Bailey. Among the guests at the wedding was none other than Charles King Mallory, the lawyer who had owned him and possibly even been his father. The white sheriff and mayor were also in the church. "Numerous presents were received by friends of both colors," said the society column of the *Hampton Home Bulletin*.[40]

Shepard Mallory never sought to shed his last name, perhaps keeping it as a mark of status, or perhaps as a kind of rebellion. Retaining the last name of a slave owner even after emancipation was common practice among Virginia enslaved people, one disliked by the average white owner, who sought a separation between the field hands and his "real family." He preferred to address enslaved people with simple, childlike first names or grandiose monikers from antiquity like Pompey or Shakespeare, meant to demean rather than elevate. Insisting on the retention of the name of the despot who had enslaved and possibly even tortured them was a way for a freed person to assert continuity in their lives and even sanctify kinship ties among those with whom they had been in bondage.

Another subversive reason for not covering up a shared last name is to point to the worst kept secret in the Tidewater: forced miscegenation. "By claiming the master's name," wrote the historian Alan Taylor, "mixed-race slaves sought to remember what the master meant to keep hidden: a blood tie as a daughter, son, niece, nephew, or cousin."[41]

Mallory learned to read and write. He found work as a school janitor and a bus driver to supplement his income as a carpenter, and bought his own house at 260 Lincoln Street, in the heart of the former Slabtown, on land that had been subdivided and sold to free Black residents. He became an ordinary citizen, busying himself with small-town activities, serving on a city fire department board, and joining the local Republican Party committee.[42]

In 1897, he spoke up at a public meeting to lament the fragmented opposition to Governor James Hoge Tyler, who had served in the Confederate army and was a descendant of the slave-owning First Families of Virginia. Mallory's own preferred candidate, William Lamb, had also served with the rebels and, oddly enough, had used enslaved labor to build up Fort Fisher, on the North Carolina coast, into the "Gibraltar of the Confederacy"—exactly the type of labor that Mallory and his two companions had sought to avoid. Mallory talked of running for Congress one day and appears to have been deep in the weeds of party intrigue. After he made a "ringing speech" at one party meeting, reported the *Daily Press* of Newport News, his allies made "a noisy demonstration in the midst of which the district chairman loudly but vainly called for order."[43]

Mallory died in 1924, well over eighty years old, though he left behind no preserved thoughts about all that he had seen or done. The lot where his home stood now abuts an open field with no historic markers. The only physical remnants of Slabtown, also called the Grand Contraband Camp, lie under this plot of earth and in other fields nearby. In 2014, the James River Institute for Archaeology excavated several trenches on the site and found "wells, privy pits, trash pits, post holes, and fence lines—all of which were representative of the types of features expected to be associated with the 1860s occupation."[44]

The U.S. Army disarmed Fort Monroe at the end of the Second World War, as gunnery defenses of river mouths were deemed obsolete in favor of more mobile sea-based defenses. Tactical responsibility for Chesapeake Bay shifted to the nearby Norfolk Naval Shipyard. The army ran a training and command center at Fort Monroe until decommissioning it entirely in 2011. That same year, it was designated a National Monument by President Barack Obama.

"The first enslaved Africans in England's colonies in America were brought to this peninsula on a ship flying the Dutch flag in

1619, beginning a long ignoble period of slavery in the colonies and, later, this Nation," Obama said in his proclamation. "Two hundred and forty-two years later, Fort Monroe became a place of refuge for those later generations escaping enslavement. . . . Thus, Old Point Comfort marks both the beginning and end of slavery in our Nation."[45]

In an upper-story conference room at Fort Monroe, Edith Taylor sat on a summer morning in 2022 to talk about her great-grandfather Robert Langley Brooks, who had come here at age seventeen seeking freedom the night before he was supposed to have been sold off to the Deep South. He was one of thousands and, like many formerly enslaved people, he never renounced the name of his old master—possibly out of pride, possibly out of spite.

Taylor was born eight years after he died in 1924, too late to have met him, but she grew up around his children, who knew him well and spoke of him with reverence. The family stories about him were legion. "I have Bob Brooks's blood in me," they would say.

"That was supposed to give the message, 'Don't bother me,'" said Taylor. "Most of them had that attitude, 'I'm a Brooks.' They were not going to be taken for granted."[46]

Taylor herself grew up in segregated Hampton, at a time when one of the only career options for Black women was to work as a maid—"cooking for white people, scrubbing floors, but we looked to better days." She started doing domestic work when she was a teenager, and for extra money taught herself how to prepare taxes and make hats. She became a notary public and put herself through college, giving what she didn't need to her relatives. Most of her six children were able to go to college, too. Eventually, she became the editor in chief of children's publications for the national conference of her Pentecostal church, in which her husband, William, was a bishop.

The legacy of slavery cast a shadow across the family. Her grandmother, one of Robert Brooks's six daughters, would shun certain dishes like pig's feet because they were "slaves' food." When things got hard, she often recited a favorite verse from Psalms: "Before the end of time, Ethiopia is going to stretch forth her hands."

"I feel blessed, very fortunate to be descendant from someone like him," Taylor said of her great-grandfather. "There was no telling what he went through, that he endured all those things, all the hardships, and was able to arise from that." It all seemed, she said, beyond imagination. She never let her children forget they were the descendants of Robert Langley Brooks, who paddled away from his cruel master toward the American flag and did not look back.[47]

Notes on Sources

Historical scholarship resembles geology. Layers rise upon older layers. No formation is ever quite complete. And every element of a mountain has some dependent relationship on neighboring stone.

I am indebted to many distinguished scholars of the formative period between 1861 and 1863, and my debts are especially great to two contemporary historians of the contraband camps. Chandra Manning's *Troubled Refuge: Struggling for Freedom in the Civil War* provides a panoramic look at the refugees from slavery throughout the war, showing how questions of citizenship emerged under military authority. Another superb view can be found in Amy Murrell Taylor's *Embattled Freedom: Journeys Through the Civil War's Slave Refugee Camps*, which provides close-up views of the experiences of several residents of the camps, pieced together through hard archival work. Taylor's nuanced portrait of Emma and Edward Whitehurst, for example, was pathbreaking scholarship, for which I am grateful.

The most complete account of the extraordinary life of Abraham Galloway was assembled by David S. Cecelski in *Fire of Freedom: Abraham Galloway & the Slaves' Civil War.* The best overview of the American Missionary Association's pivotal role in the camps is Joe M. Richardson's *Christian Reconstruction: The American Missionary Association and Southern Blacks, 1861–1890*, which also provides insight on the mercurial personality of Lewis C. Lockwood, whose own short book on Mary S. Peake is a rare glimpse of free Black life in Hampton in the early days of the Civil War. *Freedom's First Generation* by Robert Engs is also pivotal for those looking to make sense of this period.

I traveled to multiple archives in search of primary sources. The Amistad Research Center at Tulane University holds the massive collection of the American Missionary Association, previously housed at Fisk University. The clerical contributors to the *American Missionary* magazine, in particular, paid attention to the astonishing developments in the refugee camps like no other journalistic medium of the time, though three newspapers also deserve special mention. The *Anglo-African* treated the refugee influx as a major story, and I accessed its pages through digitized copies held at the University of California, Los Angeles. I also drew from background work on the Hamilton brothers by Debra Jackson. The anonymous correspondent of the *New-York Tribune* assigned to Fort Monroe wrote unusually detailed dispatches about the freed people; archived copies may be found on Newspapers.com. Finally, the short-lived *Pine and Palm* devoted many stories to the camps; its crumbling hard copies have been preserved in the Special Collections section of the Boston Public Library.

The digitized records of the Southern Claims Commission, which I accessed through the New England Historic Genealogical Society, contain the partial story of Emma and Edward Whitehurst, as well as a few other freed people discussed in this book. While the voices of the formerly enslaved were often passed through the deadening filter of military bureaucracy, valuable insights and flashes of individual personality can still be extracted from the records. The notoriously unkempt Record Group 393 at the National Archives contained memoranda of note. The diary of one of the first provost marshals to document freed people's arrival to Union lines, Roswell Farnham, is housed at the Vermont History Museum in Montpelier; I found it thanks to Amy Murrell Taylor.

I spent many hours with the personal papers of General Benjamin Butler at the Library of Congress, particularly those emerging from his brief but eventful tenure at Fort Monroe between May and August of 1861. An important supplement is the printed collection *Private and Official Correspondence of Gen. Benjamin F. Butler, During the Period of the Civil War.* A recent biography of him by Elizabeth Leonard shines further light on his famously difficult, though strangely appealing, personality. His pivotal conversation with John Baytop Cary, along with a vivid portrait of Hampton, can be found in Adam Goodheart's beautifully written *1861: The Civil War Awakening*. Butler's replacement at Fort Monroe, John Wool, did not commit much about the contraband camp to paper. His correspondence housed at the New York State Library was still insightful. The Houghton Library at Harvard University houses the correspondence of the American Freedmen's Inquiry Commission.

Historians of the Civil War invariably turn to printed compendiums of key documents, and I was no different in making use of *Abraham Lincoln, Complete Works, Comprising His Speeches, Letters, State Papers, and Miscellaneous Writings*, as well as *The War of the Rebellion: A Compilation of the Official Records of the Union and Confederate Armies*. Collections of oral testimony of enslaved people were also valuable, particularly *The Weevils in the Wheat: Interviews with Virginia Ex-slaves*, edited by Charles Perdue, Thomas Barden, and Robert Phillips, and *Slave Testimony: Two Centuries of Letters, Speeches, Interviews, and Autobiographies*, edited by John Blassingame.

I also relied on memoirs from formerly enslaved people, including *Slavery in the United States: A Narrative*, by Charles Ball; *Reminiscences of My Life in Camp*, by Susie King Taylor; *A Slave's Adventures Toward Freedom*, by Peter Bruner; *Memorys of the Past*, by John Washington; and *From Slave Cabin to Pulpit*, by Peter Randolph. Important firsthand accounts of the U.S. Colored Troops are in *The Negro's Civil War: How American Negroes Felt and Acted During the War for the Union*, edited by James McPherson, and the best overview remains *The Sable Arm*, by Dudley Taylor Cornish. I also consulted the writings of Henry McNeal Turner, collected under the title *Freedom's Witness*, edited by Jean Lee Cole and Aaron Sheehan-Dean.

Any scholar examining the growth of racialized slavery on the Virginia Peninsula of the seventeenth century must contend with *American Slavery, American Freedom*, by Edmund Morgan, and *White over Black: American Attitudes Toward the Negro, 1550–1812*, by Winthrop Jordan. Another formative title for me was Anthony Parent's *Foul Means: The Formation of a Slave Society in Virginia,*

1660–1740. Annette Gordon-Reed's *The Hemingses of Monticello: An American Family* is about so much more than its title subject and shaped my view about the development of American slavery and the complicated relationships that formed within it. A potent foreshadowing of the events at Fort Monroe and other federal positions can be found in Alan Taylor's *The Internal Enemy: Slavery and War in Virginia, 1772–1832*.

The lead-up to the Emancipation Proclamation gets detailed legal scrutiny in *The Broken Constitution: Lincoln, Slavery and the Refounding of America* by Noah Feldman. In *Freedom National: The Destruction of Slavery in the United States*, James Oakes makes a case for a tandem theory of emancipation: Lincoln, Congress, the U.S. Army, and the insistent internal movement of the enslaved people, all working in separate spheres with unstoppable combined force. An excellent window into the evolving posture of the sixteenth president was captured by his personal secretaries John Hay and John Nicolay in *Abraham Lincoln: A History*. His intellectually formative journeys down the Mississippi have been pieced together by Richard Campanella in the quirky and wonderful study *Lincoln in New Orleans: The 1828–1831 Flatboat Journeys and Their Place in History*.

I traveled to the sites of numerous contraband camps for a sense of the landscape. Although every location has been immutably altered through a century and a half of redevelopment, outlines may still be perceived. One of the handful to be preserved and marked is at Corinth, Mississippi, in the Shiloh Battlefield Unit of the National Park Service. The visitor center there maintains an archive where copies of the *Cincinnati Gazette* and *Corinth Chanticleer*—two of the key journalistic sources for the camp's development—may be accessed, along with relevant correspondence of the overseers.

A note about dialogue: Authors and journalists of the nineteenth century often employed a literary device of spelling the words of enslaved people in an onomatopoetic patois; for example, writing "massa" for master, "dey" for they, "genmum" for gentleman, and the like. This was understood by readers as an artistic method of capturing the regional flavor of African American speech, but it was done just as often for purposes of mockery or condescension. Such quotations have been rendered in standard English for this book, not just for ease of readability but to convey the clear meaning the speaker intended without creative filtration by an interlocutor. Updated spellings have also been applied to a handful of written statements made in Early Modern English by the white settlers of seventeenth-century Virginia. In no case has the diction, substantial grammar, or underlying meaning of any quote been altered. The original quotes as rendered in patois and period language may be consulted at tomzoellner.com, keyed to the numbered footnotes.

Acknowledgments

I am grateful for material support from the National Endowment for the Humanities, which funded the months of travel and research necessary to complete this book via a Public Scholar grant.

Sam Kleiner provided the initial suggestion to take a close look at the events at Fort Monroe in the summer of 1861 as a key to understanding the etiology of American emancipation.

In Hampton, Virginia, Bill Wiggins was generous with his insights and made introductions to the Contraband Historical Society. He was a careful historian and a gentleman of the first order whose career and life were driven by love. His contributions as a professor at Hampton University and as a caretaker of community history will endure. Edith Taylor told me a family story I will never forget, and Kevin Brooks also shared useful information. Ali Kolleda at the Fort Monroe Authority archives was extremely helpful in tracking down some forgotten materials, and Beth Austin at the Hampton History Center provided guidance and some informed speculation on the fire of August 7, 1861.

In Washington, DC, one of the foremost scholars of the refugee camps, Chandra Manning, gave me an invaluable education on the landscape of primary sources at the very start of this project. Cooper Wingert helped prepare me for the maze of military documents at the National Archives.

In Springfield, Illinois, I am grateful to Christian McWhirter and Meghan Harmon at the Abraham Lincoln Presidential Library and Museum for pointing me to specific documents and secondary sources.

In Cairo, Illinois, Preston Ewing Jr. gave a driving tour of what remains of the town, and showed me nineteenth-century clippings from the impressive archive he has assembled. Aaron M. Lisec pointed the way to more Cairo material in the library at Southern Illinois University. Tom Parson opened the National Park Service archive at Corinth, Mississippi. In New Orleans, Lisa C. Moore displayed grace and humor fielding my questions at the Amistad Research Center at Tulane University. Kathleen Monahan in the Special Collections division of the Boston Public Library helped me sort through the fragile pages of the only remaining copies of the *Pine and Palm* newspaper.

Amy Murrell Taylor, Manisha Sinha, Walter Johnson, Abigail Cooper, and Kate Masur provided thoughtful replies to my research queries. Megan Kate Nelson pointed me to some obscure documents and offered encouragement, along with some necessary witticisms. Marissa Jenrich of California State University, Northridge, made important narrative suggestions, as did Chandler Fritz.

At Arizona State University, Calvin Schermerhorn read drafts of some early chapters and provided an excellent critique. Catherine O'Donnell and Peter Van Cleave contributed their own valuable thoughts. I am tremendously grateful to them and to my other teachers of history—Jane Chilcott, Gary Minor, Marc Simmons, William Chaney, and William Bremer—who inspired an enchantment with the past in their students.

Mike Mungiello of InkWell Management found the book a home at The New Press under the expert watch of editor Marc Favreau and managing editor Maury Botton. Copy editor Brian Baughan gave it a thorough and professional review.

I will never be able to adequately thank my family—Erin, Peter, and Henry—who made it all worthwhile. Erin Dunkerly, my sweet love, you walked this book home.

Abbreviations and Bibliography

Abbreviations

AFIC	American Freedman's Inquiry Commission
AL	*Abraham Lincoln, Complete Works, Comprising His Speeches, Letters, State Papers, and Miscellaneous Writings.* New York: The Century Co., 1894
AMA	American Missionary Association Archives, Tulane University, Amistad Research Center, New Orleans, Louisiana
AMM	*American Missionary* magazine
BFB	Benjamin F. Butler papers, Manuscript Division, Library of Congress, Washington, DC.
CMSR	Compiled Military Service Records, National Archives and Records Administration, Washington, DC.
FMA	Fort Monroe Authority archives, Hampton, Virginia
FWP	Federal Writers Project, *Slave Narratives: A Folk History of Slavery in the United States.* Washington, DC.: Library of Congress, 1941
HHC	Hampton History Center, Hampton, Virginia
JWP	John Wool papers, New York State Library, Albany, New York
NARA	National Archives and Records Administration, Washington, DC.
NPS	Corinth Battlefield Unit archive, Shiloh National Military Park, National Park Service, Corinth, Mississippi
OR	*The War of the Rebellion: A Compilation of the Official Records of the Union and Confederate Armies.* Washington, DC.: Government Printing Office, 1880–1901
POC	*Private and Official Correspondence of Gen. Benjamin F. Butler.* Boston: The Plimpton Press, 1917

RG 393	Record Group 393: Records of U.S. Army Continental Commands, 1821–1920, National Archives and Records Administration, Washington, DC.
SCC	Southern Claims Commission, Approved Claims, 1871–1880: Virginia, series 732, M2904, RG 217: Records of the Accounting Officers of the Department of the Treasury, 1775–1927
USCT	United States Colored Troops
VMHC	Virginia Museum of History and Culture, Richmond, Virginia

Newspapers and Magazines

American Missionary
Anglo-African
Ashtabula Weekly Telegraph
The Atlantic
Baltimore Republican
Boston Daily Globe
Boston Traveler
Brooklyn Daily Eagle
Cairo City Gazette
Cairo Evening Bulletin
The Century
Charleston Mercury
Chicago Times
Chicago Tribune
Christian Advocate
Cincinnati Gazette
Cleveland Daily Leader
Commercial Advertiser
Corinth Chanticleer
Douglass Monthly
Frank Leslie's Illustrated Newspaper
Freeport Weekly Bulletin
Hampshire Gazette
Harper's
The Independent
Leavenworth Conservative
Lynchburg Virginian
Macon Telegraph
Milwaukee Free Democrat
Milwaukee Sentinel
Missouri Republican
Montgomery Daily Mail
Morning Express
National Anti-Slavery Standard
National Intelligencer
National Republican
New Orleans Times
New York Evening Post
New York Herald
New York Times
New-York Tribune
Pine and Palm
Savannah Republican
Springfield Republican
Washington Evening Star
Washington Post
Western Clarion
Wheeling Daily Intelligencer

Archives

National Archives and Records Administration
Fort Monroe Authority

Library of Congress
Houghton Library, Harvard University
Amistad Archive, Tulane University
Vermont Historical Society
Boston Public Library Special Collections
New England Historical and Genealogical Society
New York State Library
Southern Illinois University Special Collections
Corinth Battlefield Unit archive, Corinth, Mississippi

Notes

Introduction

1. Mary Frances Armstrong and Helen Wilhelmina Ludlow, *Hampton and Its Students. By Two of Its Teachers* (New York: G.P. Putnam's Sons, 1874), 111.

2. Montgomery Blair to Benjamin Butler, May 29, 1861, POC.

3. W.E.B. Du Bois, *Black Reconstruction in America, 1860–1880* (New York: Macmillan, 1935), 62; John Eaton, *Report of the General Superintendent of Freedmen, Department of the Tennessee and State of Arkansas, for 1864*, vol. 1 (Memphis, 1864), 23.

4. There is no comprehensive and widely agreed-upon determination of the total population of the camps, which fluctuated with the tides of the war. The Freedmen and Southern Society Project put the total at 474,000. Ira Berlin et al., *Slaves No More: Three Essays on Emancipation and the Civil War* (Cambridge: Cambridge University Press, 1992). But a more in-depth study of military records and participant diaries by Abigail Cooper estimates a population of eight hundred thousand freed people who experienced some contact with a Union refugee camp from 1861 to 1865. Abigail Cooper, "'Lord, Until I Reach My Home': Inside the Refugee Camps of the American Civil War" (PhD diss., University of Pennsylvania, 2015), 542–43.

5. Arthur Brooks Lapsey, ed., *The Writings of Abraham Lincoln*, vol. 5 (New York: G.P. Putnam and Sons, 1906), 447; Lapsey, *The Writings of Abraham Lincoln*, vol. 6, 88.

6. AL, vol. 2, 217.

7. James M. McPherson, *Battle Cry of Freedom: The Civil War Era* (Oxford: Oxford University Press, 1988), 835; William W. Freehling, *The South vs. the South: How Anti-Confederate Southerners Shaped the Course of the Civil War* (Oxford: Oxford University Press, 2002), xiii.

8. Joseph P. Reidy, *Illusions of Emancipation: The Pursuit of Freedom & Equality in the Twilight of Slavery* (Chapel Hill: The University of North Carolina Press, 2019), 24.

9. Elizabeth Keckly, *Behind the Scenes: Or, Thirty Years a Slave and Four Years in the White House* (New York: G.W. Carleton & Co., 1868), 112. Her last name is sometimes rendered as Keckley. As W.E.B. Du Bois concluded seventy years after emancipation, "these slaves had enormous power in their hands. Simply by stopping work, they could threaten the Confederacy with starvation. By walking into Federal camps, they showed to doubting northerners the possibility of using them as workers and as servants, as farmers, and as spies, and finally, as fighting soldiers." See Du Bois, *Black Reconstruction in America*, 121, 57.

10. Frederick Douglass, *My Bondage and My Freedom* (New York: Miller, Orton & Mulligan, 1855), 87; *Washington Evening Star*, January 2, 1863. For a discussion of this moral reversal, see Eran Shalev, *American Zion: The Old Testament as a Political Text from the Revolution to the Civil War* (New Haven, CT: Yale University Press, 2013), 181.

11. Calvin Schermerhorn, *Money Over Mastery, Family Over Freedom: Slavery in the Antebellum Upper South* (Baltimore, MD: Johns Hopkins University Press), 211.

12. Armstrong and Ludlow, *Hampton and Its Students*, 111.

13. Ibid., 114.

1. The Sound of the Hammer

1. Howard P. Nash, *Stormy Petrel: The Life and Times of Benjamin F. Butler, 1818–1893* (Rutherford, NJ: Fairleigh Dickinson University Press, 1969), 27. See also Richard S. West, *Lincoln's Scapegoat General: A Life of Benjamin F. Butler, 1818–1893* (Boston: Houghton Mifflin Company, 1965), 9–11, and Chester G. Hearn, *When the Devil Came Down to Dixie: Benjamin Butler in New Orleans* (Baton Rouge: Louisiana State University Press, 1997), 11.

2. West, *Lincoln's Scapegoat General*, 32; Hearn, *When the Devil Came Down to Dixie*, 16–17; Elizabeth D. Leonard, *Benjamin Franklin Butler: A Noisy, Fearless Life* (Chapel Hill: University of North Carolina Press, 2022), 33.

3. Hearn, *When the Devil Came Down to Dixie*, 8, 16–17.

4. At the 1860 Democratic Party convention, he cast fifty-seven ballots—one after the other—in favor of Jefferson Davis for president, reasoning he was the best choice to hold the country together. Hearn, *When the Devil Came Down to Dixie*, 26; *Massachusetts Spy*, October 19, 1859, quoted in Leonard, *Benjamin Franklin Butler*, 43; Murray M. Horowitz, "Ben Butler and the Negro: 'Miracles Are Occurring,'" *Louisiana History* 17, no. 2 (Spring 1976): 159.

5. William F. Stoddard, *Lincoln's Third Secretary* (New York: Exposition Press, 1955), 153; Hearn, *When the Devil Came Down to Dixie*, 29.

6. Winfield Scott to Cadwallader, May 15, 1861, POC, 87; Benjamin Butler to Simon Cameron, May 18, 1861, POC, 96.

7. *Boston Traveler*, May 27, 1861; Benjamin Butler to Winfield Scott, POC, 104; Worley Levi Sewell, *History of the Sewell Families in America* (Stuart, FL: privately published, 1955), 35–36. Henry Sewell's name was also spelled Seawall in some colonial documents. The term "fort" is usually applied to a single defensive structure while "fortress" means a collection of buildings. The terms were used interchangeably at Fort Monroe, which protected a multitude of buildings within a walled perimeter.

8. John Baytop Cary to Benjamin Butler, March 9, 1891, POC, 102. See also Benjamin F. Butler, *Autobiography and Personal Reminiscences of Major-General Benjamin Butler, Butler's Book*, 256–66, and Benjamin F. Butler to Winfield Scott, May 25, 1861, POC.

9. William Henry Stewart, *A History of Norfolk County, Virginia and Representative Citizens* (Chicago: Biographical Publishing Company, 1902), 71; D.G. Duncan to L.P. Walker, May 20, 1861, in OR series 1, part 2, 96.

10. *Boston Traveler*, May 27, 1861; Benjamin Butler to Winfield Scott, POC, 104. Mallory's name was sometimes misspelled as "Shepherd Mallory."

11. New York Public Library, Miriam and Ira D. Wallach Division of Art, Prints and Photographs: Picture Collection, Shelf locator: PC AFRA-H-186.

12. Benjamin Butler to Winfield Scott, May 24, 1861, POC, 106. This was not the first documented time during the secession movement that enslaved people had run for a U.S. Army position hoping for protection. Two months after Florida seceded, a group of escapees approached the walls of Fort Pickens near Pensacola. Lt. Adam Slemmer made the following brisk report: "On the morning of the 12th instant four negroes (runaways) came to the fort entertaining the idea that we were placed here to protect them and grant them their freedom." He sought to "teach them to the contrary" by escorting them to the city marshal, who returned them to slavery. He did the same with four more men who showed up that evening, not bothering to record their names. See Adam Slemmer to L. Thomas, March 18, 1861, in OR, series 1, vol. 1, 362. See also Chandra Manning, *Troubled Refuge: Struggling for Freedom in the Civil War* (New York: Vintage Books, 2016), 167.

13. John Baytop Cary to Benjamin Butler, March 9, 1891, POC, 102.

14. *New York Times*, June 2, 1861.

15. John Baytop Cary to Benjamin Butler, March 9, 1891, POC, 102. See also Butler, *Butler's Book*, 256–66, and Benjamin F. Butler to Winfield Scott, May 25, 1861, POC.

16. *New-York Tribune* report reprinted in *Andover* (MA) *Advertiser*, June 13, 1861.

17. Marion L. Starkey, *The First Plantation: History of Hampton and Elizabeth City County, Virginia, 1607–1887* (Hampton, VA: Hampton Printing and Publishing House, 1936), 78; George William Curtis, "Theodore Winthrop," *The Atlantic*, August 1861; Laura Wright Hildreth to Harriet Heard, June 6, 1861, POC, 128.

18. Benjamin F. Butler to Winfield Scott, May 27, 1861, POC, 113.

19. Benjamin F. Butler to J.W. Phelps, May 28, 1861, POC, 114. Some slaveholding families from Hampton who fled the area evidently took the most physically fit enslaved people with them, leaving behind the old and sick. See also *New York Times*, June 3, 1861.

20. Simon Cameron to Benjamin F. Butler, May 30, 1861, POC, 119.

21. *Pine and Palm*, December 21, 1861.

22. *Springfield Republican*, reprinted in *New York Evening Post*, May 30, 1861; *Missouri Republican*, June 1, 1861; *The South*, May 28, 1861; *New York World*, June 1, 1861. For speculation about the press amplification of "contraband," see James Oakes, *Freedom National: The Destruction of Slavery in the United States, 1861–1865* (New York: W.W. Norton, 2012), 102.

23. Montgomery Blair to Benjamin F. Butler, May 29, 1861.

24. Quoted in Thomas R. Flagel, "The Fortress War: Effect of Union Fortifications in the Western Theater of the U.S. Civil War" (PhD diss., Middle Tennessee State University, 2016), 35.

25. J.B. Magruder to George Deas, August 9, 1861, OR, 764. See also *Boston Globe*, August 17, 1911.

26. Magruder to Deas, August 9, 1861, OR, 764. Magruder said that the newspaper in question was the *New-York Tribune*, but archived copies of the newspaper do not contain any dispatches such as he described. It is possible he confused another discarded newspaper for the antislavery *Tribune*, a constant irritant to most Southern press watchers, or grievously misread a July 31 story about Butler's retreat from Hampton. A third possibility is that Magruder had ordered the town burned on an impulse and sought retroactively to pin it on a piece of intelligence that did not exist. As it happened, Northern newspapers were becoming an obsessively picked-over source of information by Southern military officials by this point, leading Winfield Scott to censor any telegraphic news about troop movements, remarking he would prefer a hundred Confederate spies in

any Union camp over a single reporter. See also Ernest B. Furguson, *Freedom Rising: Washington in the Civil War* (New York: Alfred A. Knopf, 2004), 118.

27. Starkey, *The First Plantation*, 82; *Christian Recorder*, August 17, 1861.

28. *Harper's Weekly*, August 31, 1861.

29. *Boston Daily Globe*, August 17, 1911; *American Missionary*, October 1861.

30. *Harper's Weekly*, August 31, 1861.

31. Starkey, *The First Plantation*, 81–82; *Farmer's Cabinet* (Amherst, NH), August 16, 1861; *Boston Daily Globe*, August 17, 1911; *Harper's Weekly*, August 31, 1861. See also Megan Kate Nelson, *Ruin Nation: Destruction and the American Civil War* (Athens: University of Georgia Press, 2012), 19–21.

32. Five thousand board feet were dragged to Slabtown every day, enough to put up at least four houses. Testimony of F.W. Bird, December 24, 1863, AFIC.

33. Quoted in Nelson, *Ruin Nation*, 26.

34. *Weekly Anglo-African*, August 17, 1861.

35. John Baytop Cary to Columbia H. Cary, January 31, 1862, Virginia Museum of History and Culture. I thank Megan Kate Nelson and Amy Murrell Taylor for pointing me toward this document.

36. Roswell Farnham to Laura Farnham, July 31, 1861; *American Missionary*, August 1862; *New York Times*, January 31, 1862.

37. *American Missionary*, October 1861, November 1861, February 1862.

38. Lewis Lockwood to American Missionary Association, March 18, 1862, AMA; *American Missionary*, July 1862.

39. Stephen Bradley, ed., *The 1860 Federal Census, Mathews County, Virginia* (Lawrenceville, VA: privately printed, 1998), 277, 76; Author interview, Edith Taylor, Fort Monroe, VA, July 18, 2022; Charles L. Perdue Jr., Thomas E. Barden, and Robert K. Phillips, eds., *The Weevils in the Wheat: Interviews with Virginia Ex-slaves* (Charlottesville: University Press of Virginia, 1976), 57.

40. *Anglo-African*, September 28, 1861.

41. Lewis Lockwood to American Missionary Association, March 20, 1862, AMA.

42. Statement of Waddy Smith, May 31, 1831, BFB.

43. Report of John Christiansen, September 17, 1861, U.S. Army Continental Commands, 1821–1920, Dept. of Virginia and North Carolina Provost Marshal, 1861, Box 15, RG 393.

44. Ibid.

45. Ibid.

46. Harvey Beals to American Missionary Association, July 25, 1864, AMA; *New-York Tribune*, August 7, 1861, reprinted in *Pine and Palm*, August 31, 1861.

47. Stephanie M.H. Camp has written of the divided self of the enslaved person: a first body of economic value for the owner, a second body experiencing pain, and a third body that was "a thing to be claimed and enjoyed" through common pleasures that might be eked out from an otherwise deprived existence. It was in this third body that they could allow their dreams of freedom to take shape, however guardedly. Stephanie M.H. Camp, *Closer to Freedom: Enslaved Woman and Everyday Resistance in the Plantation South* (Chapel Hill: University of North Carolina Press, 2005), 67–68.

48. *Pine and Palm*, August 31, 1861.

49. Richard Frederick Fuller, *Chaplain Fuller: Being a Life Sketch of a New England Clergyman and Army Chaplain* (Boston: Walker, Wise and Company, 1864), 198.

50. *Pine and Palm*, August 31, 1861.

51. Fuller, *Chaplain Fuller*, 199; *Pine and Palm*, August 31, 1861; *Douglass Monthly*, September 1861; Thomas Wentworth Higginson, *The Complete Civil War Journal and Selected Letters of Thomas Wentworth Higginson* (Chicago: University of Chicago Press, 1999), 78; *AMM*, October 1862. Higginson visited Dickinson twice in her home but found the conversations unsatisfying. "The bee himself did not evade the schoolboy more than she evaded me, and even at this day I still stand somewhat bewildered, like the boy," he wrote later. See "Emily Dickinson's Letters," *Atlantic Monthly*, October 1891.

52. Hollis Read, *The Negro Problem Solved* (New York: A.A. Constantine, 1864), 365.

53. Michael C. Cohen, *The Social Lives of Poems in Nineteenth-Century America* (Philadelphia: University of Pennsylvania Press, 2015), 115.

54. *New-York Tribune*, December 2, 1861.

55. *American Missionary*, October 1861.

2. Let No Man Put Asunder

1. William Howard Russell, *My Diary North and South* (New York: Knopf, 1988), 246.

2. Roswell Farnham to Mary Farnham, June 1, 1861, Vermont Historical Society.

3. Ibid. "Old Point" referred to Old Point Comfort, indicating that Farnham's post was located in the camps sprawling westward toward town.

4. Joseph P. Reidy, *Illusions of Emancipation: The Pursuit of Freedom and Equality in the Twilight of Slavery* (Chapel Hill: University of North Carolina Press, 2019), 24; John Hay and John Nicolay, *Abraham Lincoln: A History*, vol. 1 (New York: Century Illustrated Monthly Magazine, 1909), 441.

5. Amy Murrell Taylor, *Embattled Freedom: Journeys Through the Civil War's Slave Refugee Camps* (Chapel Hill: University of North Carolina Press, 2018), 27. This book was the first to give critical attention to the Whitehursts and their journey out of slavery.

6. Claim of Edward Whitehurst, December 5, 1877, SCC.

7. *Pine and Palm*, June 29, 1861.

8. *Genealogies of Virginia Families from the William and Mary College Quarterly* (Baltimore: Genealogical Publications, 1982), 821; W.T. Stauffer, "The Old Farms out of Which the City of Newport News Was Erected, with Some Account of the Families Which Dwelt Thereon," *William and Mary Quarterly* 14, no. 4 (October 1934): 336.

9. Stauffer, "The Old Farms," 339.

10. Lewis Lockwood to American Missionary Association, March 20, 1862, AMA.

11. Stauffer, "The Old Farms," 339.

12. Taylor, *Embattled Freedom*, 27; Claim of Edward Whitehurst, December 5, 1877, SCC.

13. *Pine and Palm*, August 31, 1861; reprinted in *American Missionary*, October 1861.

14. Claim of Edward Whitehurst, December 5, 1877, SCC.

15. Quoted in Chandra Manning, *Troubled Refuge: Struggling for Freedom in the Civil War* (New York: Vintage Books, 2016), 55.

16. Claim of Edward Whitehurst, December 5, 1877, SCC.

17. Their assets would be worth approximately $21,400 in U.S. dollars in 2025 when adjusted for inflation.

18. J.T. Schlotterbeck, "The Internal Economy of Slavery in Rural Piedmont Virginia," *Slavery & Abolition* 12, no. 1 (1991): 171.

19. Ibid., 171–74; Kathleen M. Hilliard, *Masters, Slaves, and Exchange: Power's Purchase in the Old South* (Cambridge: Cambridge University Press, 2013), 89; John J. Zaborney, *Slaves for Hire: Renting Enslaved Laborers in Antebellum Virginia* (Baton Rouge: Louisiana State University Press, 2012), 22.

20. Schlotterbeck, "The Internal Economy," 178.

21. Claim of Edward Whitehurst, December 5, 1877, SCC.

22. *Charleston Mercury*, November 30, 1861; *New York Evening Post*, reprinted in *Buffalo Courier*, November 16, 1861.

23. Report of J. Christiansen, October 2, 1861, U.S. Army Continental Commands, 1821–1920, Dept. of Virginia and North Carolina Provost Marshal, 1861, Box 15, RG 393; Claim of Edward Whitehurst, December 5, 1877, SCC. See also Taylor, *Embattled Freedom*, 33.

24. Stephanie McCurry, *Women's War: Fighting and Surviving the American Civil War* (Cambridge, MA: Harvard University Press, 2019), 85; Taylor, *Embattled Freedom*, 34–35.

25. *Boston Traveler*, July 1, 1861. The writer went on to observe: "It has often been said that slavery existed in Virginia as a mild form. Can that be a mild form of slavery where the conjugal and parental relations are thus ruthlessly sundered?"

26. Lewis Lockwood, *Mary S. Peake: The Colored Teacher at Fort Monroe* (Boston: American Tract Society, 1863), 40; *American Missionary*, October 1861.

27. *American Missionary*, November 1861.

28. Lockwood, *Mary S. Peake*, 61; *Pine and Palm*, October 5, 1861.

29. Stephanie McCurry, *Confederate Reckoning: Power and Politics in the Civil War South* (Cambridge, MA: Harvard University Press, 2010), 273. See also "'Us Never Had No Big Funerals or Weddin's on de Place': Ritualizing Black Marriage in the Wake of Freedom," in *Beyond Freedom: Disrupting the History of Emancipation*, ed. David W. Blight and Jim Downs (Athens: University of Georgia Press, 2017). Tera Hunter also makes the case that federal authorities were eager to create "self-sufficient labor units among the newly freed to perform the agricultural work so important to these new enterprises." Tera W. Hunter, *Bound in Wedlock: Slave and Free Black Marriage in the Nineteenth Century* (Cambridge, MA: Harvard University Press, 2019), 123.

30. Clara Merritt De Boer, "The Role of Afro-Americans in the Origin and Work of the American Missionary Association, 1839–1877" (PhD diss., Rutgers University, 1973), 238; Lockwood to American Missionary Association, February 24, 1862, AMA.

31. Joe M. Richardson, *Christian Reconstruction: The American Missionary Association and Southern Blacks, 1861–1890* (Tuscaloosa: University of Alabama Press, 2009), vii, 3; Acts 17:26.

32. *American Missionary*, November 1861.

33. *American Missionary*, March 1862.

34. Lockwood to William Whiting, February 21, 1862, AMA.

35. Richardson, *Christian Reconstruction*, 18.

36. Lockwood to American Missionary Association, March 15, 1862; Richardson, *Christian Reconstruction*, 6. Dr. McKay was a "doughface"—a

Northerner unopposed to slavery—who thought the contraband decision was illegal. Among other actions of apparent protest, he ordered Black women to clean the seminary at gunpoint and then withheld payment. See De Boer, "The Role of Afro-Americans," 246. Problems in the department persisted into 1863. The American Freedmen's Inquiry Commission noted several officers were "pro-slavery and scarcely loyal in sentiment, and place every obstruction in the way of benevolent and business efforts to improve the condition of the contrabands." See "Memoranda," May 1863, AFIC.

37. AMA secretary Simeon Jocelyn lobbied President Lincoln to send a doctor to look after the Hampton contrabands as an exclusive assignment. Lincoln wrote on the back of a November 26, 1861, letter sent to him by Jocelyn: "If Genl. Wool is of the opinion that the services of a surgeon are needed for the colored persons under his charge, and will select a suitable person and put him to the service, I will advise Congress that he be paid." See Richardson, *Christian Reconstruction*, 265n.

38. Charles Wilder to AFIC, August 26, 1863, AFIC.

39. Eliza Frances Andrews, *The War-Time Journal of a Georgia Girl* (Lincoln: University of Nebraska Press, 1997), 91, quoted in Eugene D. Genovese, *Roll, Jordan, Roll* (New York: Vintage, 1976), 59.

40. W.E.B. Du Bois, *The Souls of Black Folk*, 196; Genovese, *Roll, Jordan, Roll*, 236; Henry H. Mitchell, *Black Preaching: The Recovery of a Powerful Art* (Nashville: Abingdon Press, 1990), 49.

41. David Walker, *Appeal to the Coloured Citizens of the World* (Boston: revised and published by David Walker, 1830).

42. David Hackett Fischer, *African Founders: How Enslaved People Expanded American Ideals* (New York: Simon and Schuster, 2022), 343. Another enslaved person who learned to read and write used his knowledge to forge a pass and escape to Philadelphia. He then wrote his old master, George Larrimore, a "saucy letter" in gratitude for the gift of literacy (346).

43. Arthur P. Davis, "William Roscoe Davis and His Descendants," *Negro History Bulletin* 13, no. 4 (January 1950): 75.

44. *New York Times*, January 14, 1862; Davis, "William Roscoe Davis," 75. By one account, Davis managed to save $1,800 in income, most of which he spent on legal fees in a lengthy and frustrating lawsuit to free his enslaved wife, Nancy, from the conditions of the disputed will of her owner's father. The case was still unresolved when she was freed by the contraband decision in 1861. For a description of Davis, see Edward L. Pierce, "The Contrabands at Fortress Monroe," *The Atlantic*, October 1861.

45. Davis, "William Roscoe Davis and His Descendants," 75.

46. Lockwood, *Mary S. Peake*, 62.

47. *American Missionary*, October 1861.

48. Richardson, *Christian Reconstruction*, 95–96. For his part, Davis was paid $60 per month, plus expenses. Davis, "William Roscoe Davis," 80.

49. *New York Times*, January 16, 1862.

50. Ibid.

51. Henry Ward Beecher, *Freedom and War: Discourses on Topics Suggested by the Times* (Boston: Ticknor and Fields, 1863), 192.

52. William Constantine Beecher and Samuel Scoville, *Biography of Rev. Henry Ward Beecher* (New York: Charles L. Webster & Company, 1888), 294.

53. Davis, "William Roscoe Davis," 80.

54. Richardson, *Christian Reconstruction*, 92.

55. Quoted in Richardson, *Christian Reconstruction*, 59.

56. *Douglass Monthly*, March 1862. Also reprinted in *Pine and Palm*, December 21, 1861. While the Confederate army and navy made use of enslaved labor in construction and fortification projects, there is a dearth of evidence for any African American uniformed troops willingly fighting for the Confederate cause. See Kevin M. Levin, *Searching for Black Confederates: The Civil War's Most Persistent Myth* (Chapel Hill: University of North Carolina Press, 2019).

57. *Union & Advertiser*, Rochester, New York, February 12, 1862.

58. Lockwood to American Missionary Association, December 2, 1862, AMA.

59. John Oliver to William Coan, February 5, 1862, AMA.

60. *American Missionary*, May 1868; John Oliver to William Coan, February 5, 1862, AMA; Lewis Lockwood to American Missionary Association, May 5, 1862, AMA.

61. John Oliver to Simon Jocelyn, September 1862, AMA; *American Missionary*, October 1863.

62. J.N. Bebout to S.S. Jocelyn, January 8, 1862, AMA.

63. James M. McPherson, *The Negro's Civil War: How American Negroes Felt and Acted During the War for the Union* (New York: Vintage, 1965), 119.

64. John Wool to Peter H. Watson, April 8, 1862, JWP.

65. John Oliver to Simon Jocelyn, June 2 and July 27, 1862, AMA. For a description of the scene, see Betty Mansfield, "That Fateful Class: Black Teachers of Virginia's Freedmen, 1861–62" (PhD diss., Catholic University of America, 1980): 86–87, and De Boer, "The Role of Afro-Americans," 249.

66. Claim of Arthur Foreman, March 13, 1871, SCC; Fischer, *African Founders*, 635.

67. Claim of Warren White, September 8, 1871, SCC. See also Amanda Kleintop, "Networks of Resistance: Black Virginians Remember Civil War Loyalties" (honors thesis, University of Richmond, 2011).

68. Lewis Lockwood to American Missionary Association, June 2, 1864, AMA.

69. *American Missionary*, October 1861; *Union Primer; or, First Book for Children* (Philadelphia: American Sunday-School Union, 1837), 5–15.

70. John Oliver to Simon Jocelyn, July 27, 1862, AMA.

3. Away in Dixie Land

1. William Still, *The Underground Railroad: A Record of Facts, Authentic Narrative, Letters, Etc.* (Philadelphia: Porter & Coates, 1871), 151. For a vivid description of the Wilmington docks, see David S. Cecelski, *The Fire of Freedom: Abraham Galloway & the Slaves' Civil War* (Chapel Hill: University of North Carolina Press, 2012), 13–18.

2. *New National Era*, September 22, 1870; John Richard Dennett, *The South as It Is: 1865–1866* (1965; repr., Athens: University of Georgia Press, 1986), 151.

3. Cecelski, *Fire of Freedom*, 50–51. This book has done the most complete job of excavating Galloway's extraordinary story from primary documents.

4. Brigitte Fielder, Cassander Smith, and Derrick R. Spires, "*Weekly Anglo-African* and the *Pine and Palm*," *Just Teach One: Early African American Print*, no. 4 (2018): 2–4.

5. *Pine and Palm*, March 16, 1861.

6. *Anglo-African*, January 6, 1863. See also Debra Jackson, "A Black Journalist in Civil War Virginia," *Virginia Magazine of History and Biography* 116, no. 1 (2008): 45.

7. *Anglo-African*, December 26, 1863.

8. Jackson, "A Black Journalist," 53.

9. *Anglo-African*, December 26, 1863.

10. Mary Frances Armstrong and Helen Wilhelmina Ludlow, *Hampton and Its Students. By Two of Its Teachers* (New York: G.P. Putnam's Sons, 1874), 112.

11. David Chuber, "Field Fortifications During the American Civil War: A Tactical Problem" (master's thesis, U.S. Army Command and General Staff College, Fort Leavenworth, Kansas, 1996), 37.

12. Ibid. The Minié ball, which shattered bones and destroyed internal organs, was the invention of Claude-Étienne Minié, a French captain who later supervised a Remington Arms Company factory in Ilion, New York.

13. Dennis Hart Mahan, *A Treatise on Field Fortifications* (New York: John Wiley, 1861), 20, 44.

14. Earl J. Hess, *Field Armies and Fortifications in the Civil War: The Eastern Campaigns, 1861–1864* (Chapel Hill: University of North Carolina Press, 2006), 28–29, 42.

15. Leon F. Litwack, *Been in the Storm So Long: The Aftermath of Slavery* (New York: Knopf, 1979), 100; Amy Murrell Taylor, *Embattled Freedom: Journeys Through the Civil War's Slave Refugee Camps* (Chapel Hill: University of North Carolina Press, 2018), 39–40. *American Missionary*, February 1862; *Boston Journal*, June 7, 1861.

16. *Pine and Palm*, August 31, 1861; *Pine and Palm*, September 28, 1861; *Chicago Tribune*, December 30, 1861.

17. Thomas R. Flagel, "The Fortress War: Effect of Union Fortifications in the Western Theater of the U.S. Civil War" (PhD diss., Middle Tennessee State University, 2016), 70.

18. McPherson, *The Negro's Civil War*, 145.

19. *New-York Commercial Advertiser*, September 3, 1861.

20. John Wool to John A. Dix, September 16, 1861, JWP; OR, vol. 1, 775, November 1, 1861.

21. *Pine and Palm*, October 5, 1861.

22. John Wool to George McClellan, March 12, 1862, JWP.

23. *American Missionary*, December 1861.

24. *American Missionary*, November 1861.

25. Brenda E. Stevenson, *What Is Slavery?* (Malden, MA: Polity Press, 2015), 15.

26. *Pine and Palm*, September 28, 1861.

4. The Ghosts of 1619

1. Lyon Gardiner Tyler, ed., *Narratives of Early Virginia* (New York: C. Scribner's Sons, 1907), 10.

2. Ibid., 16.

3. Ibid., 11. Confusingly, John Smith named another bit of land "Point Comfort" the following year, an island off the Middle Peninsula, which came to be called New Point Comfort.

4. Arthur Charles Bevan, "Geologic Ancestry of the York-James Peninsula," *Virginia Journal of Science* 8, no. 1 (1957): 19–34. See also O.F. Evans, "The Origin of Spits, Bars, and Related Structures," *Journal of Geology* 50, no. 7 (October/November 1942): 846–65.

5. John Smith, *The Complete Works of Captain John Smith, 1580–1631*, vol. 1 (Chapel Hill: University of North Carolina Press, 2011), 37.

6. George Percy, *Observations Gathered out of a Discourse of the Plantation of the Southern Colony in Virginia by the English, 1606* (London: 1608).

7. "Instructions Given by Way, Etc.," reprinted in Ed Southern, ed., *The Jamestown Adventure: Accounts of the Virginia Colony, 1605–1614* (Winston-Salem, NC: John F. Blair, 2004), 11.

8. C.W. Poag et al., "The Chesapeake Bay Bolide Impact—a Convulsive Event in Atlantic Coastal Plain Evolution," *Sedimentary Geology* 108 (1997): 45–90. See also W.B. Rogers, "Infusorial Deposit of Virginia in the Fort Monroe Artesian Well," *The Virginias* 3, no. 10 (1882): 151–52.

9. John Smith, *The Journals of Captain John Smith* (National Geographic, 2007), 57; Percy, *Observations*, 21.

10. Percy, *Observations*, 175.

11. "Instructions for the Virginia Colony," 1606.

12. Robert Ralston Cawley, "Shakespeare's Use of the Voyagers in *The Tempest*," *PMLA* 41, no. 3 (September 1926): 688–726.

13. Ibid.

14. Everyone in the Roanoke colony disappeared, with the single enigmatic word *CROATOAN* carved into a tree trunk, left as a message for the resupply vessel arriving five years later. Raleigh had since lost his royal charter and been imprisoned in the Tower of London for conspiring against Elizabeth's successor, James I. See also Ben Jonson et al., *Eastward Hoe* (Boston: D.C. Heath and Co, 1903), 72.

15. *The Tempest*, Act II, scene i.

16. Ferrar Papers, Document 151. Transcription in Susan Myra Kingsbury, ed., *Records of the Virginia Company*, vol. 3 (Washington, DC: Government Printing Office, 1933), 241–48.

17. Alonso de Sandoval, *Treatise on Slavery: Selections from De Instauranda Aethiopum Salute* (1627), 57.

18. John Pory to Sir Dudley Carelton, September 30, 1619, in Kingsbury, *Records of the Virginia Company*, 219–22. See also Engel Sluiter, "New Light on the '20. and Odd Negroes' Arriving in Virginia, August 1619," *William and Mary Quarterly* 54, no. 2 (April 1997): 395–98.

19. Robert Rich to Nathaniel Rich, February 22, 1617, quoted in Robert Rich, *The Rich Papers: Letters from Bermuda, 1615–1646*, ed. Vernon A. Ives (Toronto: University of Toronto Press, 1984), 25.

20. Virginia Bernhard, *A Tale of Two Colonies: What Really Happened in Virginia and Bermuda* (Columbia: University of Missouri Press, 2011), 172–73. Rolfe had mentioned the arrival of the "20. and odd Negroes" at Old Point Comfort almost casually, as if trying to slip the concept into the conversation without attracting much notice. He had a personal interest to

protect as the biggest grower of the lucrative cash crop and as an "ardent smoker" of tobacco himself, as well as a family complication. The "Cape Merchant" he mentioned as one of the buyers was William Pierce, who had become his new father-in-law. After the death of Pocahontas on foreign shores, Rolfe had returned to the colony and married twenty-five-year-old Jane Pierce. A passenger on the *Treasurer*—a woman known as Angela—was listed in a muster roll six years later as a "servant" in the comparatively luxurious home of William Pierce, not five hundred yards from the site of the first rickety palisade fort at Jamestown.

21. Smith, *The Complete Works*, 468.

22. Richard Jobson, *The Golden Trade* (London, 1623), 112; Michael J. Guasco, "Settling with Slavery: Human Bondage in the Early Anglo-Atlantic World," in *Envisioning an English Empire*, ed. Robert Appelbaum and John Wood Sweet (Philadelphia: University of Pennsylvania Press, 2005), 237; *Holinshed's Chronicles of England, Scotland, Ireland*, vol. 1 (London: 1577), 25.

23. Richard Hakluyt, "Inducements to the Liking of the Voyage Intended Towards Virginia in 40. and 42. Degrees of Latitude" (1585).

24. John C. Coombs, "'Others Not Christians in the Service of the English': Interpreting the Status of Africans and African Americans in Early Virginia," *Virginia Magazine of History and Biography* 127, no. 3 (2019): 213–38.

25. 1 Timothy 6:6–19; John Donne, "A Sermon Preached to the Honorable Company of the Virginian Plantation" (London: A. Mat., 1622).

26. Bernhard, *A Tale of Two Colonies*, 170–71.

27. Pory to Carelton, September 30, 1619, in Kingsbury, *Records of the Virginia Company*, 219–22.

28. Quoted in J.H. Elliott, *Empires of the Atlantic World* (New Haven, CT: Yale University Press, 2020), 27. See also David Hackett Fischer, *Albion's Seed: Four British Folkways in America* (New York: Oxford University Press, 1989), 357.

29. William Thorndale, "The Virginia Census of 1619," *Virginia Magazine of Genealogy* 33, no. 3 (Summer 1995): 60–161. See also Fischer, *Albion's Seed*, 212.

30. William Cabel Bruce, *John Randolph of Roanoke, 1773–1833*, vol. 1 (New York: G. P. Putnam and Sons, 1922), 8. See also Fischer, *Albion's Seed*, 220, 377.

31. Winthrop D. Jordan, *White over Black: American Attitudes Toward the Negro, 1550–1812* (Chapel Hill: University of North Carolina Press, 1968), 50.

32. Anthony S. Parent Jr., *Foul Means: The Formation of a Slave Society in Virginia, 1660–1740* (Chapel Hill: University of North Carolina Press, 2003), 56; Fischer, *African Founders*, 296.

33. Quoted in Richard S. Dunn, *Sugar and Slaves: The Rise of the Planter Class in the English West Indies, 1624–1713* (Chapel Hill: University of North Carolina Press, 1972), 77.

34. Jordan, *White over Black*, xxiii. Jordan originally used the term "unthinking decision" to refer to slavery's growth; later scholars such as Peter H. Wood came to prefer the phrase "terrible transformation." See Peter H. Wood, *Strange New Land: African Americans 1617–1776* (New York: Oxford University Press, 1996).

35. James Curtis Ballagh, *A History of Slavery in Virginia* (Baltimore: Johns Hopkins Press, 1902), 46–47; Fischer, *African Founders*, 300.

36. Parent, *Foul Means*, 42–44.

37. Annette Gordon-Reed, *The Hemingses of Monticello: An American Family* (New York: W.W. Norton, 2008), 44.

38. *Journals of the House of Burgesses of Virginia*, 1619–1776, vol. 11, 197. See also Parent, *Foul Means*, 224; Elliott, *Empires of the Atlantic World*, 104.

39. James Horn, *A Land as God Made It: Jamestown and the Birth of America* (New York: Basic Books, 2005), 248; Edmund S. Morgan, *American Slavery, American Freedom* (New York: W.W. Norton, 1975), 307; William Byrd II, *The Correspondence of the Three William Byrds of Westover, Virginia, 1684–1776*, ed. Marion Tinling (Charlottesville: Virginia Historical Society, 1977), 355.

40. Fischer, *Albion's Seed*, 389. Byrd's father had used one hundred Black headrights to accumulate land in the 1690s. Parent, *Foul Means*, 44.

41. Quoted in David Herbert Donald, *Lincoln* (New York: Simon & Schuster, 1996), 166.

42. Richard Kreitner, *Break It Up: Secession, Division, and the Secret History of America's Imperfect Union* (New York: Little Brown, 2020), 45. See also "Jonathan Boucher: An American Loyalist," *Maryland Historical Magazine* (Winter 1930).

43. Quoted in James Oakes, *Freedom National: The Destruction of Slavery in the United States, 1861–1865* (New York: W.W. Norton, 2012), 3.

44. *Records of the Federal Convention*, August 29, 1787; Noah Feldman, *The Broken Constitution: Lincoln, Slavery and the Refounding of America* (New York: Farrar, Straus and Giroux, 2021), 7; Oakes, *Freedom National*, xi.

45. Kreitner, *Break It Up*, 85–86; Dennis C. Rasmussen, *Fears of a Setting Sun: The Disillusionment of America's Founders* (Princeton, NJ: Princeton University Press, 2021), 199.

46. Fischer, *African Founders*, 102.

47. Quoted in Gabriel Stepto, *The African American Years* (New York: Scribner, 2009), 153. See also Gordon-Reed, *The Hemingses of Monticello*, 124, for a perspective on how the conduct of ordinary life at Jefferson's estate suggests he did not truly believe this infamous passage in his own book.

48. Gene Williamson, *Of the Sea and Skies: Historic Hampton and Its Times* (Bowie, MD: Heritage Books, 1993), 166; William Stanhope Lovell, *Personal Narrative of Events from 1799 to 1815* (London: William Allen & Co., 1879), 152.

49. Cochrane's statements are quoted in Alan Taylor, *The Internal Enemy: Slavery and War in Virginia, 1772–1832* (New York: W.W. Norton, 2013), 209–13.

50. Dunmore's proclamation is quoted in, among other places, Glenn David Brasher, *The Peninsula Campaign and the Necessity of Emancipation: African Americans and the Fight for Freedom* (Chapel Hill: University Press of North Carolina, 2012), 11. George Washburn Smalley, *Anglo-American Memories* (New York: G.P. Putnam's Sons, 1911), 109.

51. *United Service Journal* (London: Henry Colburn, 1840), 455; Alvan Stewart, *Writings and Speeches of Alvan Stewart on Slavery*, ed. Luther Rawson Marsh (New York: A.B. Burdick, 1860), 372. See also Taylor, *The Internal Enemy*, 302–3.

52. Jamie W. Moore, *The Fortifications Board, 1816–1828, and the Definition of National Security* (Charleston: The Citadel, 1981), 24; "Information in Relation to the Progress of the Board of Engineers, in the Selection of Sites of Fortifications," February 15, 1821, U.S. Army Corps of Engineers; Robert Arthur, *History of Fort Monroe* (Fort Monroe, VA: Coast Artillery School Press, 1928), 26.

53. John R. Weaver II, *A Legacy in Brick and Stone: American Coastal Defense Forts of the Third System, 1816–1867* (McLean, VA: Redoubt Press, 2018), 16.

54. Harrison, "Simon Bernard and the American System," in *America: The Middle Period; Essays in Honor of Bernard Mayo*, ed. John B. Boles (Charlottesville, VA: University Press of Virginia, 1973), 146; William H. Carter, "Bvt. Maj. Gen. Simon Bernard," *Professional Memoirs, Corps of Engineers, United States Army, and Engineer Department at Large* 5, no. 21 (May–June, 1913): 306–14.

55. William Henry Stewart, *A History of Norfolk County, Virginia and Representative Citizens* (Chicago: Biographical Publishing Company, 1902), 78.

56. *Register of Debates in Congress*, January 25, 1826, 1150–70; "Records of the Chief of Ordnance," National Archives, RG 156, Entry 1231.

57. Edgar Allan Poe to John Allan, December 1, 1828, in *The Letters of Edgar Allan Poe*, vol. 1 (New York: Gordian Press, 1966), 65; J.S. Buckingham, *The Slaves States*, vol. 2 (London: Fisher, Son & Co., 1842), 476.

58. Charles Wyllys Betts, *Visitors' Hand-Book of Old Point Comfort, Va. and Vicinity* (Hampton, VA: Press of the Hampton Institute, 1883), 9.

59. Marion L. Starkey, *The First Plantation: History of Hampton and Elizabeth City County, Virginia, 1607–1887* (Hampton, VA: Hampton Printing and Publishing House, 1936), 74–75; Mary Frances Armstrong and Helen Wilhelmina Ludlow, *Hampton and Its Students. By Two of Its Teachers* (New York: G.P. Putnam's Sons, 1874), 10; Glenn David Brasher, *The Peninsula Campaign and the Necessity of Emancipation: African Americans and the Fight for Freedom* (Chapel Hill: University Press of North Carolina, 2012), 16–17. A vivid description of antebellum Hampton can be found in Adam Goodheart, *1861: The Civil War Awakening* (New York: Vintage, 2011), 303–12.

60. Alice Matthews Erickson, *A Chronicle of Civil War Hampton, Virginia* (Mount Pleasant, SC: Arcadia Publishing, 2014), 25; Howard P. Nash, *Stormy Petrel: The Life and Times of Benjamin F. Butler, 1818–1893* (Rutherford, NJ: Fairleigh Dickinson University Press, 1969), 76; Edward Lillie Pierce, "Contrabands at Fortress Monroe," *The Atlantic*, November 1861; Starkey, *The First Plantation*, 76.

61. Anne MacVicar Grant, *Memoirs of an American Lady: With Sketches of Manners and Scenes in America as They Existed Previous to the Revolution* (London: Longman, Hurst, Rees, and Orme, 1808), 41.

62. Robert F. Engs, *Freedom's First Generation: Black Hampton, Virginia, 1861–1890* (Philadelphia: University of Pennsylvania Press, 1979), 10. When a master near Hampton flogged one of his slaves to death in 1854, the *Norfolk Daily News* called it a "horrible crime" and the courts issued a warrant for his arrest. See William A. Link, *Roots of Secession: Slavery and Politics in Antebellum Virginia* (Chapel Hill: University of North Carolina Press, 2003), 42.

63. Engs, *Freedom's First Generation*, 9.

64. Lockwood, *Mary S. Peake*, 15; Kay Ann Taylor, "Mary S. Peake and Charlotte L. Forten," *Journal of Negro Education* 74, no. 2 (Spring 2005): 128.

65. Charles L. Perdue Jr., Thomas E. Barden, and Robert K. Phillips, eds., *The Weevils in the Wheat: Interviews with Virginia Ex-slaves* (Charlottesville: University Press of Virginia, 1976), 84.

66. Ibid., 115.

67. *America Missionary*, September 1871.

68. *Virginia Argus*, September 25, 1816.

69. Ira Berlin, *Generations of Captivity: A History of African American Slaves* (Cambridge, MA: The Belknap Press of Harvard University Press, 2003), 168.

70. Frederick Law Olmsted, *The Cotton Kingdom: A Traveller's Observations on Cotton and Slavery in the American Slave States* (London: Mason Brothers, 1861), 112; Charles Ball, *Slavery in the United States: A Narrative* (Lewistown, PA: John W. Shugert, 1836), 24; Federal Writers Project, *Slave Narratives: A Folk History of Slavery in the United States* (Washington, DC: Library of Congress, 1941), 70.

71. Elizabeth Keckly, *Behind the Scenes: Or, Thirty Years a Slave and Four Years in the White House* (New York: G.W. Carleton & Co., 1868), 28–29.

72. Calvin Schermerhorn, *Unrequited Toil: A History of United States Slavery* (Cambridge: Cambridge University Press, 2018), 40; the owner is quoted in Taylor, *The Internal Enemy*, 65.

73. Ball, *Slavery in the United States*, 60.

74. Berlin, *Generations of Captivity*, 9, 178.

75. Taylor, *The Internal Enemy*, 8.

76. Jesse Torrey, *American Slave Trade* (London: J.M. Cobbett, 1822), 23–24.

77. Sharon Ann Murphy, *Banking on Slavery: Financing Southern Expansion in the Antebellum United States* (Chicago: University of Chicago Press, 2023), 3–5; Edwin Burrows and Mike Wallace, *Gotham: A History of New York City to 1898* (Oxford: Oxford University Press, 2000), 865.

78. Schermerhorn, *Unrequited Toil*, 2. See also Kreitner, *Break It Up*, 262.

79. Quoted in Taylor, *The Internal Enemy*, 41.

80. *Southern Planter*, February 1852.

81. An older school of economic historiography, anchored in the thinking of John Stuart Mill and Adam Smith, held that the market revolution of the 1830s and the 1840s, with its associated railroads, factories, and steam engines, put slavery on a collision course with modernity. That scholarship held that an inefficient system perpetuated by the Southern elite had become an anachronism by the time of the Civil War. See Thomas N. Bonner, "Civil War Historians and the 'Needless War' Doctrine," *Journal of the History of Ideas* 17, no. 2 (April 1956): 193–216, and also Oakes, *Freedom National*, xv. But more recent scholarship has conclusively disproved this idea. Slaveholders had a market revolution of their own, adopting innovations like bank credit, insurance, steam power, management techniques, wheat reapers, telegraphs, and international shipping lanes to their own ends. As Daniel Rood has written, "Their

travels, their translations, and their conscious reworking of racial ideologies in the plantation archipelago deepened the Atlantic economy's dependence on forced labor after a few revolutionary decades when it seemed as though the institution of slavery might be destroyed." See Daniel B. Rood, *The Reinvention of Atlantic Slavery: Technology, Labor, Race, and Capitalism in the Greater Caribbean* (Oxford: Oxford University Press, 2017). See also Edward E. Baptist, *The Half Has Never Been Told: Slavery and the Making of American Capitalism* (New York: Basic Books, 2014), and Sven Beckert, *Empire of Cotton: A Global History* (New York: Knopf, 2014). The prevalence of hiring out in the mid-Atlantic was a boon to Virginia's industrializing economy and kept it formidable up until the outbreak of the war. See John J. Zaborney, *Slaves for Hire: Renting Enslaved Laborers in Antebellum Virginia* (Baton Rouge: Louisiana State University Press, 2012), 165.

5. Southern Ardor

1. George H. Reese, ed., *Proceedings of the Virginia State Convention of 1861, February 13–May 1* (Richmond: Virginia State Library, 1965), 1:410.

2. Henry Mayer, *All on Fire: William Lloyd Garrison and the Abolition of Slavery* (New York: St. Martin's Press, 1998), 143.

3. Charles Dickens, *The Letters of Charles Dickens*, ed. Madeline House and Graham Storey (Berkeley, CA: Clarendon Press, 1974), 118; William A. Link, *Roots of Secession: Slavery and Politics in Antebellum Virginia* (Chapel Hill: University of North Carolina Press, 2003), 20–21; *Lynchburg Virginian*, September 28, 1852.

4. Frederick Law Olmsted, *The Papers of Frederick Law Olmsted*, vol. 2, *Slavery and the South, 1852–1857* (Baltimore: Johns Hopkins University Press, 1977), 235.

5. Joanne B. Freeman, *The Field of Blood: Violence in Congress and the Road to Civil War* (New York: Farrar, Straus and Giroux, 2018), 38, 70, 290. In such a volatile atmosphere, prodigious drinking among members only put fuel on the fire. Committee rooms featured sideboards of liquor. A bar nicknamed Hole in the Wall operated behind the Senate post office inside the U.S. Capitol. See also Drew Gilpin Faust, *James Henry Hammond and the Old South: A Design for Mastery* (Baton Rouge: Louisiana State University Press, 1985), 355.

6. James M. McPherson, *Battle Cry of Freedom: The Civil War Era* (Oxford: Oxford University Press, 1988), 178.

7. William H. Seward, *An Autobiography*, ed. Frederick W. Seward (New York: Derby and Miller, 1891), 268.

8. *The Atlantic*, October 1860, quoted in Adam Goodheart, *1861: The Civil War Awakening* (New York: Vintage, 2011), 50.

9. Charles B. Dew, *Apostles of Disunion: Southern Secession Commissioners and the Causes of the Civil War* (Charlottesville: University of Virginia Press, 2001), 78; Horace Greeley, *A Political Text-Book from 1860* (New York: Tribune Association, 1860), 35; Jefferson Davis, *The Speeches of the Hon. Jefferson Davis* (Baltimore: John Murphy & Co, 1860), 56; Joan E. Cashin, *First Lady of the Confederacy: Varina Davis's Civil War* (Cambridge, MA: Harvard University Press, 2006), 93.

10. Paul Starobin, *Madness Rules the Hour: Charleston, 1860 and the Mania for War* (New York: PublicAffairs, 2017), 208.

11. Varina Davis, *Jefferson Davis: Ex-president of the Confederate States of America*, vol. 2 (New York: Belford Company, 1890), 31.

12. *Journal of the State Convention and Ordinances and Resolutions Adopted in January* 1861 (Jackson, MS: E. Barksdale State Printer, 1861), 87.

13. Ernest Winkler, ed., *The Journal of the Secession Convention of Texas* (Austin, TX: Austin Printing Co., 1912), 61.

14. Starobin, *Madness Rules the Hour*, 34; Henry L. Dawes, "Washington the Winter Before the War," *The Atlantic*, August 1893.

15. Daniel W. Crofts, *Reluctant Confederates: Upper South Unionists in the Secession Crisis* (Chapel Hill: University of North Carolina Press, 1993), 46; *Wheeling Daily Intelligencer*, April 20, 1861; David Herbert Donald, *Lincoln* (New York: Simon & Schuster, 1996), 290; also see John Minor Botts, *The Great Rebellion: Its Secret History, Rise, Progress, and Disastrous Failure* (New York: Harper & Bros., 1866), 194–96, for another account of the proffered bargain over Fort Sumter.

16. George S Boutwell, *Reminiscences of Sixty Years of Public Affairs* (New York: McClure, Phillips & Co., 1902), 270; Goodheart, *1861*, 87; Gary May, *John Tyler* (New York: Times Books, 2004), 141.

17. Quoted in the *Cincinnati Commercial*, July 19, 1861, the emphasis was in the original; see also Ernest B. Furguson, *Freedom Rising: Washington in the Civil* War (New York: Alfred A. Knopf, 2004), 77.

18. William W. Freehling and Craig M. Simpson, eds., *Showdown in Virginia: The 1861 Convention and the Fate of the Union* (Charlottesville: University of Virginia Press, 2010), 196–97.

19. Link, *Roots of Secession*, 187.

20. James I. Robertson Jr., "The Virginia State Convention of 1861," in *Virginia at War 1861*, ed. William C. Davis and James I. Robertson (Lexington: University Press of Kentucky, 2005), 9–13.

21. Ruffin exaggerated his role a bit. The first shot, fired an hour before dawn, was a readying signal shot touched off by Lt. Henry Farley from Fort Johnson.

22. J.B. Jones, *A Rebel War Clerk's Diary: At the Confederate States Capital, April 1861–July 1863*, vol. 1 (Philadelphia: J.B. Lippincott, 1866), 19; Elizabeth R. Varon, *Southern Lady, Yankee Spy: The True Story of Elizabeth Van Lew, a Union Agent in the Heart of the Confederacy* (Oxford: Oxford University Press, 2003), 35; Link, *Roots of Secession*, 239.

23. *Philadelphia Inquirer*, April 29, 1861. John Minor Botts, an ardent Virginia Unionist, was convinced of Henry Wise's sincerity on wanting to invade Washington. See Botts, *Great Rebellion*, 115.

24. Link, *The Roots of Secession*, 240–43; Varon, *Southern Lady*, 46. "Emotionalism, personal pride, a volatile atmosphere—all seemed to have merged into a highly inflammable situation," wrote James I. Robertson Jr. See Robertson, "The Virginia State Convention of 1861," 9. Near the end of the proceedings, Wise was sick from pneumonia and Tyler proclaimed himself too exhausted to speak. By then Tyler was suffering from dysentery and taking daily doses of quinine "spiked with a jigger of whiskey." See May, *John Tyler*, 137.

25. Marion L. Starkey, *The First Plantation: History of Hampton and Elizabeth City County, Virginia, 1607–1887* (Hampton, VA: Hampton Printing and Publishing House, 1936), 78; George Benjamin West, *When the Yankees Came: Civil War and Reconstruction on the Virginia Peninsula* (Richmond: Dietz Press, 1977), 21.

26. Edward Lillie Pierce, "The Contrabands at Fortress Monroe," *The Atlantic*, November 1861. John G. Gammons, *The Third Massachusetts Volunteer Regiment in the War of the Rebellion, 1861–1863* (Providence, RI: Snow & Farnam Co., 1906), 194.

27. Pierce, "The Contrabands at Fortress Monroe."

28. George William Curtis, "Theodore Winthrop," *The Atlantic*, August 1861.

29. George Templeton Strong, *The Diary of George Templeton Strong*, ed. Allan Nevins and Milton Halsey Thomas (New York: Macmillan, 1952), 192; Charles C. Nott, *The Coming Contraband: A Reason Against the Emancipation Proclamation* (New York: G.P. Putnam, 1862). The evolution of wartime practices had been marked by the 1625 publication of *De jure belli ac pacis*, or "the law of war and peace," by the Dutch lawyer Hugo Grotius. Foreign princes who seize private goods such as livestock and farm tools are guilty of "manifest Acts of Tyranny," he said. See Grotius, *De jure belli ac pacis*, 343n. Later military thinkers made a more fine-grained argument by distinguishing categories of *absolute* contraband—that is, obvious weap-

ons of war like gunships, muskets, and cannons whose seizure was imperative—versus *conditional* contraband, or goods that could be used to assist in warfare, such as crates of food, cannisters of fuel, civilian vehicles, and the like. Governments were advised to clear up confusion by circulating lists of what they intended to claim. For an extended discussion, see Neill H. Alford, *Modern Economic Warfare* (Washington, DC: Government Printing Office), 1967, 364–68. The paper realities of bureaucrats were often different, of course, from what happened when commanders made decisions on the spot. The lawyer Henry Wheaton made an assessment after the War of 1812 and commented: "There is some difficulty in reconciling the different authorities, which are extremely discordant and at variance with reason and justice." Henry Wheaton, *A Digest of the Law of Maritime Captures and Prizes* (New York: R. M'Dermut & D.D. Arden, 1815), 175.

30. Burrus M. Carnahan, *Act of Justice: Lincoln's Emancipation Proclamation and the Law of War* (Lexington: University Press of Kentucky, 2007), 6.

31. Orville Hickman Browning, *The Diary of Orville Hickman Browning*, vol. 1, *1850–1864*, ed. Theodore Calvin Pease and James G. Randall (Springfield: Illinois State Historical Library, 1925), 555. William F. Moore and Jane Ann Moore, *Collaborators for Emancipation: Abraham Lincoln and Owen Lovejoy* (Champaign: University of Illinois Press, 2014), 114.

32. *New York Times*, May 30, 1861; *The South*, May 28, 1861; OR, vol. 114, 755.

33. *New York Evening Post*, quoted in *Douglass Monthly*, October 1861, 536; *Missouri Daily Republican*, September 5, 1861.

34. Abraham Lincoln to Orville Browning, September 22, 1861, in AL, vol. 4, 532; Joshua Speed to Abraham Lincoln, September 1, 1863, AL, vol. 4, 506.

35. Jessie Benton Frémont, *The Letters of Jessie Benton Frémont*, ed. Pamela Herr and Mary Lee Spence (Champaign: University of Illinois Press, 1993), 266; James A. Rawley, *A Lincoln Dialogue* (Lincoln: University of Nebraska Press, 2014), 155. Jessie—the polymathic daughter of a U.S. senator—took her husband's reply to the White House herself, traveling forty-eight hours by train and arriving strung out. She asked when the president could see her, and he responded with a note sent through an aide: *Now. A Lincoln*. He then made her wait a bit in the dining room, before entering through a side door with a tight smile. She tried to make a case that her husband's bold stroke would head off the British momentum toward diplomatic recognition of the Confederacy.

Lincoln responded with an expression she described as "sneering" and without any desire to listen. "You are quite the female politician," he told her, adding that her husband "never should have dragged the Negro into the war. It is a war for a great national object and the Negro has nothing to do with it." Lincoln recalled the meeting differently and more in his own favor, saying he "had to exercise all the awkward tact I have to avoid quarreling with her." He would later acknowledge Frémont's far-sightedness in the matter, even as he questioned the timing and the politics. See John Hay, *Letters*, 134. As it happened, the official sent out to Missouri to gather evidence used against Frémont was Frank Blair, the nephew of Postmaster General Montgomery Blair, Benjamin Butler's chief ally in the administration.

36. *Liberator*, December 20, 1861, quoted in Louis P. Masur, *Lincoln's Hundred Days: The Emancipation Proclamation and the War for the Union* (Cambridge, MA: Harvard University Press, 2012), 33.

37. John Zimm, ed., *This Wicked Rebellion: Wisconsin Civil War Soldiers Write Home* (Madison: Wisconsin Historical Society Press, 2012), 118.

38. *New York Times*, August 31, 1861.

39. Zimm, *This Wicked Rebellion*, 129–30, 117. Emphasis in the original.

40. *New-York Tribune*, June 25, 1861; William Howard Russell, *My Diary North and South* (New York: Knopf, 1988), 246.

41. The Wisconsin soldier is quoted in Chandra Manning, *What This Cruel War Was Over; Soldiers, Slavery and the Civil War* (New York: Vintage, 2007), 45. Rice C. Bull is quoted in Bennett Parten, *Somewhere Toward Freedom: Sherman's March and the Story of America's Largest Emancipation* (New York: Simon and Schuster, 2025), 81. Parten notes there was an undeniable element of coercion present when Union soldiers demanded campfire entertainment from freed people.

42. Rebecca E. Zietlow, *The Forgotten Emancipator: James Mitchell Ashley and the Ideological Origins of Reconstruction* (Cambridge: Cambridge University Press, 2017), 88.

43. *New-York Tribune*, May 31, 1861.

44. *New York Times*, June 12, 1861.

45. Quoted in David S. Cecelski, *The Fire of Freedom: Abraham Galloway and the Slaves' Civil War* (Chapel Hill: University of North Carolina Press, 2012), 49; Allan Pinkerton, *The Spy of the Rebellion* (New York: G.W. Dillingham Co., 1890), 346.

46. Reprinted in the *Andover* (MA) *Advertiser*, July 13, 1861.

47. *New York Times*, June 12, 1861.

48. Pierce, "The Contrabands at Fortress Monroe."

49. "General Butler's Order for Attack on Big Bethel," POC, 132–33; Butler to Mrs. Winthrop, POC, 137; G.K. Warren to Butler, June 15, 1861, POC, 144–47.

50. *New York Times*, June 27, 1861

51. *Baltimore Republican*, June 12, 1861.

52. *Charleston Mercury*, June 15, 1861; R. Archer to Edmund Ruffin, May 31, 1842, *Journal of the House of Delegates of the Commonwealth of Virginia*, 1842, 37. The recipient of this report, Edmund Ruffin, would go on to fire one of the first shots of the Civil War at Charleston, SC.

53. Benjamin Butler to Montgomery Blair, August 11, 1861, POC, 207.

54. Benjamin Butler to Sarah Butler, August 14, 1861, POC, 215.

55. Paul Finkelman, "The Summer of '62," in *Congress and the People's Contest: The Conduct of the Civil War*, ed. Paul Finkelman and Donald R. Kennon (Athens: Ohio University Press, 2018), 88.

56. John Syrett, *The Civil War Confiscation Acts: Failing to Reconstruct the South* (New York: Fordham University Press, 2005), 3–5.

57. James Oakes, *Freedom National: The Destruction of Slavery in the United States, 1861–1865* (New York: W.W. Norton, 2012), 135.

58. Quoted in Masur, *Lincoln's Hundred Days*, 22.

59. AL, vol. 5, 329.

60. *Morning Express* (Buffalo, NY), August 3, 1861; *Brooklyn Daily Eagle*, August 7, 1861; Herman Belz, *Abraham Lincoln, Constitutionalism, and Equal Rights in the Civil War Era* (New York: Fordham University Press, 1998), 115; Ira Berlin, "Who Freed the Slaves? Emancipation and Its Meaning," in *Union and Emancipation: Essays on Politics and Race in the Civil War Era*, ed. David W. Blight and Brooks R. Simpson (Kent, OH: Kent State University Press, 1997), 292. Wisconsin soldier quoted in Zimm, *This Wicked Rebellion*, 123. See also Finkelman, "The Summer of '62."

61. John Beatty, *The Citizen-Soldier; or, Memoirs of a Volunteer* (Cincinnati, OH: Wilstach, Baldwin, 1879), 11. Halleck quoted in Elizabeth R. Varon, *Armies of Deliverance: A New History of the Civil War* (Chapel Hill: University of North Carolina Press, 2019), 36. See also William H. Freehling, *The South vs. the South: How Anti-Confederate Southerners Shaped the Course of the Civil War* (Oxford: Oxford University Press, 2002), 95–96.

62. *Burlington Weekly Free Press*, December 13, 1861; *New York Times*, also quoted in Masur, *Lincoln's Last Speech: Wartime Reconstruction and the Crisis of Reunion* (New York: Oxford University Press, 2015), 144.

63. Godfrey Weitzel to Benjamin Butler, October 29, 1862, quoted in James Parton, *General Butler in New Orleans* (Boston: Ticknor and Fields, 1866), 580.

64. *The Liberator*, January 8, 1864. Though Callahan witnessed this crowded scene after emancipation, the description lines up with other accounts of disorganization and suffering in federally occupied zones in the South, even sometimes within formal contraband camps.

65. *Cairo City Gazette*, July 25, 1861; Report of John Eaton, April 29, 1863, HL; *Frank Leslie's Illustrated Newspaper*, September 28, 1861. See also William A. Pitkin, "When Cairo Was Saved for the Union," *Journal of the Illinois State Historical Society* 51, no. 3 (Autumn 1958): 304.

66. Amy Murrell Taylor, *Embattled Freedom: Journeys Through the Civil War's Slave Refugee Camps* (Chapel Hill: University of North Carolina Press, 2018), 94; *Chicago Tribune*, October 7, 1862; Peter Hays, "Way Down in Egypt Land: Conflict and Community in Cairo, Illinois, 1850–1930" (PhD diss., University of Missouri–Columbia, 1996), 175. See also Leslie A. Schwalm, *Emancipation's Diaspora: Race and Reconstruction in the Upper Midwest* (Chapel Hill: University of North Carolina Press, 2009), 76.

67. *Chicago Times*, November 16, 1862; *Quad-City Times*, October 4, 1862; Hays, "Way Down in Egypt Land," 189. See also Alonzo M. Ward, "White Backlash in the Land of Lincoln: The Civil War Years," *Activist History Review*, October 2017, https://activisthistory.com/2017/10/18/white-backlash-in-the-land-of-lincoln-the-civil-war-years/.

68. Louis S. Gerteis, *From Contraband to Freedom: Federal Policy Toward Southern Blacks, 1861–1865* (Westport, CT: Greenwood Press, 1973), 120; Samuel Sawyer et al. to Samuel Curtis, December 29, 1862, Letters Received Relating to Military Discipline & Control, series 22, Headquarters of the Army, RG 108, National Archives and Records Administration. See also *New York Times*, December 7, 1862.

69. *Richmond Dispatch*, November 10, 1863, quoted in Jim Downs, *Sick from Freedom: African-American Illness and Suffering During the Civil War and Reconstruction* (Oxford: Oxford University Press, 2015), 40.

70. *Corinth Chanticleer*, June 12, 1863.

71. Levi Coffin, *Reminiscences of Levi Coffin* (Cincinnati: Robert Clarke & Co., 1880), 634–35.

72. George Carruthers to S.S. Jocelyn, June 12, 1863, NPS. See also *Cincinnati Gazette*, May 11, 1862, for an account of one of these raids.

73. James Alexander to Head of 1st Alabama Infantry C Troop, September 1, 1863, NPS.

74. John Eaton, "Report on Contrabands in the Department of Tennessee," April 29, 1863, NPS; Duckworth to Rosser, John A. Duckworth Papers, State Historical Society of Iowa; Duckworth quoted in "Underground Railroad: Network to Freedom," July 31, 2016, NPS; Timothy B. Smith,

Corinth 1862: Siege, Battle, Occupation (Lawrence: University Press of Kansas, 2012), 290.

75. *American Missionary*, August 1863; Eaton, "Report on Contrabands in the Department of Tennessee." See also Chandra Manning, *Troubled Refuge: Struggling for Freedom in the Civil War* (New York: Vintage Books, 2016), 115.

76. Chandra Manning, "Military Emancipation Before the Emancipation Proclamation," in Finkelman and Kennon, *Congress and the People's Contest*.

77. LeBaron Russell to Edwin Stanton, December 28, 1862, AFIC.

78. *Atlantic Messenger*, June 20, 1861.

79. *Anti-Slavery Standard*, July 13, 1861.

80. *New York Daily Herald*, July 18, 1862.

81. *Janesville Daily Gazette*, August 8, 1861.

82. *Commercial Advertiser*, May 29, 1861.

83. *New York Times*, August 31, 1861.

84. *Chicago Tribune*, June 5, 1861.

6. The Riverman

1. George Templeton Strong, *The Diary of George Templeton Strong*, ed. Allan Nevins and Milton Halsey Thomas (New York: Macmillan, 1952), 279.

2. David Herbert Donald, *Lincoln* (New York: Simon & Schuster, 1996), 332; Charles H Coleman, *Abraham Lincoln and Coles County, Illinois* (New Brunswick, NJ: Scarecrow Press, 1955), 194.

3. Strong, *Diary of George Templeton Strong*, 204.

4. John Hay and John Nicolay, *Abraham Lincoln: A History*, vol. 3 (New York: Century Illustrated Monthly Magazine, 1909), 387. William Howard Russell, *My Diary North and South* (New York: Knopf, 1988), 53. A favorite Lincoln joke involved the English noble who showed disrespect to a portrait of George Washington by hanging it in his toilet room. When Ethan Allen came for a visit, he commented that the placement made sense, for there was nothing that would make "an Englishman Shit so quick as the sight of Genl Washington." Michael Burlingame, *Abraham Lincoln: A Life* (Baltimore: Johns Hopkins University Press, 2013), 54.

5. "Reflections of Lincoln," *The Atlantic*, January 1904; Burlingame, *Lincoln*, 54.

6. Don E. Fehrenbacher and Virginia Fehrenbacher, *Recollected Words of Abraham Lincoln* (Stanford, CA: Stanford University Press, 1996), 452.

7. Abraham Lincoln to Albert Hodges, April 4, 1864, 68; James G. Blaine, *Twenty Years of Congress*, vol. 2 (Norwich: Henry Bill Publishing Company, 1886), 49. James G. Blaine related the story without revealing the name of the friend, though given that Blaine was an enthusiastic Republican supporter of Lincoln in Congress, the possibility exists that the inquisitor was Blaine himself.

8. AL, vol. 1, 12.

9. Blaine, *Twenty Years of Congress*, vol. 2, 49.

10. Richard Hofstadter, "Abraham Lincoln and the Self-Made Myth," in *The American Political Tradition and the Men Who Made It* (New York: Vintage, 1948), 93–136. See also Allen Guelzo, "The Emancipation Proclamation: Bill of Lading or Ticket to Freedom?" Gilder Lehrman Institute of American History, January 24, 2014.

11. *Century Magazine*, June 1900.

12. Ibid. See also Richard Campanella, *Lincoln in New Orleans: The 1828–1831 Flatboat Journeys and Their Place in History* (Lafayette: University of Louisiana at Lafayette Press, 2010), 227.

13. Campanella, *Lincoln in New Orleans*, 241.

14. Ibid., 57.

15. Abraham Lincoln to Mary Speed, September 27, 1841, AL, 52.

16. Abraham Lincoln to Joshua Speed, August 24, 1855, AL, 216.

17. Campanella, *Lincoln in New Orleans*, 62.

18. AL, vol. 1, 638.

19. Thomas Jefferson to Robert Livingston, April 18, 1802, in *Memoir, Correspondence, and Private Papers of Thomas Jefferson*, vol. 3 (London: Henry Colburn and Richard Bentley, 1829), 500.

20. Campanella, *Lincoln in New Orleans*, 90–95.

21. Ibid., 97. As Campanella vividly puts it: "It is safe to say that that same flatboat lumber remains in service today as studs, beams, rafters, and joists in historic New Orleans houses, frozen in place for nearly two centuries after an epic journey from virgin forest, down the Mississippi, to the flatboat wharf." His description of Hewlett's Exchange is on pages 112–17.

22. Ibid., 209.

23. For a convincing dismantling of the Hanks story, see Campanella, *Lincoln in New Orleans*, 207–21.

24. Abraham Lincoln to Alexander Stephens, January 19, 1860, *Uncollected Letters of Abraham Lincoln*, LOC, 128.

25. *Century Illustrated Magazine*, July 1891, 372; Horace Greeley, *Greeley on Lincoln* (New York: Baker & Taylor Company, 1893), 16.

26. AL, vol. 5, 288.

27. AL, 1–9; Garrison quoted in Campanella, *Lincoln in New Orleans*, 227, 242, 240.

28. Gideon Welles, *Diary of Gideon Welles: Secretary of the Navy Under Lincoln and Johnson* (New York: Houghton Mifflin, 1910), 282. See also, *The Century*, January 1890, 43. Campanella saw an unmistakable maritime aspect to this dream, plausibly linked to his early river journeys. "This recurring vision, similar to the sensation of flatboatmen navigating through darkness or mist, never failed to arrest him." Campanella, *Lincoln in New Orleans*, 191.

29. John Hay, *Inside Lincoln's White House: The Complete Civil War Diary of John Hay*, ed. Michael Burlingame and John R. Turner Ettlinger (Carbondale: Southern Illinois University Press, 1999), 19.

30. Henry Clay Whitney, *Lincoln, the President (March 4, 1861–May 3, 1865)*, 25.

31. Hay, *Inside Lincoln's White House*, 13.

32. *Messages and Papers of the President*, ed. James Richardson (Washington, DC: Government Printing Office, 1867), 627.

33. Quoted in Elizabeth D. Leonard, *Benjamin Franklin Butler: A Noisy, Fearless Life* (Chapel Hill: University of North Carolina Press, 2022), 40. Jean Baker, *James Buchanan* (New York: Times Books, 2004), 19, 89.

34. James Buchanan, *The Administration on the Eve of Rebellion* (London: Sampson Low, Son, & Marston, 1865), 10.

35. OR, vol. 1, 126.

36. Baker, *James Buchanan*, 130; Galliard Hunt, "Narrative and Letter of William Henry Trescot Concerning the Negotiations Between South Carolina and President Buchanan in December, 1860," *American Historical Review* 13, no. 3 (April 1908): 544.

37. Baker, *James Buchanan*, 133; Philip Shriver Klein, *President James Buchanan: A Biography* (University Park: Pennsylvania State University Press, 1962), 79.

38. William H. Seward, *An Autobiography*, ed. Frederick W. Seward (New York: Derby and Miller, 1891), 488.

39. Baker, *James Buchanan*, 138; George S. Boutwell, *Reminiscences of Sixty Years of Public Affairs* (New York: McClure, Phillips & Co., 1902), 275.

40. Charles Francis Adams, *The Civil War Diaries*, entry for March 4, 1861, Massachusetts Historical Society, Boston, MA.

41. John Hay, *At Lincoln's Side: John Hay's Civil War Correspondence and Selected Writings* (Carbondale: Southern Illinois University Press, 2006), 119.

42. Paul Finkelman, "The Summer of '62," in *Congress and the People's Contest: The Conduct of the Civil War*, ed. Paul Finkelman and Donald R. Kennon (Athens: Ohio University Press, 2018), 101–2.

43. *Liberator*, October 25, 1861; Henry Mayer, *All on Fire: William Lloyd Garrison and the Abolition of Slavery* (New York: St. Martin's Press, 1998), 531.

44. John C. Calhoun, *Speeches of John C. Calhoun: Delivered in the Congress of the United States from 1811 to the Present Time* (New York: Harper' and Brothers, 1843), 222; *Montgomery Weekly Mail*, October 25, 1862; Ira Berlin et al., "'To Canvass the Nation': The War for Union Becomes a War for Freedom," *Prologue: Journal of the National Archives* 20 (Winter 1988): 237; *Hartford Courant*, April 22, 1862; *New York Herald*, April 15, 1862; *Freeport Weekly Bulletin*, January 16, 1862. See also James Oakes, *Freedom National: The Destruction of Slavery in the United States, 1861–1865* (New York: W.W. Norton, 2012), 307.

45. Allen Thorndike Rice, ed., *Reminiscences of Abraham Lincoln by Distinguished Men of His Time* (New York: North American Review, 1888), 335. See also Daniel Carpenter, *Democracy by Petition: Popular Politics in Transformation, 1790–1870* (Cambridge, MA: Harvard University Press, 2021), 458.

46. *Congressional Globe*, 1862, Part 2, 1896; partially quoted in Louis P. Masur, *Lincoln's Hundred Days: The Emancipation Proclamation and the War for the Union* (Cambridge, MA: Harvard University Press, 2012), 64.

7. Exodus

1. Joanne B. Freeman, *The Field of Blood: Violence in Congress and the Road to Civil War* (New York: Farrar, Straus and Giroux, 2018), 22; Ernest B. Furguson, *Freedom Rising: Washington in the Civil* War (New York: Alfred A. Knopf, 2004), 13–14; Charles Dickens, *American Notes for General Circulation and Pictures from Italy* (London: Chapman and Hall, 1913), 138.

2. AL, vol. 1, 185; Jesse Torrey, *American Slave Trade* (London: J.M. Cobbett, 1822), 62.

3. Solomon Northup, *Twelve Years a Slave*, ed. Sue Eakin and Joseph Logsdon (Baton Rouge: Louisiana State University Press, 1996), 22.

4. Calvin Schermerhorn, *Money Over Mastery, Family Over Freedom: Slavery in the Upper Antebellum South* (Baltimore: Johns Hopkins University Press, 2011), 16; Henry Stockbridge, "Baltimore in 1846," *Maryland Historical Magazine* 6, no. 1 (March 1911): 27.

5. Calvin Schermerhorn, *The Business of Slavery and the Rise of American Capitalism, 1815–1860* (New Haven, CT: Yale University Press, 2015), 298n; Frederic Bancroft, *Slave Trading in the Old South* (Baltimore: J.H. Furst Company, 1931), 60; Stephanie E. Yuhl, "Hidden in Plain Sight: Centering the Domestic Slave Trade in American Public History," *Journal of Southern History* 79, no. 3 (August 2013): 621.

6. *Washington Post*, January 10, 1991.

7. John Washington, *John Washington's Civil War: A Slave Narrative*, ed. Crandall Shifflett (Baton Rouge: Louisiana State University Press, 2008), 36.

8. *National Republican*, March 12, 1862.

9. Reprinted in *Pine and Palm*, December 21, 1861.

10. The Library of Congress now occupies the spot where Duff Green's Row once stood.

11. *The Liberator*, September 5, 1862.

12. Ibid.

13. *Washington Post*, December 27, 1936. Iowa Circle was later renamed Logan Circle in honor of Gen. John Logan of Illinois, who during his time serving in Congress lived on the west side in a three-story house designed in the "American Steamboat Gothic" style.

14. *Wheeling Daily Intelligencer*, August 2, 1865.

15. Charles Harvey Brewster, *When This Cruel War Is Over: The Civil War Letters of Charles Harvey Brewster*, ed. David W. Blight (Amherst: University of Massachusetts Press, 1992), 57.

16. William J. Wilson, "American Freedmen's Inquiry Commission Report Preliminary," May 25, 1863, AFIC.

17. Elizabeth Keckly, *Behind the Scenes: Or, Thirty Years a Slave and Four Years in the White House* (New York: G.W. Carleton & Co. 1868), 27.

18. Keckly, *Behind the Scenes*, 69. Varina Davis believed the South would later "march on Washington," conquer it, and install Jefferson Davis in the White House. "I was bewildered with what I heard," said Keckly.

19. Keckly, *Behind the Scenes*, 85.

20. Keckly, *Behind the Scenes*, 112.

21. Ibid., 115.

22. *Christian Recorder*, March 22, 1862; James McPherson, *The Negro's Civil War: How American Negroes Felt and Acted During the War for the Union* (New York: Vintage, 1965), 133.

23. AL, vol. 1, 145. Emphasis added. See also McPherson, *The Negro's Civil War*, ix.

24. *American Missionary*, January 1863; "Preliminary Report," June 30, 1863, AFIC.

25. Joseph P. Reidy, "'Coming from the Shadow of the Past': The Transition from Slavery to Freedom at Freedmen's Village, 1863–1900," *Virginia Magazine of History and Biography* 95, no. 4 (October 1987): 411

26. *The Liberator*, September 5, 1862.

27. Keckly, *Behind the Scenes*, 142–43; Lindsey Bestebreurtje, "Beyond the Plantation: Freedmen, Social Experimentation, and African American Community Development in Freedman's Village, 1863–1900," *Virginia Magazine of History and Biography* 126, no. 3 (2018): 341–42.

28. Reidy, "'Coming from the Shadow of the Past,'" 411; *Christian Recorder*, April 26, 1862.

29. *Washington Post*, December 27, 1936.

30. John E. Washington, *They Knew Lincoln* (New York: Oxford University Press, 2018), 83.

31. Willard A. Cutter to brother, February 19, 1863, Special Collections, Pelletier Library, Allegheny College, Meadville, PA.

32. Washington, *They Knew Lincoln*, 83.

33. Ibid., 87.

34. Walt Whitman, *The Correspondence of Walt Whitman*, vol. 1, *1842–1867*, ed. Edward Haviland Miller (New York: New York University Press, 1961), 113.

35. Noah Feldman, *The Broken Constitution: Lincoln, Slavery and the Refounding of America* (New York: Farrar Straus Giroux, 2021), 128.

36. John A. Dix to Edwin M. Stanton, September 12, 1862, OR, vol. 18, 391; *Springfield Republican*, August 13, 1862; *New Bedford Mercury*, August 5, 1862. Both newspapers are quoted in Jacque V. Voegeli, "A Rejected Alternative: Union Policy and the Relocation of Southern 'Contrabands' at the Dawn of Emancipation," *Journal of Southern History* 69, no. 4 (November 2003): 775. *Cincinnati Daily Enquirer*, November 15, 1862. See also Paul Escott, *"What Shall We Do with the Negro?" Lincoln, White Racism and Civil War America* (Charlottesville: University of Virginia Press, 2009), 57.

37. Quoted in Voegeli, "A Rejected Alternative," 779, 781.

38. June 26, 1857, speech in Springfield, Illinois, AL, 235.

39. AL, vol. 5, 371.

40. *Douglass Monthly*, September 1862; *Anglo-African*, December 7, 1861. See also James McPherson, "Abolitionist and Negro Opposition to Colonization During the Civil War," *Phylon* 26, no. 4 (Winter 1965): 391–99. In a speech at Springfield on July 17, 1858, Lincoln had struck a similarly separatist chord. "All I ask for the negro is that if you do not like him, let him alone. If God gave him but little, that little let him enjoy." AL, vol. 2, 520.

41. Mary Frances Armstrong and Helen Wilhelmina Ludlow, *Hampton and Its Students. By Two of Its Teachers* (New York: G.P. Putnam's Sons, 1874), 112. McPherson, *The Negro's Civil War*, 98.

42. Michael Burlingame, *Abraham Lincoln: A Life* (Baltimore: Johns Hopkins University Press, 2013), 238; Cameron quoted in Paul Kahan, *Amiable Scoundrel: Simon Cameron, Lincoln's Scandalous Secretary of War* (Lincoln: University of Nebraska Press, 2016), 203.

43. Kahan, *Amiable Scoundrel*, 145.

44. Samuel Gridley Howe, *The Refugees from Slavery in Canada West* (Boston: Wright & Potter, 1864), 104.

45. *Douglass Monthly*, January 1862

46. "Preliminary Report," June 30, 1863, AFIC.

47. *Anglo-African*, May 11, 1861.

8. In the Cipher Room

1. Michael F. Conlin, "The Smithsonian Abolition Lecture Controversy," *Civil War History* 6, no. 4 (December 2000): 312, 314, 318.

2. Mary Henry, *The Diary of Mary Henry: The Civil War Out My Window*, ed. Jeremy T.K. Farley (Charleston, SC, privately published, 2015), 49; William Harlan Hale, *Horace Greeley: Voice of the People* (New York: Harper & Brothers, 1950), iv.

3. *New York Times*, January 4, 1862.

4. *Chicago Tribune*, January 4, 1862; Harold Holzer, *Lincoln and the Power of the Press* (New York: Simon and Schuster, 2015), 379.

5. Gregory A. Borchard, *Abraham Lincoln and Horace Greeley* (Carbondale: Southern Illinois University Press, 2019), 73.

6. *Douglass Monthly*, July 1861; Ulysses S. Grant, *Letters of Ulysses S. Grant to His Father and His Youngest Sister*, ed. Jesse Grant Cramer (New York: G. P. Putnam's Sons, 1912), 43.

7. Reprinted in the *Waynesboro* (PA) *Record*, July 18, 1862; *New York Times*, July 15, 1862.

8. Noah Feldman, *The Broken Constitution: Lincoln, Slavery and the Refounding of America* (New York: Farrar Straus Giroux, 2021), 261–65.

9. *Journal of the Senate* 54 (July 17, 1862), 872.

10. AL, vol. 2, 155.

11. Abraham Lincoln to Horace Greeley, August 22, 1862, AL, 389.

12. Michael Burlingame, *Abraham Lincoln: A Life* (Baltimore: Johns Hopkins University Press, 2013), 351.

13. Orville Hickman Browning, *The Diary of Orville Hickman Browning*, vol. 1, *1850–1864*, ed. Theodore Calvin Pease and James G. Randall

(Springfield: Illinois State Historical Library, 1925), 555; OR, series 1, vol. 11, part 3, 362–64.

14. David Herbert Donald, *Lincoln* (New York: Simon & Schuster, 1996), 345.

15. AL, vol. 5 (July 12, 1862), 317–19.

16. Ibid., 317–19.

17. Gideon Welles, *Diary of Gideon Welles: Secretary of the Navy Under Lincoln and Johnson* (New York: Houghton Mifflin, 1910), 70; AL, vol. 5 (September 13, 1862), 419–20.

18. Donald, *Lincoln*, 366. See also Louis P. Masur, *Lincoln's Hundred Days: The Emancipation Proclamation and the War for the Union* (Cambridge, MA: Harvard University Press, 2012), 84.

19. David Homer Bates, *Lincoln in the Telegraph Office: Recollections of the United States Military Telegraph Corps During the Civil War* (New York: The Century Company, 1907), 131.

20. Ibid., 141.

21. Artemus Ward, *Artemus Ward: His Book* (London: John Camden Hotten, 1865), 28.

22. Salmon P. Chase, *Inside Lincoln's Cabinet: The Civil War Diaries of Salmon P. Chase*, ed. David Herbert Donald (New York: Longmans, Green and Company, 1954), 149.

23. John Hay and John Nicolay, *Abraham Lincoln: A History*, vol. 6 (New York: Century Illustrated Monthly Magazine, 1909), 159.

24. For a discussion of the use of the passive voice and what it signified, see Feldman, *The Broken Constitution*, 279–80.

25. *Accounts and Papers of the House of Commons* 72 (January 17, 1863), 52; Charles Eliot Norton, *Letters of Charles Eliot Norton*, vol. 1, ed. Sara Norton and M.A. DeWolfe Howe (Boston: Houghton Mifflin, 1913), 252; *The Liberator*, December 5, 1862; *Die Presse*, October 12, 1862.

26. *Continental Monthly*, November 1862.

27. *New York Times*, December 4, 1862.

28. *Weekly Sentinel*, October 25, 1862; AL, vol. 2, 133; Ira Berlin et al., *Slaves No More: Three Essays on Emancipation and the Civil War* (Cambridge: Cambridge University Press, 1992), 180.

29. Douglas L. Wilson, *Lincoln's Sword: The Presidency and the Power of Words* (New York: Vintage, 2006), 142.

30. Samuel Gridley Howe to F.W. Bird, March 5, 1862, AFIC; Samuel Gridley Howe, *Letters and Journals of Samuel Gridley Howe* (Boston: Dana Estes & Co, 1906), 500.

31. *Anglo-African*, January 3, 1863; *Douglass Monthly*, October 1862.

32. John Murray Forbes, *Letters and Recollections of John Murray Forbes*, vol. 1, ed. Sarah Forbes Hughes (Boston: Houghton Mifflin and Co., 1900), 315.

33. Ibid., 318.

34. OR, vol. 2, 892.

35. AL, vol. 2, 272.

36. Austa Malinda French, *Slavery in South Carolina and the Ex-slaves* (New York: Winchell French, 1862), 14.

9. Let My People Go

1. *Douglass Monthly*, May 1861.

2. AL, vol. 5, September 13, 1862, 423.

3. Dudley Taylor Cornish, *The Sable Arm: Negro Troops in the Union Army, 1861–1865* (New York: W.W. Norton, 1966), 229.

4. Catherine Clinton, "Susie King Taylor: 'I Gave My Services Willingly,'" in *Georgia Women: Their Lives and Times*, vol. 1, ed. Ann Short Chirhart and Betty Wood (Athens: University of Georgia Press, 2009), 137; Susie King Taylor, *Reminiscences of My Life in Camp* (New York: Arno Press, 1902), 44.

5. *New York Daily Herald*, July 22, 1861.

6. *The Black Abolitionist Papers*, 138.

7. Michael Burlingame, *Abraham Lincoln: A Life* (Baltimore: Johns Hopkins University Press, 2013), 464; *Congressional Globe*, January 31, 1863, 651.

8. Leon F. Litwack, *Been in the Storm So Long: The Aftermath of Slavery* (New York: Knopf, 1979), 96; James McPherson, *The Negro's Civil War: How American Negroes Felt and Acted During the War for the Union* (New York: Vintage, 1965), 189.

9. *Corinth Chanticleer*, June 12, 1863.

10. James Redfield to wife, May 31, 1863, James Redfield Papers, Iowa State Historical Society, quoted in "National Underground Railroad: Network to Freedom," National Parks Service, July 31, 2016; *Cincinnati Gazette*, October 18, 1863.

11. *Cincinnati Gazette*, June 29, 1863.

12. Ibid., *American Missionary*, October 1863.

13. Tom Barker, "Local Historian Looks into First Lady's Family," *Southern Illinoisan*, September 12, 2010.

14. William A. Dobak, *Freedom by the Sword: The U.S. Colored Troops, 1862–1867* (New York: Skyhorse Publishing, 2013), 212–13.

15. OR, vol. 39, 93. See also John Wyeth, "Major General Forrest at Brices Cross-Roads," *Harper's New Monthly Magazine*, March 1899.

16. *Ashtabula Weekly Telegraph*, June 14, 1864; Illinois soldier quoted in Cornish, *The Sable Arm*, 270.

17. Sandy Sledge, Pension File 181318, RG 94, NARA, Washington, DC.

18. McPherson, *The Negro's Civil War*, 59.

19. Ibid.

20. Quoted in Litwack, *Been in the Storm So Long*, 75; quoted in Stephen V. Ash, "White Virginians under Federal Occupation, 1861–1865," *Virginia Magazine of History and Biography* 98, no. 2 (April 1990): 185; William K. Klingaman, *Abraham Lincoln and the Road to Emancipation, 1861–1865* (New York: Viking, 2001), 253.

21. *Brooklyn Daily Eagle*, September 8, 1910.

22. Mary Frances Armstrong and Helen Wilhelmina Ludlow, *Hampton and Its Students. By Two of its Teachers* (New York: G.P. Putnam's Sons, 1874), 112.

23. CMSR, Union, U.S. Colored Troops, Company K, Massachusetts 55th Infantry, M1801, RG 94, NARA, Washington, DC.

24. George S. Walker to Burt G. Wilder, October 1914, reprinted in Noah Andre Trudeau, ed., *Voices of the 55th: Letters from the 55th Massachusetts Volunteers, 1861–1865* (Dayton, OH: Morningside Bookshop, 1996), 134.

25. James M. Trotter to E.W. Kinsley, December 18, 1864, reprinted in Trudeau, *Voices of the 55th*, 165.

26. Armstrong and Ludlow, *Hampton and Its Students*, 112.

27. Henry Jarvis, Pension File 397995, Box 40879, RG 93, NARA, Washington, DC.

28. Quoted in James Oakes, *Freedom National: The Destruction of Slavery in the United States, 1861–1865* (New York: W.W. Norton, 2012), 402; David Herbert Donald, *Lincoln* (New York: Simon & Schuster, 1996), 431.

29. Oakes, *Freedom National*, xvii.

30. *Anglo-African*, May 14, 1864.

31. *Anglo-African*, July 2, 1864. For a reconstructed description of the meeting, see David S. Cecelski, *The Fire of Freedom: Abraham Galloway & the Slaves' Civil War* (Chapel Hill: University of North Carolina Press, 2012), 115–17.

32. William B. Gould, *Diary of a Contraband: The Civil War Passage of a Black Sailor* (Palo Alto, CA: Stanford University Press, 2002), 15–18.

33. Ibid., 18.

34. Both Ayer and White are quoted in Louis P. Masur, *Lincoln's Hundred Days: The Emancipation Proclamation and the War for the Union* (Cambridge, MA: Harvard University Press, 2012), 229–30.

35. Cornish, *The Sable Arm*, 173; Litwack, *Been in the Storm So Long*, 92–93.

36. McPherson, *The Negro's Civil War*, 221–22.

37. Quoted in Litwack, *Been in the Storm So Long*, 73.

38. Henry McNeal Turner, *Freedom's Witness: The Civil War Correspondence of Henry McNeal Turner*, ed. Jean Lee Cole and Aaron Sheehan-Dean (Morgantown: West Virginia University Press, 2013), 245.

39. George Hatton to the editor of the *Christian Recorder*, May 28, 1864, reprinted in *A Grand Army of Black Men: Letters from African-American Soldiers in the Union Army, 1861–1865*, ed. Edwin S. Redkey (New York: Cambridge University Press, 1992), 95-96.

40. *Christian Recorder*, May 26, 1864.

41. *Christian Recorder*, May 28, 1864; Ash, "White Virginians Under Federal Occupation," 188.

42. *Christian Recorder*, April 15, 1865.

43. Stephen Hurlburt to Abraham Lincoln, March 27, 1863, OR, series 1, vol. 24, 150; Thomas R. Flagel, "The Fortress War: Effect of Union Fortifications in the Western Theater of the U.S. Civil War" (PhD diss., Middle Tennessee State University, 2016), 95; *Milwaukee Daily Sentinel*, February 17, 1864.

44. McPherson, *The Negro's Civil War*, 163.

45. *Christian Recorder*, May 26, 1864.

46. Burlingame, *Lincoln*, 469.

47. Noah Brooks, *Lincoln Observed: Civil War Dispatches of Noah Brooks*, ed. Michael Burlingame (Baltimore: Johns Hopkins University Press, 2002), 17.

48. AL, vol. 5, 21.

49. AL, vol. 8, 224.

50. Noah Feldman, *The Broken Constitution: Lincoln, Slavery and the Refounding of America* (New York: Farrar Straus Giroux, 2021), 4–5.

51. Abraham Lincoln to Major General J.A. McClernand, January 8, 1863, AL, vol. 2, 296. He would later tell the journalist Joseph T. Mills that he would "be damned in time and eternity" for returning any member of the USCT to slavery. See Masur, *Lincoln's Hundred Days*, 253.

52. Abraham Lincoln to Albert G. Hodges, April 4, 1864, AL, vol. 7, 282.

53. "Lincoln, no less than the meanest slave, acted upon changing possibilities as he understood them." Ira Berlin, "Who Freed the Slaves? Emancipation and Its Meaning," in *Union and Emancipation: Essays on Politics and Race in the Civil War Era*, ed. David W. Blight and Brooks R. Simpson (Kent,

OH: Kent State University Press, 1997), 296–97. For a discussion of the tandem theory of emancipation, see Oakes, *Freedom National*, xviii–xxiv.

54. Bennett Parten, *Somewhere Toward Freedom: Sherman's March and the Story of America's Largest Emancipation* (New York: Simon and Schuster, 2025), 11.

55. *A.M.E. Review*, January 1913.

56. *Anglo-African*, January 17, 1863; *New York Times*, January 1, 1863; *American Missionary*, February 1863.

57. Thomas Wentworth Higginson, *Army Life in a Black Regiment* (Boston: Houghton Mifflin, 1900), 55–56.

58. *American Missionary*, February 1863; McPherson, *The Negro's Civil War*, 64.

59. McPherson, *The Negro's Civil War*, 65; also quoted in Masur, *Lincoln's Hundred Days*, 136; John Murray Forbes, *Letters and Recollections of John Murray Forbes*, vol. 1, ed. Sarah Forbes Hughes (Boston: Houghton Mifflin and Co., 1900), 348.

60. Author interview with Bill Wiggins, former Hampton University history professor, June 27, 2023; telegraphic dispatch reprinted in *Wisconsin State Journal*, January 3, 1863; John Oliver to S.S. Jocelyn, January 14, 1863, AMA.

61. McPherson, *The Negro's Civil War*, 63.

62. *American Missionary*, February 1863.

63. *Washington Evening Star*, January 2, 1863.

10. Who Shall We Trust?

1. Amy Murrell Taylor, *Embattled Freedom: Journeys Through the Civil War's Slave Refugee Camps* (Chapel Hill: University of North Carolina Press, 2018), 182. Camp Nelson had a reputation into 1865 for claiming the labor of male arrivals while expelling their wives and children. See also Chandra Manning, *Troubled Refuge: Struggling for Freedom in the Civil War* (New York: Vintage Books, 2016), 147–48.

2. Peter Bruner, *A Slave's Adventures Toward Freedom* (Oxford, Ohio: privately published, 1918), 43. Taylor, *Embattled Freedom*, 187.

3. John M. Palmer, *Personal Recollections of John M. Palmer* (Cincinnati: Robert Clarke Co., 1901), 242; Bruner, *A Slave's Adventures Toward Freedom*, 45.

4. Palmer, *Personal Recollections*, 225. For a slightly different account of this conversation, see *Religious Telescope*, June 15, 1898.

5. William K. Klingaman, *Abraham Lincoln and the Road to Emancipation, 1861–1865* (New York: Viking, 2001), 228; "Preliminary Report," June 30, 1863, AFIC.

6. Ulysses S. Grant to Elihu Washburne, August 30, 1863, in *General Grant's Letters to a Friend*, ed. James Grant Wilson (New York & Boston: T.Y. Crowell & Co., 1897), 28. Henry J. Raymond, *The Life and Public Services of Abraham Lincoln* (New York: Derby and Miller Publishers, 1865), 752.

7. *The Century*, October 1889.

8. John Murray Forbes to Abraham Lincoln, September 8, 1863, in *Letters and Recollections of John Murray Forbes*, vol. 2 (Boston: Houghton, Mifflin, 1899), 74. See also David Herbert Donald, *Lincoln* (New York: Simon & Schuster, 1996), 461.

9. Gary Wills, *Lincoln at Gettysburg* (New York: Simon & Schuster, 1992), 172.

10. For a discussion of religious themes in the Gettysburg address, see Noah Feldman, *The Broken Constitution: Lincoln, Slavery and the Refounding of America* (New York: Farrar Straus Giroux, 2021), 298–301.

11. William H. Seward, *The Diplomatic History of the War for the Union* (Boston: Houghton Mifflin, 1883), 163. Also quoted in Feldman, *The Broken Constitution*, 307; Michael Burlingame, *Abraham Lincoln: A Life* (Baltimore: Johns Hopkins University Press, 2013), 471.

12. Louis P. Masur, *Lincoln's Hundred Days: The Emancipation Proclamation and the War for the Union* (Cambridge, MA: Harvard University Press, 2012), 261.

13. Ronald C. White Jr., *Lincoln's Greatest Speech* (New York: Simon & Schuster, 2006), 97.

14. David Homer Bates, *Lincoln in the Telegraph Office: Recollections of the United States Military Telegraph Corps During the Civil War* (New York: The Century Company, 1907), 60.

15. *Philadelphia Press*, April 11, 12, 1865.

16. *New York Times*, April 6, 1887.

17. Ulysses S. Grant, *Personal Memoirs of U.S. Grant* (New York: Charles L. Webster and Co., 1886), 489; Bruce Catton, *The Centennial History of the Civil War: Never Call Retreat* (New York: Doubleday, 1961), 468.

18. *The Century*, May 1895.

19. William Henry Crook, *Through Five Administrations: Reminiscences of Colonel William H. Crook, Body-guard to President Lincoln* (New York: Harper & Brothers, 1910), 75.

20. *Nashville Daily Union*, February 28, 1866.

21. *Western Clarion*, December 2, 1865; November 18, 1865. The ordinance is quoted in Taylor, *Embattled Freedom*, 231.

22. *Western Clarion*, December 9, 1865.

23. *Philadelphia Inquirer*, August 9, 1865.

24. *Louisville Daily Journal*, September 4, 1865.

25. Richard D. Sears, *Camp Nelson, Kentucky: A Civil War History* (Lexington: University Press of Kentucky, 2014), 239; *Louisville Courier Journal*, May 6, 1865. See also Taylor, *Embattled Freedom*, 222. Fisk's emphasis is in the original.

26. *Cleveland Daily Leader*, September 8, 1865.

27. Manning, *Troubled Refuge*, 263.

28. *Atchison Daily Free Press*, July 22, 1865.

29. Sherman quote in William H. Freehling, *The South vs. the South: How Anti-Confederate Southerners Shaped the Course of the Civil War* (Oxford: Oxford University Press, 2002), 163–65; Henry Hitchcock, *Marching with Sherman: Passages from the Letters and Campaign Diaries of Henry Hitchcock, Major and Assistant Adjutant General of Volunteers, November 1864–May 1865* (New Haven: Yale University Press, 1927), 69. See also Bennett Parten, *Somewhere Toward Freedom: Sherman's March and the Story of America's Largest Emancipation* (New York: Simon and Schuster, 2025), 40, 52, for accounts of invasive foraging.

30. Stephanie M.H. Camp, *Closer to Freedom: Enslaved Women and Everyday Resistance in the Plantation South* (Chapel Hill: University of North Carolina Press, 2004), 138, cited in Parten, *Somewhere Toward Freedom*, 48.

31. "Minutes of an Interview," January 12, 1865, OR, series 1, vol. 47, 37.

32. Henry Halleck to William T. Sherman, December 30, 1864. William T. Sherman, *Memoirs of General W.T. Sherman*, vol. 2 (New York: D. Appleton, 1889), 245. See also, Parten. *Somewhere Toward Freedom*, 132–34.

33. William T. Sherman to Stephen Hurlbut, January 11, 1864, OR, series 1, vol. 32, 179.

34. *American Missionary*, March 1864. See also Cam Walker, "Corinth: The Story of a Contraband Camp," *Civil War History* 20, no. 1 (March 1974): 19.

35. *New Orleans Times*, June 11, 1865.

36. Manning, *Troubled Refuge*, 245.

37. William T. Sherman to Andrew Johnson, February 2, 1866, reprinted in *Army and Navy Journal*, February 10, 1866.

38. Taylor, *Embattled Freedom*, 215, 219.

39. Taylor, *Embattled Freedom*, 217; G.L. Mafley to S.C. Armstrong, September 1, 1866, Freedmen's Bureau Field Office Records, Virginia, Reports Received, Jan.–Sept. 1866, M1913, NARA.

40. "A Freeman's Speech," in Samuel Armstrong to Oliver Brown, January 26, 1867, Registered Letters Received, series 3798, Bureau of Refugees, Freedmen, and Abandoned Lands, RG 105, NARA.

Epilogue

1. *New York Times*, April 19, 1868, December 12, 2018.

2. The American Missionary Association appointed U.S. Army General Samuel Armstrong to run the Hampton Institute after the war. Among its postbellum students was an Alabamian who had grown up in slavery named Booker T. Washington.

3. Mary Frances Armstrong and Helen Wilhelmina Ludlow, *Hampton and Its Students. By Two of its Teachers* (New York: G.P. Putnam's Sons, 1874), 112.

4. Ibid.

5. Henry Jarvis, Pension File 397995, Box 40879, RG 94, NARA. He and his third wife moved to 203 S. Bethel Street in Baltimore, where he died of heart failure on March 9, 1894. At the time, her only other income was washing clothes for $2 per week. She applied for his pension benefits but denied, against the evidence, that Jarvis had been married twice before.

6. Armstrong and Ludlow, *Hampton and Its Students*, 114.

7. Elizabeth R. Varon, *Southern Lady, Yankee Spy: The True Story of Elizabeth Van Lew, a Union Agent in the Heart of the Confederacy* (Oxford: Oxford University Press, 2003), 108.

8. *American Missionary*, February 1863; James Parton, *General Butler in New Orleans* (New York: Mason Brothers, 1864), 619.

9. Elizabeth D. Leonard, *Benjamin Franklin Butler: A Noisy, Fearless Life* (Chapel Hill: University of North Carolina Press, 2022), xi.

10. Claim of Edward Whitehurst, December 5, 1877, SCC.

11. *Jones v. Clowes*, in Freedmen's Bureau Field Office Records, Virginia, Reports Received, Jan.–Sept. 1866, M1913, NARA; Amy Murrell Taylor, *Embattled Freedom: Journeys Through the Civil War's Slave Refugee Camps* (Chapel Hill: University of North Carolina Press, 2018), 240.

12. George Benjamin West, *When the Yankees Came: Civil War and Reconstruction on the Virginia Peninsula* (Richmond: Dietz Press, 1977), 39.

13. Robert F. Engs, *Freedom's First Generation: Black Hampton, Virginia, 1861–1890* (Philadelphia: University of Pennsylvania Press, 1979), 90.

14. West, *When the Yankees Came*, 109.

15. *True Southerner*, December 7, 1865, quoted in Taylor, *Embattled Freedom*, 219.

16. Arthur P. Davis, "William Roscoe Davis and His Descendants," *Negro History Bulletin* 13, no. 4 (January 1950): 80.

17. Ibid., 82.

18. *Brooklyn Daily Eagle*, September 8, 1910.

19. Susie King Taylor, *Reminiscences of My Life in Camp* (New York: Arno Press, 1902), 54.

20. Ibid., 61.

21. *New York Times*, September 17, 1865.

22. John Richard Dennett, *The South as It Is* (Athens: University of Georgia Press, 1986), 152. See also David Zucchino, *Wilmington's Lie: The Murderous Coup of 1898 and the Rise of White Supremacy* (New York: Grove Press, 2020), 32.

23. Quoted in Zucchino, *Wilmington's Lie*, 43.

24. Debra Jackson, "A Black Journalist in Civil War Virginia," *Virginia Magazine of History and Biography* 116, no. 1 (2008): 67.

25. Peter Bruner, *A Slave's Adventures Toward Freedom* (Oxford, Ohio: privately published, 1918), 52.

26. *Bedford Inquirer*, June 9, 1865.

27. *Brooklyn Daily Eagle*, August 12, 1865.

28. William Harlan Hale, *Horace Greeley: Voice of the People* (New York: Harper & Brothers, 1950), 322. When some Republican members of New York's Union Club demanded he answer for his actions, Greeley responded: "You evidently regard me as a weak sentimentalist, misled by a maudlin philosophy. I arraign you as narrowheaded blockheads who would like to be useful to a great and good cause but don't know how."

29. Markinfield Addey, *Life and Imprisonment of Jefferson Davis* (New York: M. Doolady, 1866), 92–93. Shelby Foote ended his three-volume history *The Civil War: A Narrative* with a version of these words, supposedly spoken to a newspaper reporter who visited Davis at Beauvoir, his Biloxi estate, shortly before his death: "His was a different style, though it too had its beauty and its uses: as in his response to a recent Beauvoir visitor, a reporter who hoped to leave with something that would help explain to readers the underlying motivation of those crucial years of bloodshed and division. Davis pondered briefly, then replied. 'Tell them—' He paused as if to sort the words. 'Tell the world that I only loved America,' he said." See Shelby Foote, *The Civil War, A Narrative, Volume 3: Red River to Appomattox* (New York: Vintage Books, 1974), 1060. Foote gave no citation, and no evidence of the late-life quote from Davis can be found in American or British newspapers. Foote, who described himself as a "novelist-historian," appears to have been reappropriating the earlier, less compact, statement given to Dr. John Craven in his prison cell on July 11, 1865.

30. John Russell Young, *Around the World with General Grant*, vol. 1 (New York: The American News Company, 1879), 416–17. An illustration of the meeting appears on page 411.

31. "Down Town," by Paul Turner, *Chicago Reader*, June 17, 1999.

32. Ron Powers, *Far from Home: Life and Loss in Two American Towns* (New York: Anchor, 1992), 8; Jan Peterson Roddy and Preston Ewing Jr., *Let My People Go: Cairo, Illinois, 1967–1973* (Carbondale: Southern Illinois University Press, 1996).

33. Author interview, Preston Ewing Jr., Cairo, Illinois, May 3, 2023.

34. Engs, *Freedom's First Generation*, 75. John Townsend Trowbridge, *The South: A Tour of its Battlefields and Ruined Cities in 1865* (Hartford, CT.: L. Stebbins, 1866), 220.

35. *Philadelphia Inquirer*, June 13, 1865.

36. Engs, *Freedom's First Generation*, 69.

37. Ibid., 139–40; *Harper's Weekly*, September 1865.

38. *San Francisco Evening Bulletin*, October 3, 1865; Engs, *Freedom's First Generation*, 139–40.

39. *Memphis Daily Avalanche*, April 7, 1866.

40. *Hampton Home Bulletin*, January 19, 1889, quoted in Engs, *Freedom's First Generation*, 146.

41. Alan Taylor, *The Internal Enemy: Slavery and War in Virginia, 1772–1832* (New York: W.W. Norton, 2013), 258.

42. Adam Goodheart, *1861: The Civil War Awakening* (New York: Vintage, 2011), 382.

43. *Portsmouth Star*, August 27, 1897; *Newport News Daily Press*, May 20, 1934; *Baltimore Sun*, November 17, 1897; *Newport News Daily Press*, September 6, 1898. See also Rod Gragg, *Confederate Goliath: The Battle of Fort Fisher* (Baton Rouge: Louisiana State University Press, 2006), xiv, 100.

44. Matthew Laird and Sean P. Romo, "Searching for Slabtown: A Preliminary Archeological Investigation of the Grand Contraband Camp Site," James River Institute for Archaeology, Williamsburg, VA, January 2015, p. ix. At St. John's Church in the center of Hampton, one of the only buildings to survive the fire of 1861, the graffitied name *Shep. Mallory* is carved into an exterior brick of the south transept, hard to spot, with an old-style serif on the *S*. The vestry of St. John's commissioned an investigation to examine the possibility that the pioneering fugitive might have risked punishment in the Jim Crow era to carve his name on one of the most historic structures in town. They concluded it was unlikely, and that the carving was a creative historical gag pulled off by an unknown individual. See "Background: Shep. Mallory Brick on Wall of St. John's Church,"

Heritage Working Group of St. John's, 2011. Author interview, Rev. Samantha Vincent-Alexander, July 19, 2022, Hampton, VA.

45. The White House, President Barack Obama, "Presidential Proclamation—Establishment of the Fort Monroe National Monument," November 1, 2011, NARA.

46. Author interview, Edith Taylor, Fort Monroe, VA, July 18, 2022. See also "Oral History Interview with Edith Taylor," February 3, 2013, CC2013.42.1, Hampton History Museum, Hampton, VA.

47. Author interview, Edith Taylor, Fort Monroe, VA, July 18, 2022.

Image Sources

vi–vii: map by Joe LeMonnier

viii: map by Joe LeMonnier

11: Reading Room 2020/Alamy Stock Photo

17: Mouseion Archives / Alamy Stock Photo

41: Library of Congress

53: Library of Congress

83: Library of Congress

116: Library of Congress

150: National Archives

191: Library of Congress

199: Universal Images Group North America LLC/Alamy Stock Photo

Index

About the Author

Tom Zoellner is the author of nine nonfiction books, including *Island on Fire: The Revolt That Ended Slavery in the British Empire*, winner of the National Book Critics Circle Award for the best nonfiction book of 2020. He works as a professor at Chapman University and as an editor-at-large for the *Los Angeles Review of Books*.